Legends of Saints and Sinners

Legends of
Saints and Sinners

collected and translated from the Irish

by

DOUGLAS HYDE

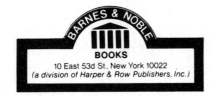

BOOKS
10 East 53d St., New York 10022
(a division of Harper & Row Publishers, Inc.)

First published Dublin 1915

This IUP reprint is a photolithographic facsimile
of the text of the first edition.

Published in the U.S.A. 1973 by:
Harper & Row Publishers, Inc.
Barnes & Noble Import Division

ISBN 06-493110-2

PRINTED IN THE REPUBLIC OF IRELAND AT SHANNON

CONTENTS.

v

INTRODUCTION.

I HAVE called the present volume "Legends of Saints and Sinners," which to a certain extent it is ; but I mean it for a book of Irish Christian folk-lore. My idea in compiling it has been to give for the first time a collection of genuine Irish folk-lore which might be called " Christian." By this I mean folk-stories and folk-poems which are either entirely founded upon Christian conceptions, or else are so far coloured by them, that they could never have been told—at least in their present shape—had not Christianity established itself in Ireland. Every one of these stories conforms fairly to this standard, except one or two, which I give as necessary corollaries. They are all translations from the Irish. I have found hardly any such stories in English. They were mostly collected by myself from the mouths of native speakers, but three or four of them I have taken from Irish MSS. in my own possession, and a few more were given me by my friends. Not one of these stories was ever translated into English before, with the exception of those which I have taken from my own "Religious Songs of Connacht."[1] Many of

---

[1] And " Teig O'Kane," which I translated for Mr. Yeats nearly twenty years ago.

these I decided to republish here, as they were practically
lost amongst the heterogeneous mass of poems, prayers,
charms, etc., in which they were embedded ; and, as the
Religious Songs are little known, these stories which I
have excerpted from them will be new to nineteen-twen-
tieths of my readers. Several of these pieces have never
been printed even in Irish, but I hope to shortly publish
the original text of these, especially the Adventures of
Léithin, which seems to belong to a strange and weird
cycle of beast and bird-lore, now lost or almost lost, but
of which we find hints here and there though we know
nothing certain.

Most of these pieces may be said to be in a true sense
" folk-lore," seeing that they have almost all lingered
more or less vividly in the memory of people who for the
most part could neither read nor write. Some of them
obviously come from Continental sources, though how they
first found their way into Ireland is obscure, and the
derivation of some of them cannot now be traced ; others,
however, are of a purely native invention ; while a third
class engrafts native traits and ideas upon foreign subject
matter.

The stories in this collection cover a good deal of ground
and present many various aspects of folk tradition and folk
belief. Of native Saints we find legends concerning
Patrick, Columcille, Deglan, Moling and Ciaran ; of
foreign Saints we find legends of St. Peter, St. Paul and
St. Martin ; of unknown or mythical characters we find
tales of Grainne Oïgh, Friar Brian, The Old Woman
of Beare, and Mulruana.   Of other well-known names,
Oisín and Oscar and Solomon appear. Curiously enough

I have not chanced upon any folk-tale told about Saint Brigit, the "Mary of the Gael." There is, for some reason or other, a distinct predominance of Petrine stories among these legends.

When we consider the collection as a whole, we find that its purely Irish aspect is apparent in many ways, and in none more than in the very characteristic dovetailing of what is Pagan into what is Christian. But its omissions are even more distinctly Irish than its inclusions.

In most countries, for instance, the Devil is the great outstanding anthropomorphic conception added to the folk-lore of Europe by the introduction of Christianity ; and later the belief in Witches, who trafficked directly or indirectly with the Evil One, became extraordinary prevalent and powerful. Now the most striking fact about our collection is that the Devil personified rarely appears in it at all, and Witches never. The belief in Witches, and in Witches' Sabbaths, with which other nations were positively obsessed, and which gave rise to such hecatombs of unhappy victims in almost all the Protestant and in some of the Catholic countries in Europe, as well as in America, never found its way into native Ireland at all, or disturbed Gaelic sanity, although a few isolated instances occurred amongst the English settlers. The Highland Gaels, to whom the idea of witches was more familiar owing to their proximity to the Scottish Lowlands, which was one of the most witch-ridden countries in Europe, simply borrowed the English word for witch under the form "buitseach," and from that they coined the word "buitseachas" for witchcraft.

The Irish, however, did not borrow even the name— they had never heard of the thing itself, and had naturally no name for a class of creatures with whom they had no acquaintance

It is true that the Evil Eye was known in Ireland, and I have found one or two prayers or charms against it ;[1] but so far as I have collected, I have not been able to find it made the basis of any story.

In ancient times, however, there were creatures known in Ireland who appear to have had some of the characteristics of the Christian witches, but their conception is purely Pagan and owes nothing to Christianity. Their Irish name was *amait*, and it was applicable to both sexes. In the old translation of the " Cath catharda " (the Irish version of Lucan's Pharsalia), Medea is called the chief *amait* or witch of the world. In the " Agallamh na Senorach " or Dialogue between St. Patrick on one side, and Oisín and Caoilte[2] on the other, we read of nine women *amaits* who were engaged in " amaidecht," and who used never allow a man or woman to escape them. " And they were not long there," says the thirteenth (?) century text," until they saw the nine black gloomy witches (*amaits*) coming to meet them ; and if the dead ever arose out of the ground the yells which they used to utter round them on all sides would have brought them forth [from their tombs]. And Patrick takes the holy water

---

[1] See " Religious Songs of Connacht," vol. II., p. 52.
[2] Pronounce Ussheen and Cweeltia. Oisín is better known as Ossian in Scotland.

and sprinkles it on the *amaits*, and they fled away from him
until they reached Inis Guil, which is called the island
of the shrine or the White Lake of Ceara.[1]   And it was
there they heard the last cry from them.   And the people
seated themselves on the sodded sward, and the King of
Connacht spake then, 'that is the chasing of a good-cleric
that thou hast given to the demons,' said he.' "

This word *amait*, though lost in folk-speech, and never
now used in the sense of witch, has nevertheless perpetu-
ated itself in an extraordinary tradition in parts of Connacht.   The appellation for the Fairy Palace, where the
Good People or Tuatha De Danann dwell, is *bruidhean*
(pronounced Breean with the b broad), and there is a
belief that there is a denizen of the bruidhean called
" amadán na bruidhne," which seems to mean the " fool
of the palace " whose lightest touch is death.   From the
other creatures of the bruidhean one may escape scathe-
less, but never from the " amadán."   This " amadán " I
take to be a folk perversion or a diminutive of *amait*, and
to have nothing at all to say to the word " amadán," " a
fool."

The *amait* owes nothing to Christianity, but her equivalent in modern folk-lore would rather be found in the
story of "Conn among the goats," where the woman whom

---

[1] Now Loch Carra, in Co. Mayo. The bottom of this lake consists
of white marl, which gives the water an extraordinary light green
appearance; hence it is called in old Irish documents Fionnloch
Ceara, or the " white lake of Carra." The metrical Dinnsenchus,
however, caimly ignoring this obvious physiological reason, evident
to anyone who had ever examined the lake, gives a fantastic account
of the white wings of angels, from which it says the water derived
its name.

all thought dead comes back from the grave, and kills her
husband, or in the story of the Priest and Bishop, where
the hanged woman comes back as a malevolent spirit to
claim the priest ; or in some of the stories that Curtin
collected around Dingle.

It is quite true that there are many current tales or
beliefs concerning more or less malignant old women who
steal butter from their neighbours' churns by charms
or exorcisms, who turn themselves into hares and suck the
cows, and who are supposed to possess certain more or
less supernatural powers. These old women, however,
seldom or never figure in regular stories, nor have they
given rise to a type or even to a common appellation.
They are just known as " cailleacha " or hags. There is
absolutely nothing in Irish folk-lore, so far as I am
acquainted with it, to suggest the disgusting and obscene
orgies of the witches' sabbaths, as we find them in other
countries, or of incubi or succubi, or of intercourse with
the devil, or of riding on broomsticks to keep appointments
with the Evil One, or of conjuring up the dead, or even
of producing wasting diseases in enemies, or making
waxen or clay images of those whom they wished to
injure.[1]

The Devil, too, in so far as he comes into Irish folk-
lore, is a much less grotesque figure than the usual
mediaeval conception of him, such as we see with
horns and hooves in Albrecht Dürer's pictures. He
is usually designated as the " Old Devil " or the

---

[1] I am not quite so certain about this last having never been prac-
tised in Ireland, but I have certainly never been told any story about
it, nor seen it mentioned in MSS.

Aidhbherseoir, often contracted to Airseoir from the Latin Adversarius. He does not generally appear as roaming through the world seeking whom he may devour, but mostly keeps to his own abode in the Infernal Regions, where he must be sought. We meet him in both forms, as a wandering person and as king of the Lower Regions in my late friend's, Mr. Larminie's, very curious and interesting story of the woman who went to hell. He is not the popular or common character in our folk-lore that he is in Teutonic legend. He does not construct bridges, nor hold high festival on hill tops, and few or none of the curious freaks of nature as seen in rocks, chasms, and the like are attributed to him. The Devil's Bit and the Devil's Punch Bowl, so common in Anglo-Irish nomenclature, do not always correspond to the original Irish appellation.

When the survivors of the old Fianna, Oisín (or Ossian), Caoilte and the rest, were told about Hell and the Devil by St. Patrick and his clergy, they could not, according to the Ossianic legends, comprehend it in the least, and the misunderstandings which the doctrine gave rise to were taken full advantage of by the composers of the Ossianic ballads. The idea of bringing the last great figure of Paganism, the warrior and poet Ossian, into contact with the first great Christian figure in Ireland, St. Patrick, was a brilliant one, and it gave birth to whole volumes of badinage and semi-comic wrangling in the popular ballads which told of the warrior and the cleric. These ballads used to be in great vogue at one time, and any seanchuidhe worthy of the name used to be able to repeat

by heart many hundreds of lines of the dialogue between
Patrick and Oisín. This is now nearly a thing of the past,
but the poems exist in numberless manuscripts, and are
not yet forgotten by the older Irish speakers, though the
only specimen I have given in this volume is the Baptism
of Oisín, and it is in prose. St. Patrick displays in places
an excess of priestly rigour, but this is always done to set
off the naïveté of Oisín's answers.

> ı n-ıfṗeann na bpıan aṗ láıṁ
> Acá an feaṗ ráıṁ ʋo ḃṗonnaʋ an c-óṗ,
> Imċeóċaıʋ cuṗa maṗ ʋ'ımċıᵹ an ḟıann,
> Aᵹuṗ cṗáċcamaoıṗ aṗ Ḋıa ᵹo fóıl.¹

But Oisín could not understand how Patrick's God could
get the better of his Fianna, or why He should try to
put them in hell at all.

> Were God and my son Oscar seen
>   On Knocknaveen in combat long,
> And I saw my Oscar on the sod,
>   It's then I'd say that God was strong.

> How is your God a better man
>   (Or all your clan of clerics there)
> Than Finn, our Fenian chief, so great,
>   So straight, so generous, so fair?

The spirit of banter in which St. Patrick and the Church
are treated, and which just stops short of irreverence, is,
of course, a mediaeval and not a primitive trait. My
friend, the late Mr. Nutt, thought that it is a trait more

---

¹ I wrote down this from the recitation of an old man near Monivea,
Co. Galway. I have not seen it in MS. Literally, " In hell of the
pains in bondage is the gentle man (Fionn) who used to bestow the
gold. You will go as the Fianna have gone, and let us talk about
God yet awhile."

characteristic of the twelfth than of any succeeding century.

It would be exceedingly easy to fill volumes with stories from the lives of Saints which exist either in old vellum or in paper MSS., but this has not been my aim. I have kept to actual folk survivals, and have drawn upon MSS. of Saints' lives only for the elucidation of the folktale.

Finally, I should say that after having collected Irish folk-lore for a quarter of a century, the amount of folk-stories which are wholly conditioned by Christianity or largely based upon Christian conceptions would be, in my opinion, about one story in four, or one story in five. There still remains the fascinating problem of their sources. If foreign, what was their origin and who brought them here ; if native, who invented them, and when, and with what purpose ? I have prefixed a few notes to each of the following stories which possibly may not be wholly uninteresting to the reader who has an eye for these problems.

LEGENDS OF SAINTS AND SINNERS.

[*FROM THE IRISH.*]

ST. PATRICK AND CROM DUBH.

PREFACE.

This legend, told by Michael Mac Ruaidhri of Ballycastle, Co. Mayo, is evidently a confused reminiscence of Crom Cruach, the great pagan idol which was overthrown by St. Patrick.[1] Though Crom appears as a man in this story, yet the remark that the people thought he was the lord of light and darkness and of the seasons is evidently due to his once supposed Godhead. The fire, too, which he is said to have kept burning may be the reminiscence of a sacrificial fire.

From a letter written to Sir Samuel Ferguson[2] by the late Brian O'Looney, concerning Mount Callan in the Co. Clare, we see that this legend of Crom was widely circulated. "Domnach Lunasa or Lammas Sunday," says O'Looney, "the first Sunday of the month of August was the first "fruits' day, and a great day on Buaile-na-greine. On "Lammas Sunday, called Domnach Crom Dubh, and "anglicised Garland Sunday, every householder was sup- "posed to feast his family and household on the first "fruits, and the farmer who failed to provide his people

[1] See my "Literary History of Ireland," pp. 84-88. Also Stokes edition of the "Tripartite Life," p. 92.

[2] See the paper read by Sir Samuel before the Royal Irish Academy, April 28, 1873.

" with new potatoes, new bacon and white cabbage on that
" day was called a *felemuir gaoithe*, or wind farmer ; and if
" a man dug new potatoes before Crom Dubh's day he
" was considered a needy man. . . . . . . The
" assemblage of this day was called *comthineol Chruim*
" *Dhuibh*, or the congregation or gathering of Crom Dubh,
" and the day is called from him *Domnach Chrom Dubh*,
" or Crom Dubh's Sunday, now called Garland Sunday by
" the English-speaking portion of the people of the sur-
" rounding districts. This name is supposed to have been
" derived from the practise of strewing garlands of flowers
" on the festive mound [or Mount Callan] on this day, as
" homage to Crom Dubh—hence the name Garland Sunday.
    " Assuredly I saw blossoms and flowers deposited upon
" it on the first Sunday of August, 1844, and put some upon
" it myself, as I saw done by those who were with me.
  .   .   .   .
    " If you ask me who Crom Dubh was, I can only tell you
" I asked the question myself on the spot. I was told that
" Crom was a god and that Dubh or Dua meant *a sacrifice,*
" which in combination made Crom Dubh, or Crom Dua,
" that is, Crom's Sacrifice ; and this Sunday was set apart
" for the feast and commemoration of this Crom Dubh,
" whoever he may have been."
    It is interesting to find O'Looney's old-time experiences
in Co. Clare so far borne out by this legend from North
Mayo.
    The name Téideach given to Crom's son, is, as Mr. Lloyd
acutely points out, founded upon a misunderstanding
of the name of the hole which must have been " poll an
t séidte," the puffing or blowing hole. Downpatrick, where
these events are supposed to have taken place, is at the ex-
treme northern extremity of Tyrawley, Co. Mayo, and all
the other places are in its neighbourhood.
    For the *leannán sidhe,* or fairy sweetheart (often supposed
to be the muse of the poets), see O'Kearney's " Feis tighe
Chonáin." Oss. Soc. Publ. vol. II., pp. 80-103. For the
Irish of this story, see " Lúb na Caillighe," p. 33.

THE STORY

BEFORE St. Patrick came to Ireland there lived a chieftain in the Lower Country[1] in Co. Mayo, and his name was Crom Dubh. Crom Dubh lived beside the sea in a place which they now call Dún Patrick, or Downpatrick, and the name which the site of his house is called by is Dún Briste, or Broken Fort. My story will tell why it was called Dún Briste.

It was well and it was not ill, brother of my heart! Crom Dubh was one of the worst men that could be found, but as he was a chieftain over the people of that country he had everything his own way; and that was the bad way, for he was an evil-intentioned, virulent, cynical,[2] obstinate man, with desire to be avenged on every one who did not please him. He had two sons, Téideach and Clonnach, and there is a big hollow going in under the road at Gleann Lasaire, and the name of this hollow in Poll a' Téidigh or Téideach's hole, for it got its name from Crom Dubh's son, and the name of this hole is on the mouth of [*i.e.*, used by] English-speaking people, though they do not know the meaning of it. Nobody knows how far this hole is going back under the glen, but it is said by the old Irish speakers that Téideach used to go every day in his little floating curragh into this hole under the glen, and that this is the reason it was called Téideach's Hole.

It was well, my dear. To continue the story, Crom

---

[1] Lower means " northern." It means round the Lagan, Creevagh and Ballycastle.
[2] Literally " doggish." The meaning is rather " snarling " or " fierce " than cynical.

Dubh's two sons were worse than himself, and that leaves them bad enough! Crom Dubh had two hounds of dogs and their names were Coinn Iotair and Saidhthe Suaraighe,¹ and if ever there were [wicked] mastiffs these two dogs were they. He had them tied to the two jaws of the door, in order to loose them and set them to attack people according as they might come that way ; and, to go further, he had a big fire kindled on the brink of the cliff so that any one who might escape from the hounds he might throw into the fire ; and to make a long story short, the fame of Crom Dubh and his two sons, and his two mastiffs, went far and wide, for their evil-doing ; and the people were so terrified at his name, not to speak of himself, that they used to hide their faces in their bosoms when they used to hear it mentioned in their ears, and the people were so much afraid of him that if they heard the bark of a dog they would go hiding in the dwellings that they had underground, to take refuge in, to defend themselves from Crom Dubh and his mastiffs.

It is said that there was a linnaun shee² or fairy sweetheart walking with Crom Dubh, and giving him knowledge according as he used to require it. In place of his inclining to what was good as he was growing in age, the way he went on was to be growing in badness every day, and the wind was not quicker than he, for he was as nimble as a March hare. When he used to go out about the country he used to send his two sons and his two mastiffs before him, and they announcing to the people according as

---

¹ Pronounced like " Cunn eetir " and " sy-ha soory "—hound of rage and bitch of wickedness ?
² Linnaun shee, a fairy sweetheart ; in Irish spelt " leannán sidhe."

they proceeded, that Crom Dubh was coming to collect his standing rent, and bidding them to have it ready for him. Crom Dubh used to come after them, and his trickster (?) along with him, and he drawing after him a sort of yoke like a wheelless sliding car, and according as he used to get his standing-rent it used to be thrown into the car, and every one had to pay according to his ability. Anyone who would refuse, he used to be brought next day before Crom Dubh, as he sat beside the fire, and Crom used to pass judgment upon him, and after the judgment the man used to be thrown into the fire. Many a plan and scheme were hatched against Crom Dubh to put him out of the world, but he overcame them all, for he had too much wizardry from the [fairy] sweetheart.

Crom Dubh was continuing his evil deeds for many years, and according as the story about him remains living and told from person to person, they say that he was a native of hell in the skin of a biped, and through the horror that the people of the country had for him they would have given all that ever they saw if only Crom Dubh and his company could have been put-an-end-to ; but there was no help for them in that, since he and his company had the power, and they had to endure bitter persecution for years, and for many years, and every year it was getting worse ; and they without any hope of relief because they had no knowledge of God or Mary or of anything else which concerned heaven. For that reason they could not put trust in any person beyond Crom Dubh, because they thought, bad as he was, that it was he who was giving them the light of the day, the darkness of the night, and the change of seasons.

It was well, brother of my heart. During this time St. Patrick was going throughout Ireland, working diligently and baptizing many people. On he went until he came to Fo-choill or Foghill ; and at that time and for long afterwards there were nothing but woods that grew in that place, but there is neither branch nor tree there now. However, to pursue the story, St. Patrick began explaining to the Pagans about the light and glory of the heavens. Some of them gave ear to him, but the most of them paid him no attention. After he had taken all those who listened to him to the place which was called the Well of the Branch to baptize them, and when he had them baptized, the people called the well Tobar Phadraig, or Patrick's Well, and that is there ever since.

When these Pagans got the seal of Christ on their forehead, and knowledge of the Holy Trinity, they began telling St. Patrick about the doings of Crom Dubh and his evil ways, and they besought him if he had any power from the All-mighty Father to chastise Crom Dubh, rightly or wrongly, or to give him the Christian faith if it were possible.

It was well, brother, St. Patrick passed on over through Tráigh Leacan, up Béal Trághadh, down Craobhach, and down under the Logán, the name that was on Crom Dubh's place before St. Patrick came. When St. Patrick reached the Logán, which is near the present Ballycastle, he was within a quarter of a mile of Crom Dubh's house, and at the same time Crom Dubh and Téideach his son were trying a bout of wrestling with one another, while Saidhthe Suaraighe was stretched out on the ground from ear to tail. With the squeezing they were giving

one another they never observed St. Patrick making
for them until Saidhthe Suaraighe put a howling bark
out of her, and with that the pair looked behind them and
they saw St. Patrick and his defensive company with
him, making for them ; and in the twinkling of an eye
the two rushed forward, clapping their hands and setting
Saidhthe Suaraighe at them and encouraging her.

With that Téideach put his fore finger into his mouth
and let a whistle calling for Coinn Iotair, for she was at
that same time hunting with Clonnach on the top of Glen
Lasaire, and Glen Lasaire is nearly two miles from Dun
Phadraig, but she was not as long as while you'd be saying
De' raisias [Deo Gratias] coming from Glen Lasaire when
she heard the sound of the whistle. They urged the two
bitches against St. Patrick, and at the same time they did
not know what sort of man St. Patrick was or where he
came from.

The two bitches made for him and coals of fire out of
their mouths, and a blue venemous light burning in their
eyes, with the dint of venom and wickedness, but just as
they were going to seize St. Patrick he cut [marked] a ring
round about him with the crozier which he had in his
hand, and before the dogs reached the verge of the ring
St. Patrick spoke as follows :—

A lock on thy claws, a lock on thy tooth,
A lock on Coinn Iotair of the fury.
A lock on the son and on the daughter of Saidhthe Suaraighe.
A lock quickly, quickly on you.

Before St. Patrick began to utter these words there
was a froth of foam round their mouths, and their hair
was standing up as strong as harrow-pins with their fury,

but after this as they came nearer to St. Patrick they
began to lay down their ears and wag their tails. And
when Crom Dubh saw that, he had like to faint, because he
knew when they laid down their ears that they would not
do any hurt to him they were attacking. The moment
they reached St. Patrick they began jumping up upon
him and making friendly with him. They licked both
his feet from the top of his great toe[1] to the butt of his
ankle, and that affection [thus manifesting itself] is
amongst dogs from that day to this. St. Patrick began
to stroke them with his hand and he went on making
towards Crom Dubh, with the dogs walking at his heels.
Crom Dubh ran until he came to the fire and he stood up
beside the fire, so that he might throw St. Patrick
into it when he should come as far as it. But as St.
Patrick knew the strength of the fire beforehand he lifted
a stone in his hand, signed the sign of the cross on the
stone, and flung the stone so as to throw it into the middle
of the flames, and on the moment the fire went down to the
lowest depths of the ground, in such a way that the hole
is there yet to be seen, from that day to this, and it is called
Poll na Sean-tuine, the hole of the old fire (?), and when
the tide fills, the water comes in to the bottom of the hole,
and it would draw " deaf cows out of woods "—the
noise that comes out of the hole when the tide is coming
in.

It was well, company[2] of the world ; when Crom Dubh
saw that the fire had departed out of sight, and that the dogs
had failed him and given him no help (a thing they had

---

[1] Rather " the space between the toes."
[2] A variant of " it was well, my dear."

never done before), he himself and Téideach struck out like a blast of March wind until they reached the house, and St. Patrick came after them. They had not far to go, for the fire was near the house. When St. Patrick approached it he began to talk aloud with Crom Dubh, and he did his best to change him to a good state of grace, but it failed him to put the seal of Christ on his forehead, for he would not give any ear to St. Patrick's words.

Now there was no trick of deviltry, druidism, witchcraft, or black art in his heart, which he did not work for all he was able, trying to gain the victory over St. Patrick, but it was all no use for him, for the words of God were more powerful than the deviltry of the fairy] sweetheart.

With the dint of the fury that was on Crom Dubh and on Téideach his son, they began snapping and grinding their teeth, and so outrageous was their fury that St. Patrick gave a blow of his crozier to the cliff under the base of the gable of the house, and he separated that much of the cliff from the cliffs on the mainland, and that is to be seen there to-day just as well as the first day, and that is the cliff that is called Dún Briste or Broken Fort.

To pursue the story. All that much of the cliff is a good many yards out in the sea from the cliff on the mainland, so Crom Dubh and his son had to remain there until the midges and the scaldcrows had eaten the flesh off their bones. And that is the death that Crom Dubh got, and that is the second man that midges ate,[1] and our ancient shanachies say that the first man that midges ate was Judas

---

[1] See the story of Mary's Well, p. 17.

after he had hanged himself ; and that is the cause why the bite of the midges is so sharp as it is.

To pursue the story still further. When Clonnach saw what had happened to his father he took fright, and he was terrified of St. Patrick, and he began burning the mountain until he had all that side of the land set on fire. So violently did the mountains take fire on each side of him that himself could not escape, and they say that he himself was burned to a lump amongst them.

St. Patrick returned back to Fochoill and round through Baile na Pairce, the Town of the Field, and Bein Buidhe, the Yellow Ben, and back to Clochar. The people gathered in multitudes from every side doing honourable homage to St. Patrick, and the pride of the world on them that an end had been made of Crom Dubh.

There was a well near and handy, and he brought the great multitude round about the well, and he never left mother's son or man's daughter without setting on their faces the wave of baptism and the seal of Christ on their foreheads. They washed and scoured the walls of the well, and all round about it, and they got forked branches and limbs of trees and bound white and blue ribbons on them, and set them round about the well, and every one of them bowed down on his knees saying their prayers of thankfulness to God, and as an entertainment for St. Patrick on account of his having put an end to the sway of Crom Dubh.

After making an end of offering up their prayers every man of them drank three sups of water out of the well, and there is not a year from that out that the people used not to make a *turus* or pilgrimage to the well, on the

anniversary of that day ; and that day is the last Sunday
of the seventh month, and the name the Irish speakers
call the month by in that place is the month of Lughnas
[August] and the name of the Sunday is Crom Dubh's
Sunday, but, the name that the English speakers call
the Sunday by, is Garland Sunday. There is never a
year from that to this that there does not be a meeting
in Cill Chuimin, for that is the place where the well is.
They come far and near to make a pilgrimage to the well ;
and a   number of other people go there too, to amuse
themselves and drink and spend.   And I believe that the
most of that rakish lot go there making a mock of the
Christian Irish-speakers who are offering up their prayers
to their holy patron Patrick, high head of their religion.

Cuimin's well is the name of this well, for its name was
changed during the time of Saint Cuimin on account of
all the miraculous things he did there, and he is buried
within a perch of the well in Cill Chuimin.

There does be a gathering on the same Sunday at
Dún Padraig or Downpatrick at the well which is called
Tobar Brighde or Briget's Well beside Cill Brighde, and
close to Dún Briste ; but, love of my heart, since the
English jargon began a short time ago in that place the
old Christian custom of the Christians is almost utterly
gone off.

There now ye have it as I got it, and if ye don't like it
add to it your complaints.[1]

---

[1] Apparently tell it with your complaint added to it.

MARY'S WELL.

PREFACE.

The following story I got from Proinsias O'Conchubhair when he was in Athlone about fifteen years ago, and he heard it from a woman who herself came from Ballintubber, Co. Mayo. This Ballintubber is not to be confounded with the Roscommon place of the same name, which is called in Irish Baile-an-tobair Ui Chonchubhair, or O'Conor's Ballintubber. The Mayo Ballintubber is celebrated for its splendid Abbey, founded by one of the Stauntons, a tribe who took the name of Mac a mhilidh (Mac-a-Veely or Mac Evilly) in Irish. The prophesy is current in Mayo that when the abbey is re-roofed Ireland will be free. My friend, Colonel Maurice Moore, told me that when he was a young boy he often wondered why the people did not roof the abbey, and so free Ireland without any more trouble. The tomb of the notorious Shaun na Sagart, the priest-hunter, which is not far away from it, is still pointed out by the people. It is probably he who is the " spy " in the following story, although his name is not mentioned. He belonged to a class who appear to have made it their business to track down priests and friars, which is alluded to in the following lines :

> It is no use for me to be saying it,
> Seeing your kinship with Donough-of-the-priest
> And with Owen-of-the-cards his father,
> With the people who used to cut off heads
> To put them into leather bags,
> To bring them down with them to the ci'y,
> And to bring home the gold they got for them,
> For sustenance for wives and children.

It will be noticed that it was Mary Mother who put the curing of the Blind into this well, and Owen O Duffy, the poet, says of her that she is

> A woman who put a hedge round every country.
> A woman to whom right inclines.
> A woman greatest in strength and power,
> A woman softest (*i.e.*, most generous) about red gold.
> A woman by whom is quenched the anger of the king.
> A woman who gives sight to the blind.

For the Irish text of this story, see " Religious Songs of Connacht," vol. I., p. III.

The abbey where the holy well broke out was, according to some, founded by Cathal O Conor in 1216, for the Augustinians, and was dedicated to the Holy Trinity.

THE STORY.

LONG ago there was a blessed well in Ballintubber (*i.e.*, town of the well), in the county Mayo. There was once a monastery in the place where the well is now, and it was on the spot where stood the altar of the monastery that the well broke out. The monastery was on the side of a hill, but when Cromwell and his band of destroyers came to this country, they overthrew the monastery, and never left stone on top of stone in the altar that they did not throw down.

A year from the day that they threw down the altar— that was Lady Day in spring—the well broke out on the site of the altar, and it is a wonderful thing to say, that there was not one drop of water in the stream that was at the foot of the hill from the day that the well broke out.

There was a poor friar going the road the same day, and he went out of his way to say a prayer upon the site of the blessed altar, and there was great wonder on him when he saw a fine well in its place. He fell on his knees and began to say his paternoster, when he heard a voice saying : " Put off your brogues, you are upon blessed ground, you are on the brink of Mary's Well, and there is the curing of thousands of blind in it ; there shall be a person cured by the water of that well for every person who heard mass in front of the altar that was in the place where the well is now, if they be dipped three times in it, in the name of the Father, the Son, and the Holy Spirit."

When the friar had his prayers said, he looked up and saw a large white dove upon a fir tree near him. It was the dove who was speaking. The friar was dressed in false clothes, because there was a price on his head, as great as would be on the head of a wild-dog [wolf].

At any rate, he proclaimed the story to the people of the little village, and it was not long till it went out through the country. It was a poor place, and the people in it had nothing [to live in] but huts, and these filled with smoke. On that account there were a great many weak-eyed people amongst them. With the dawn, on the next day, there were above forty people at Mary's Well, and there was never man nor woman of them but came back with good sight.

The fame of Mary's Well went through the country, and it was not long till there were pilgrims from every county coming to it, and nobody went back without being cured ; and at the end of a little time even people from other countries used to be coming to it.

There was an unbeliever living near Mary's Well. It

was a gentleman he was, and he did not believe in the cure. He said there was nothing in it but pishtrogues (charms), and to make a mock of the people he brought a blind ass, that he had, to the well, and he dipped its head under the water. The ass got its sight, but the scoffer was brought home as blind as the sole of your shoe.

At the end of a year it so happened that there was a priest working as a gardener with the gentleman who was blind. The priest was dressed like a workman, and nobody at all knew that it was a priest who was in it. One day the gentleman was sickly, and he asked his servant to take him out into the garden. When he came to the place where the priest was working he sat down. "Isn't it a great pity," says he, "that I cannot see my fine garden ? "

The gardener took compassion on him, and said, " I know where there is a man who would cure you, but there is a price on his head on account of his religion."

" I give my word that I'll do no spying on him, and I'll pay him well for his trouble," said the gentleman.

" But perhaps you would not like to go through the mode of curing that he has," says the gardener.

" I don't care what mode he has, if he gives me my sight," said the gentleman.

Now, the gentleman had an evil character, because he betrayed a number of priests before that. Bingham was the name that was on him. However, the priest took courage and said, " Let your coach be ready on to-morrow morning, and I will drive you to the place of the cure ; neither coachman nor anyone else may be present but myself, and do not tell to anyone at all where you are going, or give anyone a knowledge of what is your business."

On the morning of the next day Bingham's coach was ready, and he himself got into it, with the gardener driving him. " Do you remain at home this time," says he to the coachman, " and the gardener will drive me." The coachman was a villain, and there was jealousy on him. He conceived the idea of watching the coach to see what way they were to go. His blessed vestments were on the priest, inside of his other clothes. When they came to Mary's Well the priest said to him, " I am going to get back your sight for you in the place where you lost it." Then he dipped him three times in the well, in the name of the Father, the Son, and the Holy Spirit, and his sight came to him as well as ever it was.

" I'll give you a hundred pounds," said Bingham, " as soon as I go home."

The coachman was watching, and as soon as he saw the priest in his blessed vestments, he went to the people of the law, and betrayed the priest. He was taken and hanged, without judge, without judgment. The man who was after getting back his sight could have saved the priest, but he did not speak a word in his behalf.

About a month after this another priest came to Bingham, and he dressed like a gardener, and he asked work of Bingham, and got it from him ; but he was not long in his service until an evil thing happened to Bingham. He went out one day walking through his fields, and there met him a good-looking girl, the daughter of a poor man, and he assaulted her and left her half dead. The girl had three brothers, and they took an oath that they would kill him as soon as they could get hold of him. They had not long to wait. They caught him in the same place where he assaulted the girl, and hanged him on a tree, and left him there hanging.

On the morning of the next day millions of flies were gathered like a great hill round about the tree, and nobody could go near it on account of the foul smell that was round the place, and anyone who would go near it the midges would blind them.

Bingham's wife and son offered a hundred pounds to anyone who would bring out the body. A good many people made an effort to do that, but they were not able. They got dust to shake on the flies, and boughs of trees to beat them with, but they were not able to scatter them, nor to go as far as the tree. The foul smell was getting worse, and the neighbours were afraid that the flies and noisome corpse would bring a plague upon them.

The second priest was at this time a gardener with Bingham, but the people of the house did not know that it was a priest who was in it, for if the people of the law or the spies knew, they would take and hang him. The Catholics went to Bingham's wife and told her that they knew a man who would banish the flies. "Bring him to me," said she, "and if he is able to banish the flies, that is not the reward he'll get, but seven times as much."

" But," said they, " if the people of the law knew, they would take him and hang him, as they hung the man who got back the sight of his eyes for him before." " But,"

said she, " could not he banish the flies without the knowledge of the people of the law ? "

" We don't know," said they, " until we take counsel
with him."

That night they took counsel with the priest and told
him what Bingham's wife said.

" I have only an earthly life to lose," said the priest,
" and I shall give it up for the sake of the poor people,
for there will be a plague in the country unless I banish the
flies.   On to-morrow morning I shall make an attempt
to banish them in the name of God, and I have hope
and confidence in God that he will save me from my
enemies.   Go to the lady now, and tell her that I shall be
near the tree at sunrise to-morrow morning, and tell her
to have men ready to put the corpse in the grave."

They went to the lady and told her all the priest
said.

" If it succeeds with him," said she, " I shall have the
reward ready for him, and I shall order seven men to be
present."

The priest spent that night in prayer, and half an hour
before sunrise he went to the place where his blessed vestments were hidden ; he put these on, and with a cross in
one hand, and with holy-water in the other, he went to
the place where were the flies. He then began reading out
of his book and scattering holy-water on the flies, in the
name of the Father, the Son, and the Holy Ghost. The
hill of flies rose, and flew up into the air, and made the
heaven as dark as night. The people did not know
where they went, but at the end of half an hour there was
not one of them to be seen

There was great joy on the people, but it was not long till they saw the spy coming, and they called to the priest to run away as quick as it was in him to run. The priest gave to the butts (took to his heels), and the spy followed him, and a knife in each hand with him. When he was not able to come up with the priest he flung the knife after him. As the knife was flying out past the priest's shoulder he put up his left hand and caught it, and without ever looking behind him he flung it back. It struck the man and went through his heart, so that he fell dead and the priest went free.

The people got the body of Bingham and buried it in the grave, but when they went to bury the body of the spy they found thousands of rats round about it, and there was not a morsel of flesh on his bones that they had not eaten. They would not stir from the body, and the people were not able to rout them away, so that they had to leave the bones over-ground.

The priest hid away his blessed vestments and was working in the garden when Bingham's wife sent for him, and told him to take the reward that was for banishing the flies, and to give it to the man who banished them, if he knew him.

"I do know him, and he told me to bring him the reward to-night, because he has the intention of leaving the country before the law-people hang him."

"Here it is for you," said she, as she handed him a purse of gold.

On the morning of the next day the priest went to the brink of the sea, and found a ship that was going to France. He went on board, and as soon as he had left

the harbour he put his priest's-clothes on him, and gave
thanks to God for bringing him safe. We do not know
what happened to him from that out.

After that, blind and sore-eyed people used to be
coming to Mary's Well, and not a person of them ever
returned without being cured. But there never yet was
anything good in this country that was not spoilt by somebody, and the well was spoilt in this way.

There was a girl in Ballintubber and she was about to be
married, when there came a half-blind old woman to her
asking alms in the honour of God and Mary.

" I've nothing to give to an old blind-thing of a hag,
it's bothered with them I am," said the girl.

" That the marriage ring may never go on you until
you're as blind as myself," says the old woman.

Next day, in the morning, the young girl's eyes were
sore, and the morning after that she was nearly blind,
and the neighbours said to her that she ought to go to
Mary's Well.

In the morning, early, she rose up and went to the
well, but what should she see at it but the old woman
who asked the alms of her, sitting on the brink, combing
her head over the blessed well.

" Destruction on you, you nasty hag, is it dirtying
Mary's Well you are ? " said the girl. " Get out of that
or I'll break your neck."

" You have no honour nor regard for God or Mary, you
refused to give alms in honour of them, and for that
reason you shall not dip yourself in the well."

The girl caught a hold of the hag trying to pull her

from the well, and with the dragging that was between them, the two of them fell into the well and were drowned.

From that day to this there has been no cure in the well.

———

HOW COVETOUSNESS CAME INTO THE CHURCH.

PREFACE.

I heard this story from a workman of the late Mr. Reding-
ton Roche, of Rye Hill (in Irish, Druim an tseagail) near
Monivea, Co. Galway. It was in Irish prose, but it re-
minded me so strongly of those strange semi-comic mediæval moralities common at an early date to most European
languages—such pieces as Goethe has imitated in his poem
of "St. Peter and the Horse Shoe"—that I could not
resist the temptation to turn it into rhyme. I have heard
a story something like this in the County Tipperary, only
that it was told in English. This story is the reason (I
think the narrator added) of the well-known proverbial
rann :

> Four clerks who are not covetous
> Four Frenchmen who are not yellow,
> Four shoemakers who are not liars,
> Those are a dozen who are not in the country.

More than one piece of both English and French literature
founded upon the same motif as this story will occur to the
reader. The original will be found at p. 161 of "The
Religious Songs of Connacht," vol I.

THE STORY

> As once our Saviour and St. Peter
> Were walking over the hills together,
> In a lonesome place that was by the sea,
> Beside the border of Galilee,
> Just as the sun to set began
> Whom should they meet but a poor old man !

His coat was ragged, his hat was torn,
He seemed most wretched and forlorn,
Penury stared in his haggard eye
And he asked an alms as they passed him by.

Peter had only a copper or two,
So he looked to see what the Lord would do.
The man was trembling—it seemed to him—
With hunger and cold in every limb.
But, nevertheless, our Lord looked grave,
He turned away and he nothing gave.
And Peter was vexed awhile at that
And wondered what our Lord was at,
Because he had thought him much too good
To ever refuse a man for food.
But though he wondered he nothing said,
Nor asked the cause, for he was afraid.

It happened that the following day
They both returned that very way,
And whom should they meet where the man had been
But a highway robber gaunt and lean !
And in his belt a naked sword—
For an alms he, too, besought the Lord.
" He's a fool," thought Peter, " to cross us thus,
He won't get anything from us."
But Peter was seized with such surprise
He scarcely could believe his eyes,
When he saw the Master, without a word,
Give to the man who had the sword.

After the man was gone again
His wonder Peter could not restrain
But turning to our Saviour said :
" Master, the man who asked for bread,
The poor old man of yesterday,
Why did you turn from him away ?
But to this robber, this shameless thief,
Give, when he asked you for relief.
I thought it most strange for *you* to do ;
We needn't have feared him, we were two.
I have a sword here, as you see,
And could have used it as well as he ;
And I am taller by a span,
For he was only a little man."

" Peter," said the Lord, " you see
Things but as they *seem* to be.
Look within and see behind,
Know the heart and read the mind,
'Tis not long before you know
Why it was I acted so."

After this it chanced one day
Our Lord and Peter went astray,
Wandering on a mountain wide,
Nothing but waste on every side.
Worn with hunger, faint with thirst,
Peter followed, the Lord went first.
Then began a heavy rain,
Lightning gleamed and gleamed again,
Another deluge poured from heaven,
The slanting hail swept tempest-driven.
Then when fainting, frozen, spent,
A man came towards them through the bent.
And Peter trembled with cold and fright,
When he knew again the robber wight.
But the robber brought them to his cave,
And what he had he freely gave.
He brought them wine, he gave them bread,
He strewed them rushes for a bed,
He lent them both a clean attire
And dried their clothes before the fire,
And when they rose the following day
He gave them victuals for the way,
And never left them till he showed
And put them on the straightest road.

" The Master was right," thought Peter then,
" The robber is better than better men.
" There's many an honest man," thought he,
" Who never did as much for me."

They had not left the robber's ground
Above an hour, when, lo, they found
A man upon the mountain track
Lying dead upon his back.
And Peter soon, with much surprise,
The beggarman did recognize.
" Ochone ! " thought Peter, " we had no right
To refuse him alms the other night.
He's dead from the cold and want of food,
And we're partly guilty of his blood."
" Peter," said our Lord, " go now
Feel his pockets and let us know
What he has within his coat."
Peter turned them inside out,
And found within the lining plenty
Of silver coins, and of gold ones twenty.
" My Lord," said Peter, " now I know
Why it was you acted so.
Whatever you say or do with men,
I never will think you wrong again."
" Peter," said our Saviour, " take
And throw those coins in yonder lake,

That none may fish them up again,
For money is often the curse of men."

Peter gathered the coins together,
And crossed to the lake through bog and heather.
But he thought in his mind " It's a real sin
To be flinging this lovely money in.
We're often hungry, we're often cold,
And money is money—I'll keep the gold
To spend on the Master, he needs the pelf,
For he's very neglectful of himself."
Then down with a splash does Peter throw
The *silver* coins to the lake below,
And hopes our Lord from the splash would think
He had thrown the whole from off the brink.
And then before our Lord he stood
And looked as innocent as he could.

Our Lord said : " Peter, regard your soul ;
Are you sure you have now thrown in the whole ? "
" Yes, all," said Peter, " is gone below,
But a few gold pieces I wouldn't throw,
Since I thought we might find them very good
For a sup to drink, or a bite of food.
Because our own are nearly out,
And they're inconvenient to do without.
But, if you wish it, of course I'll go
And fling the rest of the lot below."

" Ah, Peter, Peter," said our Lord,
" You should have obeyed me at my word.
For a greedy man you are I see,
And a greedy man you will ever be ;
A covetous man you are of gain,
And a covetous man you will remain."

So that's the reason, as I've been told,
All clergy are since so fond of gold.

KNOCK   MULRUANA.

PREFACE.

This story was told by my friend, Mr. Peter McGinley,
who printed it in 1897 in the " Gaelic Journal " of that year.
He told me that though the story came from the Irish
speaking part of the country it was in English it was first
repeated to him when he was a young boy, and he retold
it in Irish, without any change in the story itself.   He says
that he feels sure it is just as he heard it.   The story comes
from Gleann Domhain, which is near Gartan, in Donegal,
celebrated as the birthplace of Colmcille, and Cnoc Mhaoil-
ruandha is near at hand, and the lake is a little below it.
The proverb, " as I have burned the candle I'll burn the
inch," does not, he says, always signify impenitence, but
means rather to hold out in any course, good or evil, until
the last.   The name Maolruanadha, which I have shortened
into Mulruana, is variously anglicised Mulroney and
Moroney.   This story may remind the reader a little of
Lewis's ', Monk."

THE   STORY.

On this side of Glen Domhain, there is a little hill
whose name is Mulroney's Hill, and this is the reason
why it was given that name.

In old times there was a man living in a little house
on the side of the hill, and Mulruana was his name.
He was a pious holy man, and hated the world's vanities

so much that he became a hermit, and he was always alone in that house, without anyone in his neighbourhood. He used to be always praying and subduing himself. He used to drink nothing but water, and used to eat nothing but berries and the wild roots which he used to get in the mountains and throughout the glens. His fame and reputation were going through the country for the holy earnest life that he was living.

However, great jealousy seized the Adversary at the piety of this man, and he sent many evil spirits to put temptations on him. But on account of all his prayers and piety it failed those evil-spirits to get the victory over him, so that they all returned back to hell with the report of the steadfastness and loyalty of Mulruana in the service of God.

Then great anger seized Satan, so that he sent further demons, each more powerful than the other, to put temptation on Mulruana. Not one of them succeeded in even coming near the hut of the holy man. Nor did it fare any better with them whenever he came outside, for he used always to be attentive to his prayers and ever musing on holy things. Then every evil-spirit of them used to go back to hell and used to tell the devil that there was no use contending with Mulruana, for that God himself and His angels were keeping him and giving him help.

That account made Satan mad entirely, so that he determined at last to go himself, hoping to destroy Mulruana, and to draw him out of the proper path. Accordingly he came one evening at nightfall, in the guise of a young woman, and asked the good man for lodging. Mulruana rudely refused the pretended woman, and banished her away from his door, although he felt a compassion for her because the night was wet and stormy, and he thought that the girl was without house and shelter from the rain and cold. But what the woman did was to go round to the back of the house and play music, and it was the sweetest and most melancholy music that man ever heard.

Because Mulruana had had a pity for the poor girl at the first, he listened now to her music, and took great delight in it, and had much joy of it, but he did not allow her into his hut. At the hour of midnight the devil went back to hell, but he had a shrewd notion that he had won the game and that he had caught the holy man. Mulruana had quiet during the remainder of the night, but instead of continuing at his prayers, as was his custom, he spent the end of the night, almost till the dawn of day, thinking of the beauty of the girl and of the sweetness of her music

The day after that the devil came at the fall of night in the same likeness, and again asked lodging of Mulruana. Mulruana refused that, although he did not like to do it, but he remembered the vow he had made never to let a woman or a girl into his hut. The pretended woman went round to the back of the house, and she was playing music that was like fairy music until it was twelve o'clock, when she had to go away with herself to hell. The man inside was listening to the playing and taking great delight in it, and when she ceased there came over him melancholy and trouble of mind. He never slept a wink that night, and he never said a word of his prayers either, but eagerly thinking[1] of the young woman, and his heart going astray with the beauty of her form and the sweetness of her voice.

On the morning of the next day Mulruana rose from his bed, and it is likely that it was the whisper of an angel he heard, because he remembered that it was not right for him to pay such heed to a girl and to forget his prayers. He bowed his knees and began to pray strongly and earnestly, and made a firm resolve that he would not think more about the girl, and that he would not listen to her music. But, after all, he did not succeed in obtaining a complete victory over his thoughts concerning the young woman, and consequently he was between two notions until the evening came.

When the night was well dark the Adversary came again in the shape of the girl, and she even more beautiful and more lovely than she was before, and asked the man for a night's lodging. He remembered his vow and the resolve he had made that day in the morning, and he refused her, and threatened her that she should not come again to trouble him, and he drove her away with rough sharp words, and with a stern, churlish countenance, as though there were a great anger on him. He went into his hut and the girl remained near the hut outside, and she weeping and lamenting and shedding tears.

When Mulruana saw the girl weeping and keening piteously he conceived a great pity for her, and compassion for her came to him, and desire, and he did not free his heart from those evil inclinations, since he had

---

[1] This idiom, borrowed from the Irish, is very common in Anglo-Irish. It is not governed by the rules of English grammar.

not made his prayers on that day with a heart as pure as
had been his wont, and he listened willingly and gladly.
It was not long until he came out, himself, in spite of his
vow and his good resolutions, and invited the pretended
woman to come into his hut. Small delay she made in
going in !

It was then the King of Grace took pity at this man
being lost without giving him time to amend himself,
since he had ever been truly pious, diligent, humane,
well disposed and of good works, until this great temptation
came over him. For that reason God sent an angel to
him with a message to ask him to repent. The angel
came to Mulruana's house and went inside. Then the
devil leapt to his feet, uttered a fearful screech, changed
his colour, his shape, and his appearance. His own
devilish form and demoniac appearance came upon him.
He turned away from the angel like a person blinded with
a great shining or blaze of light, and went out of the
hut.

His senses nearly departed from Mulruana with the
terror that overcame him. When he came to himself
again the angel made clear to him how great was the sin
to which he had given way, and how God had sent him
to him to ask him to repent. But Mulruana never
believed a word he said. He knew that it was the devil
who had been in his company in the guise of a young
woman. He remembered the sin to which he had con-
sented, so that he considered himself to be so guilty that it
would be impossible for him ever to obtain forgiveness
from God. He thought that it was deceiving him the
angel was, when he spoke of repentance and forgiveness.

The angel was patient with him and spoke gently. He
told him of the love and friendship of God and how He
would never refuse forgiveness to the truly penitent,
no matter how heavy his share of sins. Mulruana did not
listen to him, but a drowning-man's-cry issued out of his
mouth always, that he was lost, and he ever-cursing God,
the devil and himself. The angel never ceased, but entreating and beseeching him to turn to God and make repentance—but it was no use for him. Mulruana was as
hard and as stubborn as he was before, all the time taking
great oaths and blaspheming God.

All the time the angel was speaking he had the appearance of a burning candle in his hand. At long last, when
the candle was burnt all but about an inch, a gloom fell
over the countenance of the angel and he stood out from
Mulruana, and threatened him, and told him that his term
of grace was almost expired, and, said he, unless you make
repentance before this inch of candle is burnt away, God
will grant you no more respite, and you will be damned
for ever.

Then there came silence on Mulruana for a while,
as though he were about to follow the advice of the
angel. But then on the spot he thought of the sin
that he had done. On that, despair seized him, and the
answer he gave the angel was, " as I have burned the
candle I'll burn the inch." Then the angel spoke to
him with a loud and terrible voice, announcing to
him that he was now indeed accursed of God, and,
said he, " thou shalt die to-morrow of thirst." Mulruana answered him with no submission, and said, " O
lying angel, I know now that you are deceiving me. It

is impossible that I should die of thirst in this place, and
so much water round about me.   There is, outside there,
a well of spring water that was never dry, and there is a
stream beside the gable of the house which would turn the
wheel of a great mill no matter how dry the summer day,
and down there is Loch Beithe on which a fleet of ships
might float.   It is a great folly for you to say that anybody
could die of thirst in this place."   But the angel departed
from him without an answer.

Mulruana went to lie down after that, but, if he did, he
never slept a wink through great trouble of spirit.   Next
morning, on his rising early, the sharpest thirst that man
ever felt came upon him.   He leapt out of his bed and
went to the stoap [pail] for water, but there was not a
drop in it.   Out with him then to the well, but he did not
find a drop there either.   He turned on his foot towards
the stream that was beside the house, but it was dry before
him down to the gravel.   The banks and the pebbles
in the middle of it were as dry as though they had never
seen a drop of water for a year.   Mulruana remembered
then the prophecy of the angel and he started.   A quaking
of terror came upon him, and his thirst was growing every
moment.   He went running at full speed to Loch Beithe,
but when he came to the brink of the lake he uttered one
awful cry and fell in a heap on the ground.   Loch Beithe
too was dry before him

That is how a cowherd found him the next day, lying
on the brink of the lake, his eyes starting out of his head,
his tongue stretched out of his throat, and a lump of white
froth round his mouth.   His awful appearance was such
that fear would not let the people go near him to bury

him, and his body was left there until birds of prey and
wild dogs took it away with them.

That is how it happened Mulruana as a consequence
of his sin, his impenitence, and his despair, and that is
the reason why it is not right for any one to use the old
saying, " As I've burnt the candle I'll burn the inch,"
and yonder is " Cnoc Mhaoilruanadha," Mulruana's Hill,
as a witness to the truth of this story

THE STONE OF TRUTH OR THE MERCHANT OF THE SEVEN BAGS.

PREFACE.

The Stone of Truth is as old as the times of the Druids. The celebrated Lia Fail was a stone of truth. Certain stones were oracles in old times. There was a stone in Oriel, and a celebrated stone called Cloeh Labhrais in the south which were oracular. A man who suspected his wife made her stand upon the southern stone to swear that she had not wronged him. She spied a man she knew too well far away upon the mountain, and swore she had never done anything she ought not to have done—no more than with that man on the skyline. The heart of the stone was broken with this equivocation, and it burst asunder exclaiming bíonn an fírinne féin searb, " even truth itself is bitter." The idea is Pagan, but this story is motivated in a Christian manner, by alleging that the stone derived its miraculous power from St. Patrick's having knelt on it in prayer. I got this story from Francis O'Conor. For the original Irish, see " Religious Songs of Connacht," vol. II., p. 230.

THE STORY.

THERE was a man in it, hundreds and hundreds of years ago, whose name was Páidin[1] O Ciarbháin [Keerwaun, or Kerwin] and he was living close to Cong in West Connacht. Páidin was a strange man ; he did not believe in God or in anything about him. It's often the priest thought to bring

---

[1] Pronounced " Paudyeen."

him to Mass, but it was no use for him, for Páidin would not take the advice of priest or bishop. He believed that man was like the beast, and he believed that when man died there was no more about him.

Páidin lived an evil life ; he used to be going from house to house by day, and stealing in the night.

Now, at the time that St. Patrick was in West Connacht seeking to make Christians of the Pagans, he went down one day upon his knees, on a great flag stone, to utter prayers, and he left after him a great virtue in the same stone, for anybody who might speak above that stone, it was necessary for him to tell the clear truth, he could not tell a lie, and for that reason the people gave the name to that flag of the Stone of Truth

Páidin used always to have a great fear of this stone, and it's often he intended to steal it. One night when he found an opportunity he hoisted the stone on his back, took it away with him, and threw it down into a great valley between two hills, seven miles from the place where it used to be, and the rogue thought that he was all right ; but the stone was back in its old place that same night without his knowing.

Another night after that he stole the geese of the parish priest, and as the people doubted him, they said that they would bring him to the Stone of Truth. Páidin was laughing in his own mind, for he knew that he had the stone stolen ; but great was the surprise that was on him when he saw the stone before him in its own place. When he was put above the stone he was obliged to tell that he had stolen the geese, and he got a great beating from the priest. He made a firm resolution then that if he got an opportunity at the stone again, he would put it in a place that it would never come out of.

A couple of nights after that he got his opportunity again, and stole the stone a second time. He threw it down into a great deep hole, and he went home rejoicing in himself. But he did not go a quarter of a mile from the place until he heard a great noise coming after him. He looked behind him and he saw a lot of little people, and they dressed in clothes as white as snow. There came such fear over Páidin that he was not able to walk one step, until the little people came up with him, and they carrying the Stone of Truth with them. A man of them spoke to him and said : " O accursed Páidin, carry this stone back to the place where you got it, or you shall pay dearly for it."

" I will and welcome," said Páidin.

They put the stone upon his back and they returned the road on which they had come. But as the devil was putting temptation upon Páidin, he went and threw the stone into a hole that was deeper than the first hole, a hole which the people made to go hiding in when the war would be coming. The stone remained in that hole for more than seven years, and no one knew where it was but Páidin only.

At the end of that time Páidin was going by the side of the churchyard, when he looked up at a cross that was standing there, and he fell into a faint. When he came to himself, there was a man before him and he clothed as white as the snow. He spoke to him and said : "O accursed Páidin, you are guilty of the seven deadly sins, and unless you do penance you shall go to hell. I am an angel from God, and I will put a penance on you. I will put seven bags upon you and you must carry them for one and twenty years. After that time go before the great cross that shall be in the town of Cong, and say three times, ' My soul to God and Mary,' spend a pious life until then, and you will go to heaven. Go to the priest now, if you are obedient (and ready) to receive my counsel."

" I am obedient," said Páidin, " but the people will be making a mock of me."

" Never mind the mock, it won't last long," said the angel.

After this conversation a deep sleep fell upon Páidin, and when he awoke there were seven bags upon him, and the angel was gone away. There were two bags on his right side, two bags on his left side, and three others on his back, and they were stuck so fast upon him that he thought that it was growing on him they were. They were the colour of his own skin, and there was skin on them. Next day when Páidin went among the people he put wonder on them, and they called him the Merchant of the Seven Bags, and that name stuck to him until he died.

Páidin began a new life now. He went to the priest, and he showed him the seven bags that were on him, and he told him the reason that they were put on him. The priest gave him good advice and a great coat to cover the seven bags with ; and after that Páidin used to be going from house to house and from village to village asking alms, and there used never be a Sunday or holiday that he would not be at Mass, and there used to be a welcome before him in every place.

About seven years after that Páidin was going by the side of the hole into which he had thrown the Stone of Truth. He came to the brink of the hole, went down on his two knees and asked God to send him up the stone. When his prayer was ended he saw the stone coming up, and hundreds of white doves round about it. The stone was rising and ever rising until it came into Páidin's presence on the ground, and then the doves went back again. The next day he went to the priest and told him everything about the Stone of Truth, and the way it came up out of the hole. " I will go with you," said the priest, " until I see this great wonder." The priest went with him to the hole and he saw the Stone of Truth. And he saw another thing which put great wonder on him ; thousands and thousands of doves flying round about the mouth of the hole, going down into it and coming up again. The priest called the place Poll na gColum or the Dove's Hole, and that name is on it until the present day. The blessed stone was brought into Cong, and it was not long until a grand cross was erected over it, and from that day to this people come from every place to look at the Doves' Hole, and the old people believed that they were St. Patrick's angels who were in those doves.

The Stone of Truth was for years after that in Cong, and it is certain that it did great good, for it kept many people from committing crimes. But it was stolen at last, and there is no account of it from that out.

Páidin lived until he was four score years of age, and bore his share of penance piously. When the one and twenty years that the angel gave him were finished, and he carrying the seven bags throughout that time, there came

a messenger in a dream to say to him that his life in this
world was finished, and that he must go the next day
before the Cross of Cong and give himself up to God and
Mary. Early in the morning he went to the priest and
told him the summons he had got in the night. People
say that the priest did not believe him, but at all events
he told Páidin to do as the messenger had bidden him.

Páidin departed, and left his blessing with his neighbours and relations, and when the clock was striking
twelve, and the people saying the Angelical Salutation,
Páidin came before the cross and said three times, " My
soul to God and to Mary," and on the spot he fell dead.

That cross was in the town of Cong for years. A bishop,
one of the O'Duffy's, went to Rome, and he got a bit of the
true Cross and put it into the Cross of Cong. It was there
until the foreigners came and threw it to the ground. The
Cross of Cong is still in Ireland, and the people have an
idea that it will yet be raised up in the town of Cong with
the help of God.

THE ADVENTURES OF LÉITHIN

PREFACE.

The following interesting story, which, so far as I
know, has never been noted, has come down to us in
a late Middle Irish text from which I now translate
it for the first time. My attention was first called to
it years ago by my friend, Dr. Nicholas O'Donnell
of Melbourne, an Australian born and bred, but a
good Irish scholar, who made a transcript of the
story for me from an Irish MS. which he picked up in
Australia. It may well have been taken from a vellum,
for the initial letter is omitted and a great space left for
the scribe to insert it in colours later on. I have
carefully compared the copy of the Australian text
with four other copies which I find in the Royal
Irish Academy, the oldest of which however only dates
from 1788, but I found virtually no difference between
them, and it is evident that they are all drawn from
the same original. There seems to be no variant
known. There is an ancient poem of great interest bearing
on this story, called the Colloquy between Fintan and the
Hawk of Achill. It is in Egerton, 1782, and the text
was published in " Anecdota from Irish MSS." vol. I.,
p. 24, but has never been translated. Fintan, who sur-
vived the flood, holds colloquy with the bird, which asked
him about his life, and Fintan asks the bird's age. " O
hawk from cold Achill take a benison and a victory, from
the time you were born of an egg, tell the number of
[the years of] your life."

" I am of the same age as thou, O Fintan, son of Bochra."
The Bird asks Fintan " since he was a poet and a prophet "

to tell him the greatest evils he had ever experienced.
We learn from the answer that the ancient salmon in our
story was really a rebirth of Fintan himself, and it is
exceedingly interesting to find the wily old crow[1] who ate
Léithin's young ones, appear upon the scene again, as a
leading personage in another drama. Fintan tells how the
Creator placed him in the cold streams in the shape of a
salmon, how he frequented the Boyne, the Bush, the Bann,
the Suck, the Suir, the Shannon, the Slaney, the Liffey,
etc., etc. At last he came to Assaroe.

"A night I was on the wave in the north and I at seal-
frequented Assaroe. I never experienced a night like that
from the beginning to the end of my time.[2]

"I could not remain in the waterfall. I give a leap—
it was no luck for me—the ice comes like blue glass between
me and the pool of the son of Modharn.

"There comes a crow out of cold Achill, above the
inver of Assaroe, I shall not hide it, though it is a thing
to keep as a secret. He swept away with him one of my
eyes.

"The Goll or Blind One of Assaroe has clung to me [as
a name] from that night. Rough the deed. I am ever
since without my eye. No wonder for me to be aged."

THE BIRD.

"It was I who swallowed thy eye, O Fintan. I am the
grey Hawk, who be's alone in the waist of Achill."

Fintan demands eric [recompense] for his eye, but the
implacable old crow answers :

"Little eric would I give thee, O Fintan, son of Bochra
the soft, but that one remaining eye in the withered
head quickly would I swallow it of one morsel."

The bird goes on to tell Fintan about the various battles
it had seen in Ireland. As for the battle of Moytura in
Cong :

---

[1] The word "préachan," though it usually means crow, is applied
to the seabhac or hawk in this poem. In Co. Roscommon I always
heard the Marsh Harrier (or Kite as they called him in English),
termed "préachan gcearc" in Irish.

[2] Literally "of the world."

" It was there thy twelve sons fell ; to see them, aw-
some was the blow, and I gnawed off each fresh body[1] either
a hand or one foot or one eye."

The old crow it was who carried off the hand of Nuadh
covered with rings, which had been lopped off in the slaughter, and which was replaced later on by a silver hand,
whence the King of the Tuatha De Danann received the
cognomen of Nuadh of the silver hand, but his real hand
was the plaything of the crows' young for seven years. He
recounts all the eyes he had picked out of heroes' heads
after famous fights. It was he too who perched upon
Cuchulainn's shoulder, when, dying, he had bound himself
to the standing stone,[2] but though his life had almost departed from him the hero pierced him with his *cletin
curad* or hero's little quill. " I came above the hero as
his countenance was darkening in death to eat his eyes,
it was not an errand of luck, I stoop my head. He feels
me on his face, he raises up his weakening hand, he puts
his hero's little quill through my body at the first effort (?)
I take a troubled flight to Innis Geidh across the valleyed
sea and draw forth from myself, rough the task, the hard
tough shaft of the dartlet. The head remains in my body.
It tortured my heart sorely : sound I am not since that day,
and I conceal it not since I am old. It was I who slew, great
the tidings, the solitary crane that was in Moy Leana and
the eagle of Druim Breac, who fell by me at the
famous ford.

It was I who slew, pleasant the supper, the solitary crane
of blue Innis Géidh. IT WAS I WHO CHEWED BENEATH
MY COMB THE TWO FULL-FAT BIRDS OF LEITHIN. It
was I who slew, royal the rout, THE SLENDER BLACKFOOT
of Slieve Fuaid ; the BLACKBIRD of Drum Seghsa of the
streams died in the talons of my daughter."

It is plain then that this ancient poem, found in
Egerton 1782, and in the Book of Fermoy, actually pre-
supposes our story, and has a close connection with it.

---

[1] Literally " limb."
[2] See my " Literary History of Ireland," p. 351.

THE STORY.

A GENTLE, noble, renowned patron there was of a time in the land of Ireland, whose exact name was Ciaran of Cluan.[1] A good faith had he in the mighty Lord.

One day Ciaran bade his clerics to go look for thatch for his church, on a Saturday of all days,[2] and those to whom he spake were Sailmin, son of Beogan, and Maolan, son of Naoi, for men submissive to God were they twain, so far as their utmost diligence went, and many miracles were performed for Maolan, as Ciaran said in the stanza,

> Maolan, son of Naoi the cleric,
> His right hand be for our benison
> If the son of Naoi desired it
> To work miracles like every saint.

And, moreover, Sailmin, son of Beogan, he was the same man of whom, for wisdom, for piety, and for religion, Ciaran spake the stanza,

> Sailmin melodious, son of Beogan.
> A faith godlike and firm.
> No blemish is in his body.
> His soul is an angel.

He was the seventh son of the sons of Beogan of Burren,[3] and those men were the seven psalmists of Ciaran, so that from them are the " Youth's Cross " on the Shannon, and the [other] " Youth's Cross " on the high road to Clonmacnoise [named].

Howsoever the clerics fared forth alongside the Shannon, until they reached Cluain Doimh. There they cut the full of their little curragh of white-bottomed

---

[1] *i.e.,* Clonmacnoise.   [2] Literally " especially."   [3] In West Clare.

green-topped rushes. But [before they had done] they heard the voice of the clerics' bell at the time of vespers on Sunday, so they said that they would not leave that place until the day should rise on them on Monday, and they spake the lay as follows :

> The voice of a bell I heard in Cluan[1]
> On Sunday night defeating us,
> I shall not depart since that has been heard,
> Until Monday, after the Sunday.
>
> On Sunday did God shape-out Heaven,
> On that day was the King of the apostles born ;
> On Sunday was born Mary
> Mother of the King of Mercy.
>
> On Sunday, I say it,
> Was born victorious John Baptist.
> By the hand of God in the stream in the East
> Was he baptised on Sunday.
>
> On Sunday, moreover, it is a true thing,
> The Son of God took the captivity out of hell.
> On a Sunday after the battle   . . . ?
> Shall God deliver the judgment of the last day.
>
> On a Sunday night, we think it melodious,
> The voice of the cleric I hear,
> The voice I hear of a bell
> On Drum Diobraid above the pool.
>
> The voice of the bell I hear
> Making me to postpone-return
> The voice of the bell I hear
> Bringing me to Cluan.
>
> By thy hand O youth,
> And by the King who created thee,
> My heart thinks it delightful
> The bell and the voice.

Howbeit the clerics abode that night [where they were] for the love of the King of Sunday. Now there occurred, that night, a frost and a prolonged snow and a rigour of

---

[1] *i.e.*, Clonmacnoise.

cold, and there arose wind and tempest in the elements
for their skaith, without as much as a bothy or a lean-
to of a bed or a fire for them, and surely were it not for
the mercy of God protecting them round about, it was
not in the mind of either of them that he should be alive
on the morrow after that night, with all they experienced
of oppression and terror from the great tempest of that
wild-weather, so that they never remembered their acts
of piety or to say or sing a prayer (?) Nor could they
sleep or rest, for their senses were turned to foolishness,
for they had never seen the like or the equal of that storm,
and of the bad weather of that night, for the venom of
its cold and moreover for the bitterness of the morning
[which followed it]. And as they were there on the
morning of the next day they heard a gentle, low, lament-
able, woe-begone conversation of grief above their heads
on high, on a tall, wide-extended cliff. And [the meaning]
was revealed to them through the virtue of their holiness,
and although much evil and anxiety had they suffered,
[still] they paid attention to the conversation and observed
it. And they between whom the conversation was,
were these, namely an eagle who was called Léithín[1]
and a bird of her birds[2] in dialogue with her, piteously
and complainingly lamenting their cold-state, pitifully,
sadly, grievously; and said the bird to the eagle :

" Léithín," said he, " do you ever remember the like
of this morning or of last night to have come within
thy knowledge before ? "

---

[1] Apparently " the little grey one," from " liath"-grey; pronounced
" Lay-heen." I have made her feminine and called her " she "
in the translation, but the Irish makes her masculine.

[2] *i.e.*, one of its own young eagles, or nestlings.

" I do not remember," said Léithin, " that I ever heard
or saw the like or the equal of them, since the world was
created, and do you yourself remember, or did you ever
hear of such [weather] ? " said the eagle to the bird.

" There are people who do remember," said the bird.

" Who are they ? " said the eagle.

" Dubhchosach, the Black-footed one of Binn Gulban,[1]
that is the vast-sized stag of the deluge,[2] who is at Binn
Gulban ; and he is the hero of oldest memory of all those
of his generation (?) in Ireland.

" Confusion on thee and skaith ! surely thou knowest
not that ; and now although that stag be far away from
me I shall go to see him, to find if I may get any knowledge from him ! "

Therewith Léithin went off lightly, yet was she scarcely
able to rise up on high with the strength of the bad weather,
and no more could she go low with the cold of the . . .?
and with the great abundance of the water, and, though
it was difficult for her, she progressed lightly and low-
flying, and no one living could reveal or make known
all that she met of evil and of misery going to Ben Gulban
looking for the Blackfoot. And she found the small-
headed swift-footed stag scratching himself against a
bare oak rampike. And Léithin descended on a corner
of the rampike beside him. And she saluted the stag in
his own language and asks him was he the Blackfoot.
The stag said that he was, and Léithin spoke the lay :

> Well for you O Blackfoot,
> On Ben Gulban high,
> Many moors and marshes,
> Leap you lightly by.

---

[1] Now Ben Bulben in Co. Sligo.   [2] *i.e.,* " As old as the deluge."

Hounds no more shall hunt you
Since the Fenians fell,
Feeding now untroubled
On from glen to glen.

Tell me stag high-headed,
Saw you ever fall
Such a night and morning?
You remember all.

[The Stag Answers.]
I will give you answer
Léithin wise and gray,
Such a night and morning
Never came my way.

" Tell me, Blackfoot," said Léithin, " what is thy
age ? "

" I shall tell thee," said the Blackfoot. " I remember
this oak here when it was a little sapling, and I was born
at the foot of the oak sapling, and I was reared upon that
couch [of moss at its foot] until I was a mighty-great
stag, and I loved this abode [ever], through my having
been reared here. And the oak grew after that till it
was a giant oak (?) and I used to come and constantly
scratch myself against it every evening after my journeyings and goings [during the day] and I used [always]
to remain beside it in such wise till the next morning,
and if I had to make a journey or were hotly hunted I
used to reach the same tree, so that we grew up with one
another, until I became a mighty-great stag, and this
tree became the bare withered rampike which you see,
so that it is now only a big ruined shapeless-stump without
blossom or fruit or foliage to-day, its period and life
being spent. Now I have let a long period of years[1] go

---

[1] Or, " a cargo of five hundred years."

by me, yet I never saw and never heard tell-of, in all that time, the like of last night."

Léithin departs [to return] to his birds after that, and on his reaching home the other[1] bird spoke to him, " have you found out what you went to inquire about ? "

" I have not," said Léithin, and she began to revile the bird for all the cold and hardships she had endured, but at last she said, " who do you think again would know this thing for me ? " said Léithin.

" I know that," said the bird, " Dubhgoire the Black caller of Clonfert[2] of Berachan."

" Well then I shall go seek him."

And although that was far away from her, yet she proceeded until she reached Clonfert of St. Berachan, and she was observing the birds until they had finished their feeding [and were returning home], and then Léithin saw one splendid bird beautifully-topped, victorious-looking, of the size of a blackbird, but of the brightness of a swan, and as soon as it came into its presence Léithin asks it whether it were Dubhgoire. It said that it was. It was a marvel [to Léithin] when it said that it was, namely that the blackbird should be white, and Léithin spake the lay.

"How is that O Dubhgoire, sweet is thy warbling, often hast thou paid thy calls throughout the blue-leaved forest.

" In Clonfert of the bright streams and by the full plain of the Liffey, and from the plain of the Liffey coming from the east to Kildare behind it.

---

[1] Literally " second."
[2] Perhaps " Cluansost." There is no Berachan in Clonfert in the martyrologies. See " The Death of Bearachan," p. 63.

" From that thou departest to thy nest in the Cill which Brigit blessed. Short was it for thee to overleap every hedge till thou camest to the townland in which Berachan was.

" O Dubhgoire tell to me—and to count up all thy life—the like of yesterday morning, didst thou ever experience it, O Dubhgoire ? "

[DUBHGOIRE ANSWERS.]

" To me my full life was three hundred years before Berachan, the lifetime of Berachan I spent [added thereto], I was enduring in lasting happiness.

" Since the time that Lughaidh of the Blades was for a while in the sovereignty of all Ireland I never experienced by sea or by land such weather as that which Léithin mentions in his lay." [1]

" Well, then, my own errand to thee," said Léithin, " is to enquire if thou didst ever experience, or remember to have seen or [to have heard] that there ever came such a morning as yesterday for badness."

" I do not remember that I ever saw such," said Dubhgoire, " or anything like it."

As for Léithin, she was sad and sorrowful, for those tidings did not help (?) her, and she proceeded on her way till she reached her nest and birds.

" What have you to tell us to-day ? " said the bird.

" May you never have luck nor fortune," said Léithin. " I have no more news for you than I had when departing, except all my weariness from all the journeyings and

---

[1] Literally, " I never got on sea or land a knowledge of that lay of Léithin's,"

wanderings which you contrive to get me to take, without my getting any profit or advantage out of you," and with that she gave a greedy venemous drive of her beak at the bird, so that she had like to have made a prey and flesh-torn spoil ef it, with vexation at all the evil and misery she had experienced going to Kildare, so that the bird screeched out loudly and pitifully and miserably.

[A while] after that Léithin said, " It's a pity and a grief to me if any one in Ireland knows [that there ever came a night worse than that night] that I myself do not know of it."

" Well, then, indeed, there is one who knows," says the bird, " Goll of Easruaidh (*i.e.*, the Blind One of Assaroe) and another name of him is the Éigne[1] of Ath-Seannaigh (*i.e.*, the salmon of Ballyshannon), and it is certain that he knows about that, if any one in the world knows about it."

" It is hard for me to go the way you tell me," said Léithin, " yet should I like exceeding well to know about this thing."

Howsoever she set out, and she never came down until she reached Assaroe of Mac Modhuirn, and she began observing and scrutinizing Assaroe until she saw the salmon feeding near the ford, and she saluted him and said, " Delightful is that O Goll, it is not with thee as with me, for our woes are not the same," and she spake the lay :

[LEITHIN SPEAKS.]

" Pleasant is that [life of thine] O Goll with success (?) many is the stream which thou hast adventured, not the

---

[1] This is an old poetic word for a salmon.

same for thee and for us, if we were to relate our wander-ings.

"It is to thee that I have come from my house, O Blind one of Assaroe, how far doth thy memory go back, or how far is thy age to be reckoned ? "

[THE SALMON ANSWERS.]

"As for my memory, that is a long one. It is not easy to reckon it. There is not on land or in bush a person like me—none like me but myself alone !

"I remember, it is not a clear-cut remembrance, the displacing showers of the Deluge, four women and four men, who remained after it in the world.

"I remember Patrick of the pens coming into the land of Ireland, and the Fir Bolg, manful the assembly, coming from Greece to take possession of it.

"Truly do I mind me of Fintan's coming into the country close to me. Four men were the crew of his ship, and an equal number of females.

"I remember gentle Partholan's taking the kingship over Ulster. I remember, a while before that, Glas, son of Aimbithe in Emania.

"I chanced to be one morning that was fair, on this river, O Léithin, I never experienced a morning like that, either before it or after it.

"I gave a leap into the air under the brow of my hard rock [here], and before I came down into my house [of water] this pool was one flag of ice.

"The bird of prey[1] seized me above the land with a

---

[1] Literally "eagle," but this is a mistake, it was not an eagle.

furious ungentle onslaught, and bore away my clear blue
eye. To me it was not a pleasant world."

" Well now, my own object in coming to thee," said
Léithin, " was to enquire of thee whether thou dost ever
remember such a morning as was yesterday ? "

" Indeed saw I such a morning," quoth Goll. " I
remember the coming of the deluge, and I remember the
coming of Partholan and of Fintan and the children of
Neimhidh and the Fir Bolg and the Tuatha De Danann,
and the Fomorians and the sons of Milesius and Patrick
son of Alprunn, and I remember how Ireland threw off
from her those troops, and I remember a morning
that was worse than that morning, another morning
not speaking of the great showers out of which the deluge
fell. And the deluge left only four men and four women,
namely, Noe, son of Laimhfhiadh and his wife, and Sem,
Cam and Japhet, and their three wives, for in truth that
was the crew of the ark, and neither [church] man nor
canon reckon that God left undestroyed in the world
but those four. However, wise men truly recount that
God left another four keeping knowledge and tribal-
descent and preserving universal genealogies, for God
did not wish the histories of the people to fade, and so
he left Fintan son of Laimhfhiadh towards the setting
of the sun, south, keeping an account of the west of the
world, and, moreover, Friomsa Fhurdhachta keeping
the lordship of the north, and the prophet and the
Easba ? duly ordering [the history of the] south. And
those are they who were alive outside of the ark, and I
remember all those people. And Léithin," said Goll,

" I never saw the like of that morning for vemon except
one other morning that was worse than the morning that
you speak of, and worse than any morning that ever came
before it.   It was thus.   One day I was in this pool and
I saw a beautifully coloured butterfly with purple spots
in the air over my head.   I leapt to catch it, and before
I came down the whole pool had become one flag of ice
behind me, so that [when I fell back] it bore me up   And
then there came the bird of prey[1] to me, on his seeing
me [in that condition], and he gave a greedy venemous
assault on me and plucked the eye out of my head, and
only for my weight he would have lifted me, and he threw
the eye into the pool, and we both wrestled together
until we broke the ice with the violence of the struggle,
and with the [heat of the] great amount of crimson-red
blood that was pouring from my eye, so that the ice was
broken by that, so that with difficulty I got down into the
pool [again], and that is how I lost my eye.   And it is
certain O Léithin," said Goll, " that that was by far the
worst morning that I ever saw, and worse than this morning that thou speakest of."

Now as for the clerics, they took council with one
another, and determined to await [the eagle's return] that
they might know what she had to relate.   However
they experienced such hardships and anguish from the
cold and misery of the night, and they could not [despite
their resolution] endure to abide [the eagle's return].   So
Maolan, the cleric, said, " I myself beseech the powerful

---

[1] Literally " eagle."   MSS. reads " fiolar "—" the eagle," which
is evidently a mistake.

Lord, and the chosen Trinity, that the eagle, Léithin, may come with the knowledge she receives to Clonmacnoise and tell it to Ciaran," [and therewith they themselves departed.]

Now as for Goll [the salmon], he asked Léithin, after that, who was it that sent her in pursuit of that knowledge.

" It was the second bird of my own birds."

" That is sad," said Goll, " for that bird is much older than thou or than I either, and that is the bird that picked my eye out of me, and if he had desired to make thee wise in these things it would have been easy for him. That bird," said he, " is the old Crow of Achill. And its talons have got blunted with old age, and since its vigour and energy and power of providing for itself have departed from it, its way of getting food is to go from one nest to another, smothering and killing every bird's young, and eating them, and so thou shalt never overtake thy own birds alive. And O beloved friend, best friend that I ever saw, if thou only succeedest in catching him alive on thy return, remember all the tricks he has played thee, and avenge thy birds and thy journeyings and thy wanderings upon him, and then too mind thee to avenge my eye."

Léithin bade farewell to Goll, and off she went the selfsame way she had come, in a mighty swift course, for she felt certain [now] that she would not overtake her birds alive in her nest. And good cause had she for that dread, for she only found the place of the nest, wanting its birds, they having been eaten by the Crow of Achill. So that all Léithin got as the result of her errand was the loss of her birds.

But the old Crow of Achill had departed after its despoiling [the nest], so that Léithin did not come upon it, neither did she know what way it had gone.

Another thing, too, Léithin had to go every Monday, owing to the cleric's prayer, to Clonmacnoise. There the eagle perched upon the great pinnacle of the round tower[1] of Clonmacnoise, and revealed herself to the holy patron, namely Ciaran. And Ciaran asked her for her news. And Léithin said she was [not ?] more grieved at her wanderings and her loss than at that. Thereupon Ciaran said that he would give her the price and reward of her storytelling ; namely, every time that her adventures should be told, if it were stormy or excessive rain that was in it at the time of telling, it should be changed into fine sky and good weather.

And Léithin said that it was understood by her [all along] that it was not her birds or her nest she would receive from him ; and since that might not be, she was pleased that her journeyings and wanderings should not go for nothing.

And [thereupon] Léithin related her goings from the beginning to the end, just as we have told them above. So those are the adventures of Léithin. Thus far.

---

[1] Literally " Bell-house."

THE COMPARISON AS TO AGE BETWEEN THE FOUR ELDERS; NAMELY, THE CROW OF ACHILL, THE GREAT EAGLE OF LEAC NA BHFAOL, THE BLIND TROUT OF ASSAROE, AND THE HAG OF BEARE.

PREFACE.

This is the folk-lore version of the last story, and it is very interesting because it lends strength to the assumption that the story may be a piece of pre-Christian folk-lore, and probably very much older than any documents. I think it is pretty obvious that St. Ciaran and his clerics were brought into the written version simply to insure the tale against any clerical hostility which might be displayed by well-intentioned friars or others who would say—" those are only foolish tales, let them be." But the presence of St. Ciaran and his two clerics would be sure to disarm hostility, if any such were attempted. The whole of mediaeval Irish literature is full of examples of such forethought.

This story was told by Joyce or Seoigtheach, of Poll na bracha, in Co. Galway, some years ago, for the Oireachtas. There are a great number of stories in Irish with regard to old age. A common saying which I have often heard, but with variants, is the following, which purports to tell the life of those things in the universe which will last longest :

> Tri cuaille fáil, cú.
> Tri cú, each.
> Tri eich, duine.
> Tri daoine, iolar.
> Tri iolair, bradán.
> Tri bradáin, iubhair (pronounced " úr.")
> Tri iubhair, eitre,
> Tri eitreacha o thús an domhain go deireadh an domhain

i.e., " Three wattles (such as are placed in a hedge to fill a gap)=a hound's life, three hounds a steed, three steeds a man, three men an eagle, three eagles a salmon, three salmon a yew tree, three yew trees a ridge, three ridges from the beginning to the end of the world." " Eitre " has been explained to me as the old very wide ridges that used to be used in ancient times which left an almost indelible track in the ground. But my friend Mr. Hodgson took down a different explanation from Mathias O'Conor, and a different version, after " tri ur, eitre," came " tri eitre, ' eye-ar'." and 'eitre' he explained as the mark of a plough on land, and ' aidhear' or " eye-ar " as the mark of a spade.

The Crow of Achill is a bird that every Irish speaker in the West has heard of, but Raftery curiously made him a " raven." In one of his poems he says of a place in his beloved Mayo where birds delighted to resort :

Ta an fiach dubh as Acaill ann
Ta an seabhac as Loch Erne ann,
Ta an t-iolrach o'n nGreig ann
Agus an eala on Roimh.

i.e., the Raven out of Achill is there, the Hawk from Lough Erne is there, the Eagle out of Greece and the Swan from Rome !

THE STORY.

IN the Island of Achill the Crow lived   He never frequented wood, tree or bush, but an ancient forge in which he spent his time every evening throughout the year, and every year of his lifetime, lying on the anvil. And as it is the custom of birds usually to rub their beaks to the thing that is nearest to them, the Crow used to give an odd rub, now and again, to the horn of the anvil. At long last, in the end, the horn grew to be as thin and worn away as a knitting needle, by the continuous rubbing.

One night there happened to be a great storm. There came frost, snow and wind, very violent. The roofing was swept away off the forge, and along with it went the plumage and feathers of the crow, and the poor crow was left in the morning after that dreadful night, and he without a feather or any plumage on his body, but just as much as if he had been scalded with boiling water.

When the sun rose after that in the morning there came a rest and a calm, but the poor crow was afraid to go out, and [*i.e.*, after] the flaying that had been done upon him during the night. " Oh," said he, " it's a long time I'm in this world, and I never felt a single other night of such bad weather as the night last night. It is my own opinion that there is not a single living creature in the entire world older than myself, unless it be the great Eagle of Leac-na-bhfaol,[1] and I'm in doubt but that the eagle is the older. I'll go to himself now until I get knowledge from him if he ever felt a night as cold and as venemous as the night we had last night."

When the light of day came and the heat of the sun was right, my crow slipped off with the intention of journeying to the eagle. He was going and ever-going as well as he was able, seeing he was without feathers, until he came in the end, at long last, as far as the nest of the Eagle.

" Aroo ! " says the Eagle ; " O Crow of my heart, what has happened to you, or where have your plumage and your feathers gone ? "

" Oh, don't ask me that," said the Crow, " didn't yourself feel the cold and ill weather of last night ? "

---

[1] Pronounce L'ock-na-weel.

" Well, indeed," said the Eagle, " I didn't notice one jot of the wild weather that you're talking of."

" Heavy was your slumber then," said the Crow. " I never experienced any night myself that was one half as venemous as it was—and signs on me ! I am come now to you to find out from you did there ever come any night in your time that was colder than it ; because I was laying out in my own mind that you are older than I am."

" I have no right-certainty as to my own age," said the Eagle ; but even if I had, I know that there is another creature who is still alive in the world and who is very much older than I am."

" Who is that ? " said the Crow.

" He is the Blind Trout of Assaroe," said the Eagle. " Go you, now, to that Trout, and perhaps you might get the solving of your question from him."

The Crow went off and he never stopped nor stayed until he came as far as Assaroe, and he found out the Trout. He told his story then to the Trout, and told him that he came to find out from him if there had ever come a night in the world that was as cold as last night.

" There did, and a thousand times colder," said the Trout.

" I'd scarcely believe you,"[1] said the Crow.

" Why, then," said the Trout, " if you don't believe me, you can go to an older authority than I."

" And who is that authority ? " said the Crow.

" The Old Woman of Beare," said the Trout.

---

[1] Literally " it's badly I'd believe you."

" I'll go right away to her this moment,"[1] said the Crow.

" Wait yet," said the Trout, " until I tell you my own story. I was swimming on the surface of this pool one fine calm evening, as calm and as fine as any evening that ever I saw. There were thousands of flies above the pool. I sprang upward to catch the full of my mouth of them, and before I reached back again into the water there was ice on the [surface of the] water, and I was jumping and floundering on the flag of ice until the raven[2] came and picked the eyes out of my head. My share of blood began running fast[3] out of me, and I was there until the heat of the blood melted the flag of ice that was on the water, down through it, and let me down into the water again. That was the coldest night that I ever felt myself, and that is the way I lost my sight. I was christened the Blind Trout of Assaroe ever since, but some of the people call me the Old Trout of Assaroe. Alas, my bitter misfortune! I am ever since without sight."

The Crow heard him out, but he would not be easy or satisfied in his own mind until he should go on a visit to the Old Woman of Beare.

" Farewell, Trout," said he, " I must go to the Old Woman now until I hear her own story."

" May your journey succeed with you Crow, you will have neither loss nor hurt in the house of the Old Woman," said the Trout.

---

[1] Literally " now itself."
[2] Notice the use of the definite article.
[3] Literally " thickly."

The Crow went off then, and he never stopped nor stayed until he came to the Old Woman's house.

"Welcome, O Crow out of Achill," said she. "What is this has happened to you, or where are your plumage and feathers?"

"They are gone with the big wind," said he; and with that he told his story to the Old Woman from beginning to end, and he put the same question to her that he had put before that to the Eagle and to the Trout—Did she ever feel any night that was as sore and venemous as last night?

"That's true for you," said she; "I did feel a little stroke of cold at the beginning of the night, but I drew a wool pack over my head then, and I never felt anything but moonogues[1] of perspiration running off me again until morning."

"Are you very old?" said the Crow; "or what age are you?"

"I have no certain date with regard to my age," said the Old Woman—"only this much. My father used to kill a beef every year, on the day I was born, in honour of my birthday, as long as he lived, and I followed the same custom, from that day to this. All the horns [of the beeves I killed] are on the loft in the barn and do you remain in my house until to-morrow, and if you like I'll send the servant boy to count them and you yourself can keep account of them [as he numbers them aloud.][2]

On the morrow with the rise of day the servant went

---

[1] Literally "little bog-berries"
[2] See the story of "The Old Woman of Beare."

up to count the horns, and he spent one full year, and a day over, at that work, and after all that there was only one corner of the loft emptied.

And during all that time the Crow was taking his ease, and there was neither thirst nor hunger on him [so well was he treated] and his plumage and his feathers grew on him again.

But even so, he got tired of keeping count.

" I give you the branch " [palm of victory] said he to the Old Woman ; " you are as old as the old grandmother long ago, who ate the apples," and he sped forth from the Old Woman and went home.

———————

THE DEATH OF BEARACHAN

PREFACE.

The following little story, taken down in Irish by my friend Father Kelleher from the dictation of Mary Sweeney, aged 82, of Coolea, Ballyvourney, Co. Cork, and sent me by Miss G. Schoepperle, who published the text in the revue Celtique in 1911, is of great interest, because it is almost unique as showing a point of contact—one of the exceedingly few points of contact—between Breton and Irish folk-lore. " Il n'est, que je sache, d'autre example en Irlande d'un messager surnaturel, tel que l'enfant mystérieux qui parait dans le conte qui suit," says Miss Schoepperle, truly, but in Brittany, she goes on to say, the " buguel (Irish, buᴀċᴀıll) noz," *i.e.*, the boy or herdsman of the night, is well known. It is generally described as a little child with its head too large for its body, which only seldom appears, but which is heard to cry and lament in fields or on deserted roads. Its apparition is a presage of death. Lebraz in his Légende de la Mort has more than one story of its appearance. The salient points in the following story which seem to connect it with the Breton legend are : (1) The gradual growth in size of the being which was at first small ; (2) the lamentations and cries which it utters, and (3)—most remarkable of all—that it described itself as a herdsman, and was a presage of death.

The Bearchan of this story must have been the bishop of Cluᴀın-ꝼoꞃcᴀ in Uí ꝼᴀılᵹe (King's County) about the year 690. He was of the race of the Oᴀlꝼıᴀoᴀ or Scoto-Irish, and was 21st in descent from Cᴀıꞃbꞃe Rıᴀoᴀ who fought in the battle of Ceᴀnn ꝼeᴀḃꞃᴀc in 186 A.D. I have seen his pedigree in MS. There are about six other St. Bearchans, but so far as I know the only one who would have been at

all likely to have attracted a body of legend to himself
was this Bearchan of Cluᴀın-ꞃoꞃᴛᴀ, who was esteemed as
a prophet and poet. Besides I find this very curious note
in the Martyrology of Donegal compiled by Brother Michael
O'Clery from the old books of Ireland in 1630 :

Ɗoƀᴀᴄ ƀeꞃᴄᴀın ᴅᴀ ꞃꞃıoᴛ ᴣo nuᴀıꝺe ın Uıƀ Pᴀıłᴣı 1
ƀꞃeꞃonn ó Uı ƀeꞃᴄᴀın, ᴀn mᴀıꝺı ꞃóꞃ ᴛımᴄıoł ᴀn uıꞃᴣe.
Ann ꞃın ᴀᴛᴀ́ cluᴀınꞃoꞃᴛᴀ 7 ᴀnn ꞃın ᴀᴛᴀ́ ᴛempᴀłł
ƀeꞃᴄᴀın ᴀcuꞃ ꝺo ƀí, i.e., " Berchan's vat has been
found new in Ui Failgi in the territory of the Ui
Berchain. The timber was still round the water
[*i.e.*, was still good enough to hold water.] It is
there Cluainsosta is, and there Berchan's church is and
was." So, then, there must have been some well-known
story connected with Berchan's vat. The list of the great
Earl of Kildare's library, which was drawn up in 1518, con-
tained a " St. Berchan's Book." Poems ascribed to him
are found in the " Wars of the Gael and Gall." For other
references to him, see my " Literary History of Ireland,"
210-11.[1] " Bearachán " is the modern pronunciation of the
older Berchán.

THE STORY.

BEARACHAN of Glen Flesk[2] had a dream or vision that
there was no danger of his ever dying until three kings

---

[1] See also O'Curry MS. Materials p. 412.—418 and 432. Fer-da-
lethe, or the "man of two halves," was another name for him,
"because he spent half of his life in the world and half on pilgrimage ut ferunt periti." An old rann runs :

Ceıᴛꞃı ꞃᴀıꝺe ᴣᴀıƀel n-ᴄłᴀn
ꞃeıꞃꝺı ᴀn ᴛíꞃ ᴀ ꝺᴛᴀnᴣᴀꝺᴀꞃ,
Colum cıłłe Molınᴣ łᴀn
ƀꞃeꞃᴀınn ƀıoꞃꞃᴀ ᴀᴣuꞃ ƀeꞃᴄᴀn.

i.e., "Four prophets of the clean Gael. The country from which
they sprang was the better for them. Columbcille, full Moling,
Brendan of Birr and Berchan."

[2] Near Killarney in Co. Kerry. But, as I have shown, he was
probably Bearchan of Cluainsosta. There is no Berchan of Glenflesk
in any of the Irish martyrologies.

THE THREE KINGS ADMIT THE "POOR LITTLE CREATURE"

should come to his house without asking or invitation. On a certain night they did pay him a visit. He told them that there would not be a bit of him alive in the morning. They passed a good part of the night eating and drinking away, and they making a jest of him [saying] that so long as they themselves were in the house there would be no danger of [anything happening] him.

They got hold of a big dabhach or vat, and [they put] Bearachan in under the mouth of the vat [to protect him] and they three were round about it.

He had not been long placed there by them when they heard a very clear little voice outside, and it crying ; and there was snow outside, and cold.

They asked it, "what was outside and what it wanted."

It said that it was a cow-herd and that it was perished.

They left him outside for a good space of time. At last they let him in. He came in and sat down beside the fire, a poor little creature, and he shaking with the cold. They gave him food and drink, but he told them that he was too much frightened, and that he would not eat it.

They had a fine red-hot fire, and he was warming himself at the fire. He was a very short time there till he began swelling with the [heat of the] fire and growing big. He drew a little musical instrument out of his pocket and started to play on it. And according as the music was a-playing by him the others were inclining to weaken and fall asleep, until they [all, at last] fell softly in a dead sleep.

And when they awoke in the morning, they had no music and no Bearachan—nothing but his bones left bare and naked underneath the vat.

STORY OF SOLOMON.

PREFACE.

How Solomon comes into Irish folk-lore is hard to say,
but I have heard at least three stories about him, of which
the present is the most interesting. I wrote it down, word
for word, from the mouth of Michael Mac Ruaidhri, in 1896.
There is an undoubtedly Eastern flavour about it, but how
it came to the County Mayo I cannot imagine, for I have
not been able to trace it to any known source.

Solomon's name was better known in the middle ages
in connection with the conjuration of spirits. "Für solche
halbe Hexenblut Ist Salomonis Schlüssel gut," says Faust
in the study scene, when threatened by the demon dog.
Josephus mentions Solomon's power over ghosts, and a book
of conjurations in Hebrew which was ascribed to Solomon
was translated into Latin, French, Italian, German and
Spanish. The best known German edition according to Zerfi
(one of Faust's editors) is called " clavicula Salomonis et
theosophia pneumatica."

THE STORY.

WHEN Solomon's mother was sick, Solomon used to
send a man from the village in which he was, to watch
her every night ; and every man who used to be watching
her had to come before sunrise next morning with word
to Solomon of how his mother was, and the first man who
would say that his mother was dead, his head was to be

whipt off him, and hung upon a spear that was above the Great Door. And they used to go, man after man, each night in their turn, and five pounds was the reward for their work, which they used to get each night. It was well, and it was not ill, until it came to the turn of a widow's son to go to watch the mother of Solomon ; and the night that he was going to watch her she was very weak and overcome, and given up for death.

When the account came to the widow's son to go and watch Solomon's mother, there came the weakness and the sweat of death upon him, and his mother began to keene for him, because she had no one but him. And as he was going home from the day's work that he had, that evening, he was weeping and troubled ; and there met him a half-fool, and he asked the widow's son for what cause was he weeping, and the widow's son told him as I am telling it to you.

" What is the reward that you will get ? " said the half-fool to the widow's son.

" Five pounds," says he to him.

" My soul to God of the graces," says the half-fool, " but I'll go in your place to night, if you give me the five pounds."

" I'll give you five pounds, and something over," says the widow's son, " if you go there."

True was the story. The half-fool went to watch Solomon's mother that night, and she was in the last agony when he went into the room, and he was watching her until after the hour of twelve at night ; and he heard a noise at the big door, and he rose upon his feet and walked to the big door, and there was a man at the big door, and he watching, looking in on a window that was in the big door. And the man who was in it was a body-servant of Solomon ; and Solomon had a great regard for this man, and he used to send this man every night to bring him word privately—to tell him if the man who was taking care of his mother was doing his business right. Now, there was none of the men who were watching his mother for a year so keenly-watchful as the half-fool who was watching her that night. No man of them heard the man who was at the big door any night except him.

The half-fool opened the big door then, and thère was an old sword hung up over the big door. When the big door was opened the body-servant thought to come in, but the half-fool drew the sword, and threw the head off him. He left him there and went to the sleeping-room where Solomon's mother was, and he was not long in it until Solomon's mother died.

Solomon was getting very uneasy about his servant as to what was the reason that he was not coming to him with tidings, as he used to come every other night. But, howsoever, Solomon did not leave the house till morning, and he did not go to look for him. [He waited], but he did not come. And when the day came, the widow's son was not with Solomon before the rising of the sun, as the other men had been. Solomon did not go to rest, but he ever looking out through the window, and at long last he saw the widow's son—for he thought it was he was in it— coming to the palace. And when he came in to Solomon they saluted one another. And says the half-fool—

it was he was in it—to Solomon, " I am asking pardon of you, O king and prince."

" Why say you that ? " said Solomon.

" I knocked the hat off your body-servant yesterday," said the half-fool.

" You have your pardon got," said Solomon.

" But, O thou best of the kings," said the half-fool, " the head was with the hat." And as Solomon was after giving him his pardon, he could not go back of his word.

" Have you any other tidings with you ? " said Solomon.

" I have," said he.

" Tell them," said Solomon.

" God's brightness is on the earth," said he.

" The sun is risen," said Solomon.

" It is," said the half-fool.

" The stones that were above yesterday," said he, " they are going below now."

" The plough is ploughing, then," said Solomon.

" It is," said he, " and the first house in which you were reared, it is overthrown."

" Then my mother is dead," said Solomon.

" She is," said the half-fool.

" I shall have your head on the spear," said Solomon.

" You shall not, O honest noble king," said the half-fool, " you yourself were the first man who said it."

" By my honour," said Solomon, " it was I."

Ye see now, that, as wise as Solomon was, the half-fool got the victory over him in wisdom. " There be's luck on a fool." [1]

---

[1] A common proverb.

CHRISTMAS ALMS.

PREFACE.

There are many rhyming petitions and prayers amongst the " Askers of Alms " to be recited at the door of those from whom they crave assistance.   One of the virtues most insisted upon in prayers and didactic poems is almsgiving. The following story was probably invented with a deliberately didactic purpose.   It was told by Mary Gowlan, Cathair-na-Mart (Westport), some twenty years ago. The Dardeels, or Dharadeels which came out of the mouth of the dying woman are the most loathsome insects known to the Irish peasant. They are black beetles with cocked tails. See the " Legend of the Dardeel, the Keerogue and the Prumpolaun."

THE STORY.

IN the old time there was a married couple living near Cauher-na-Mart,[1] in the County Mayo. They had seven of a family, but God sent them worldly means, and they wanted for nothing but the love of God.

The man was a pious and generous person, and was good to the poor, but the wife was a hard miser without mercy, who would not give alms to man or stranger, and after refusing the poor man she used not to be satisfied with that, but she used to give him abuse also. If a person able to do work were to come looking for alms from

---

[1] Westport.

her, she would say, " Unless you were a lazy vagabone you would not be here now looking for alms and bothering my head with your talk ; " but if an old man or an old woman who could do no work would come to her, it is what she would say to them that they ought to be dead long before that.

One Christmas night there was frost and snow on the ground. There was a good fire in Patrick Kerwan's house—that was the man's name—and the table was laid. Patrick, his wife and his family were sitting down at the table, and they ready to go in face of a good supper when they heard a knock at the door. Up rose the wife and opened it. There was a poor man outside, and she asked him what he was looking for.

" I'm looking for alms in the honour of Jesus Christ, who was born on this festival night, and who died on the Cross of passion for the human race."

" Begone, you lazy guzzler," she said, " if you were one half as good at working as you are at saying your prayers, you would not be looking for alms to-night, nor troubling honest people," and with that she struck the door to, in the face of the poor man, and sat down again at the table.

Patrick heard a bit of the talk she gave the poor man, and he asked who was at the door.

" A lazy good-for-nothing, that was looking for alms," said she, " and if it wasn't that it was a lazy vagabone that was in it, he would not come looking for alms from people who are earning their share of food hardly, but he would sooner be saying his old prayers than working for meat."

Patrick rose. " Bad was the thing you did," said he, " to refuse anyone for a morsel of meat, and especially to refuse him on Christmas night. Isn't it God that sent us everything that we have ; there is more on this table than will be eaten to-night ; how do you know whether we shall be alive to-morrow ? "

" Sit down," says she, " and don't be making a fool of yourself ; we want no sermons."

" May God change your heart," says Patrick, and with that he got the full of his two hands of bread and food, and out with him, following the poor man, going on the track of his feet in the snow as quick as he could, till he came up with him. He handed him the food then, and told him he was sorry for his wife's refusing him. " But," says he, " I'm sure there was anger on her."

" Thank you for your food," said the poor man. He handed the food back again to him, and said " [there], you have your food and your thanks, [both]. I am an angel from heaven who was sent to your wife in the form of a poor man, to ask alms of her in the honour of Jesus Christ, who was born this night, and who suffered the passion of the Cross for the human race. She was not satisfied with refusing me, but she abused me also. You shall receive a great reward for your alms, but as for your wife she shall not be long until she is standing in the presence of Jesus Christ to give Him an account of the way in which she spent her life on this world."

The angel departed, and Patrick returned home. He sat down, but he could neither eat nor drink.

" What's on you ? " says the wife, " did that stroller do anything to you ? "

" My grief ! it was no stroller was in it, but an angel from heaven who was sent to you in the shape of a man to

ask alms of you, in honour of Jesus Christ, and you were
not satisfied with refusing him, but you must abuse him
with bad names. Now, your life on this world is not long,
and in the name of God, I beseech you, make a good use of
it."

" Hold your tongue," she said, " I think that you saw a
ghost, or that you lost your senses, and may God never
relieve you, nor anyone else who would leave a good fire,
and a good supper, running out in the snow after a lazy
rap ; but the devil a much sense was in you ever."

" If you don't take my advice, you'll repent when you'll
be too late," said Patrick ; but it was no use for him to be
talking.

When Little Christmas [New Year's Day] came, the
woman was not able to get dinner ready ; she was deaf and
blind. On the Twelfth Night she was not able to leave
her bed, but she was raving and crying, " give them alms,
alms, alms, give them everything in the house in the name
of Jesus Christ."

She remained for a while like that, between the death
and the life, and she without sense. The priest came
often, but he could do nothing with her. The seventh
day the priest came to her, and he brought the last oil
to anoint her with.

The candles were lit, but they were quenched upon the
spot. They tried to light them again, but all the coals
that were in the county Mayo would not light them. Then
he thought to put the oil on her without a candle, but on
the spot the place was filled with a great smoke, and it was
little but the priest was smothered. Patrick came to the
door of the room, but he could go no further. He could

hear the woman crying, " a drink, a drink, in the name of Christ ! "

She remained like this for two days, and she alive, and they used to hear her from time to time crying out, " a drink, a drink," but they could not go near her.

Word was sent for the Bishop O'Duffy, and he came at last, and two old friars along with him. He was carrying a cross in his right hand. When they got near Patrick's house, there came down on them with one swoop a multitude of kites, and it was little but they plucked the eyes out of the three.

They came then to Patrick's door and they lit the candles. The bishop opened a book and said to the friars, " When I shall begin reading the prayers do ye give the responses." Then he said, " Depart, O Christian soul —— "

" She is not a Christian soul," said a voice, but they saw no one.

The Bishop began again, " Depart, O Christian soul, out of this world, in the name of the all-powerful Father who created you." Before he could say more there came great thunder and lightning. They were deafened with the thunder ; the house was filled with smoke. The lightning struck the gable of the house and threw it down. The deluge came down so that the people thought it was the end of the world that was in it.

The Bishop and the two friars fell to their prayers again. " O Lord, according to the abundance of Thy mercy, look mercifully upon her," said the Bishop. " Amen," said the friars. There came a little calm and the Bishop went over to the bed. Poor Patrick came to

the other side of the bed, and it was not long until the
woman opened her mouth and there came a host of
dardeels out of it. Patrick let a screech and ran for fire
to put on them. When he came back the woman was
dead, and the dardeels gone.

The Bishop said prayers over her, and then he himself
went away and the two friars, and Patrick went out to get
women to wash the corpse, but when he came back the
body was not to be found either up or down. There was
a purse of gold round its neck, and the purse went with the
body, and there is no account of either of them from that
out.

Many was the story and version that the neighbours had
about Patrick Kerwan's wife. Some of them say that the
devil took her with him. Others said that the good people
carried her away. At all events there is no account of her
since.

At the end of a month after that the speckled disease
(smallpox) broke out amongst the children and they all
died. There was very great grief on Patrick. He was
alone, by himself, without wife, without children, but he
said : " Welcome be the will of God."

A short time after that, he sold all that he had and went
into a monastery. He spent his life piously and died a
happy death. May God grant us a good death and the
life that is enduring.

THE BURIAL OF JESUS.

PREFACE.

The first time I heard this poem was at the Galway Feis many years ago. A poor old man, called the Ceannuidhe Cóir (Canny Core) or Honest Merchant—I don't know what his real name was—recited it. I took him aside in the interval during the competitions and wrote the most of it down from his recitation. My friend, Eoghan O Neachtain, wrote the rest of it down for me from the old man's mouth later on, but with the greatest difficulty as he had lost his teeth and pronounced very badly. Neither of us ever heard the poem before, and it is obviously only a fragment of a long piece, now, I fear, hopelessly lost, in common with many others, once popular. Indeed, I have seen a copy of this poem written down by a man called Hessian some eighty years ago, who called it the Assire [=Aiseirghe], but it is hopelessly undecipherable. This curious piece refers to a story once so commonly known in Ireland that it may almost be said to have formed part of the regular account of the crucifixion. It is celebrated even more in Irish art than in Irish story and song. When examining a few years ago the remains of the beautiful abbey which gives to Ennis its Irish name of Mainistir na h-Innse, I saw where a portion of the stone carving had recently been laid bare, and there, as plain as though it had been carved yesterday, was a very spirited picture of the cock rising up out of the pot and getting ready to crow. This was included with the other symbols of the crucifixion. I have seen the same thing on old wooden crucifixes, and elsewhere. There seems to have been a body of legend in some way or other connecting the cock with the history of the Passion. A Coptic legend tells us that on the day of the betrayal a roasted cock had been served up to our Lord, who bade it rise up and follow Judas, who was then upon his way to make his bargain with the chief priests. The cock rose up and did what it was ordered, and brought back word to our Lord that the arch-traitor had sold Him, "and for this that cock shall enter Paradise." Thevonet Voyages II. 75, quoted in Journal for Apocrypha.

It is more likely, however, that the legend as we know it came from the second Greek form of the Gospel of Nico-demus, certain MSS. of which contain the following passage : "And when the Jews refused to receive again from Judas the thirty pieces of silver for which he had betrayed his Master, he threw them in their midst and went away. And he came home to make a halter out of a cord to hang himself with. There he found his wife sitting and roasting a cock upon the coals. And he said unto her : ' Rise wife and get a rope ready for me because I mean to hang myself as I deserve.' But his wife said unto him, ' Why speakest thou like that ? ' And Judas replied, ' Know then that I have unjustly betrayed my master, Jesus, to the evil-doers who have taken him before Pilate to put Him to death ; but He will rise again on the third day, and then woe to us." But his wife said unto him, ' Speak not so, and believe it not. For it is just as likely that this cock roasting on the coals will crow as that Jesus will rise, as thou sayest.' And while she was thus speaking the cock flapped his wings and crew thrice. Then was Judas yet the more convicted, etc." (Tischendorff, p. 289). The legend found its way into Scotland also. It is told in a bald version in Scotch Gaelic of only four verses, recovered by Carmichael (" Carmina Gadelica," vol. II., p. 176) : " That cock which you have in the pot pounded as fine as cabbage, the liar shall not leave the tomb until it crows upon the beam." For the original and literal translation, see " Religious Songs of Connacht."

THE STORY.

Virgin gentle, courteous, gracious,
Whose goodness, which my soul embraces,
A shaft of light through time and space is
To lead it into heavenly places.

Thy Holy Son, the King of Angels,
Suffered passion, wounds, estrangement,
In satisfaction for the ailments
Of the sins which here assail us.

*   *   *   *   *   *   *

He was laid in the tomb at the will of the King,
    He died with pains unstinted,
The blood of His heart on the point of the dart,
    And death on His cold face printed.

At the door of the tomb was a stone of gloom,
    Not a hundred men could heave it,
But an angel came from heaven like flame
    To raise it and to leave it.

The Magdalen came, and she came in her haste
    To wash His wounds in a minute,
She searched through the gloom of the rock-hewn tomb,—
    No trace of the Lord was in it.

She saw by the wall the grave clothes all
    Lying empty there, and started,
And timidly asked of the soldier guard,
    " Where has our Lord departed."

" I was here," said the guard, " I kept watch and kept ward,
    Why seek ye the truth to smother ?
I've a nice little cock who boils here in my pot—
    And the one is as dead as the other."

" I've a nice little cock who boils here in my pot,
    While the camp looks on and sees us,
And until the cock rises out of the pot,
    He never shall rise, your Jesus."

With that the dead cock flew out of the pot,
    And clapped with his wings loud crowing,
" Ochone " ! cried the man, and his features grew wan,
    " Then Jesus is up and doing."

[SPAKE THE VIRGIN.]
" I sicken, I sigh, with longing I die,
  If ye show me not where to find Him,
To put balm in the cuts and the stabs and the wounds,
  Wherewith in His side they signed Him."

He is gone where are gone the Apostles, and soon
  In Galilee thou shalt find him.

[SPAKE CHRIST.]
By Peter my Church has been holily built
  With flame of faithful endeavour,
Though the body be stricken the soul hath no guilt,—
  Confess ye My name for ever.

Here is another melodious little piece about the two
Marys which I got from my friend Miss Agnes O'Far-
relly, who got it from a young gossoon in Inismaan, or
in Aranmore, I do not know which.

UPROSE THE TWO MARYS.

Uprose the two Marys,
  Two hours ere day,
And they went to the temple
  To keene and to pray.

There came in the angel
  With candle so bright,
" All hail to thee, Mary,"
  Said God full of light.

" And dost thou forget it,
  Thy passion and pain,
And dost thou forget it,
  Thy slaying by men ?

" And dost thou forget it,
  The spear and the threat,
Which no children of Adam
  Could ever forget ? "

  *   *   *   *

Remember me, children
  Of Adam and Eve,
And the heavens of God
  Ye shall surely receive.

SAINT PETER.

PREFACE.

An old woman named Bridget Casey, from near Baile-
'dir-dhá-abhainn or Riverstown, Co. Sligo, told this story
to F. O'Conor in Athlone, from whom I got it. For the
original see " Religious Songs of Connacht," vol. 1, p. 192.

THE STORY.

AT the time that St. Peter and our Saviour were walking
the country, many was the marvel that his Master showed
him, and if it had been another person who was in it
and who had seen half as much, no doubt his confidence
in his Master would have been stronger than that of
Peter.

One day they were entering a town, and there was a
musician sitting half-drunk on the side of the road and he
asking for alms.   Our Saviour gave him a piece of money,
going by of him. There came wonder on Peter at that,
for he said to himself, " many's the poor man in great want
that my Master refused, but now He has given alms to this
drunken musician ; but perhaps," says he to himself,
" perhaps He likes music."

Our Saviour knew what was in Peter's mind, but he
did not speak a word about it.

On the next day they were journeying again, and a poor friar (*sic*) met them, and he bowed down with age and almost naked. He asked our Saviour for alms, but He took no notice of him, and did not answer his request.

"There's another thing that's not right," said Peter in his own mind. He was afraid to speak to his Master about it, but he was losing his confidence in Him every day.

The same evening they were approaching another village when a blind man met them and he asking alms. Our Saviour talked with him and said, "What do you want?" "The price of a night's lodging, the price of something to eat, and as much as I shall want to-morrow: if you can give it to me you shall get great recompense, and recompense that is not to be found in this sorrowful world."

"Good is your talk," said the Lord, "but you are only seeking to deceive me, you are in no want of the price of a lodging or of anything to eat, you have gold and silver in your pocket, and you ought to give thanks to God for your having enough to do you till [next] day."

, The blind man did not know that it was our Saviour who was talking to him, and he said to him, "It is not sermons but alms I'm asking for, I am certain that if you did know that there was gold or silver about me you would take it from me. Get off now, I don't want your talk."

"Indeed you are a senseless man," said the Lord, "you will not have gold or silver long," and with that He left him.

St. Peter was listening to the discourse, and he had a wish to tell the blind man that it was our Saviour who was talking to him, but he got no opportunity. But there was another man listening when our Saviour said that the blind man had gold and silver. It was a wicked plunderer who was in it, but he knew that our Saviour never told a lie. As soon as He and St. Peter were gone, the robber came to the blind man and said to him, " give me your gold and silver or I'll put a knife through your heart."

" I have no gold or silver," said the blind man, " if I had, I wouldn't be looking for alms." But, with that, the robber caught hold of him, put him under him, and took from him all he had. The blind man shouted and screamed as loud as he was able, and our Saviour and Peter heard him.

" There's wrong being done to the blind man," said Peter.

" Get treacherously and it will go the same way," said our Saviour, " not to speak of the Day of Judgment."

" I understand you, there is nothing hid from you, Master," said Peter.

The day after that they were journeying by a desert, and a greedy lion came out. " Now, Peter," said our Saviour, " you often said that you would lose your life for me, go now and give yourself to the lion, and I shall escape safe."

Peter thought to himself and said, " I would sooner meet any other death than let a lion eat me ; we are swift-footed, and we can run from him, but if I see him coming up with us I'll remain behind, and you can escape safe."

" Let it be so," said our Saviour.

The lion gave a roar, and off and away with him after them, and it was not long till he was gaining on them and close up to them.

"Remain behind, Peter," said our Saviour, but Peter let on that he never heard a word, and went running out before his Master. The Lord turned round and said to the lion, "go back to the desert," and so he did.

Peter looked behind him, and when he saw the lion going back, he stood till our Saviour came up with him.

"Peter," said He, "you left me in danger, and—what was worse than that—you told lies."

"I did that," said Peter, "because I knew that you have power over everything, not alone over the lion of the wilderness."

"Silence your mouth, and do not be telling lies ; you did *not* know, and if you were to see me in danger to-morrow you would forsake me again. I know the thoughts of your heart."

"I never thought that you did anything that was not right," said Peter.

"That is another lie," said our Saviour. "Do you not remember the day that I gave alms to the musician who was half drunk, there was wonder on you, and you said to yourself that many's the poor man in great want, whom I refused, and yet that I gave alms to a drunken man because I liked music. The day after that I refused the old friar, and you said that that was not right ; and the same evening you remember what happened about the blind man. I will explain to you now why I acted like that. That musician did more good than twenty friars of his sort since ever they were born. He saved a girl's soul from the pains of hell. She wanted a piece of money, and was going to commit a deadly sin to get it, but the musician prevented her and gave her the piece of money, though he himself was in want of a drink at the same time. As for the friar, he was not in want at all ; although he had the name of friar he was a limb of the devil, and that was why I paid him no heed. As for the blind man, his God was in his pocket, for the old word is true, ' where your store is your heart will be with it.' "

A short time after that Peter said, " Master, you have a knowledge of the most lonesome thoughts in the heart of man, and from this moment out I submit to you in everything."

About a week after that they were travelling through hills and mountains, and they lost their way. With the fall of the night there came lightning, thunder, and heavy rain. The night was so dark they could not see a sheep's path. Peter fell against a rock and hurt his foot so badly that he was not able to walk a step.

Our Saviour saw a little light under the foot of a hill, and he said to Peter, " remain where you are, and I will go for help to carry you."

" There is no help to be found in this wild place," said Peter, " and don't leave me here in danger by myself."

" Be it so," said our Saviour, and with that he gave a whistle, and there came four men ; and who was captain of them but the person who robbed the blind man a while before that ! He recognized our Saviour and Peter, and told his men to carry Peter carefully to the dwelling-place

they had among the hills. " These two put gold and
silver in my way a short time ago," said he.

They carried Peter into a chamber under the ground.
There was a fine fire in it, and they put the wounded
man near it, and gave him a drink. He fell asleep,
and our Saviour made the sign of the cross with his
finger above the wound, and when he awoke he was
able to walk as well as ever. There was wonder on
him when he awoke, and he asked " what happened to
him." Our Saviour told him each thing and how it
occurred.

" I thought," said Peter, " that I was dead, and that I
was up at the gate of heaven, but I could not get in, for
the door was shut, and there was no doorkeeper to be
found."

" It was a vision you had," said our Saviour, " but it is
true. Heaven is shut and is not to be opened until I die
for the sin of the human race who put anger on My Father.
It is not a common but a shameful death I shall get, but I
shall rise again gloriously and open the heaven that was
shut, and you shall be doorkeeper."

" Ora ! Master," said Peter, " it cannot be that you
would get a shameful death. Would you not allow me to
die for you ? I am ready and willing."

" You think that," said our Saviour.

The time came when our Saviour was to get death. The
evening before that He Himself and His twelve disciples
were at supper, when He said, " There is a man of you
going to betray Me." There was great trouble on them,
and each one of them said, " Am I he ? " But He said,

" He who dips with his hand in the dish with Me, he is the man who shall betray Me."

Peter said then, " If the whole world were against you," said he, " I will not be against you." But our Saviour said to him, " Before the cock crows to-night you will reneague (deny) Me three times."

" I would die before I would reneague you," said Peter ; " indeed I shall not reneague you."

When death-judgment was passed upon our Saviour, His enemies were beating Him and spitting on Him. Peter was outside in the court, when there came a servant-girl to him and said to him, " You were with Jesus." " I don't know," says Peter, " what you are saying."

Then when he was going out the gate another girl said, " There's a man who was with Jesus," but he took his oath that he had no knowledge at all of Him. Then some of the people who were listening said, " There is no doubt at all but you were with Him ; we know it by your talk." He took the great oaths, then, that he was not with Him. And on the spot the cock crew, and then he remembered the words our Saviour said, and he wept the tears of repentance, and he found forgiveness from Him whom he denied. He has the keys of heaven now, and if we shed the tears of repentance for our faults, as he shed them, we shall find forgiveness as he found it, and he will welcome us with a hundred thousand welcomes when we go to the door of heaven.

LEGENDS OF ST. DEGLAN.

PREFACE

I wrote down the following legend of St. Deglan, word for word, in Irish, from the telling of my friend, Padraig O'Dalaigh, who comes himself from the Decies.

THE STORY

WHEN Deglan was leaving Rome he held his bell in his hand, but as he was going into the ship he left the bell upon a rock that was by the harbour, and forgot to bring it with him. The ship put out to sea, with the bell left on the rock behind it.

When Deglan was coming near Ireland he remembered the bell, and knew that he had left it on the rock behind him in Rome. Old people say that long ago there used not to be much good in "a cleric without a bell." [1] Deglan knew that he would want the bell when he would land in Ireland, and he prayed God to send it to him.

At the end of a little time what should be seen swimming behind the ship but the rock and the bell on it, just as

---

[1] "A cleric without a bell," and "the forgetting his bell by the cleric," are common proverbs in Irish.

Deglan had left it at Rome. And when the vessel came
to land, then the stone came into the harbour at Ardmore,
and the stone comes up on the shore, and it is there yet.
The stone is set high up on the top of two smaller stones,
and room between the two for a man to pass out under
them. If you were to see the hole you would feel certain
that even a cat could not pass out through it, and yet a
big man can pass through.

Every Deglan's Day, the 24th of July, and the Sunday
nearest to it, thousands of people come from all over
the Decies, from twenty miles away, to the " pattern,"
and anyone who has anything the matter with him,
either disease or pain or sickness, goes in under that
stone, and believes firmly in his mind that he will be
healed. Hundreds do that yet, up to the present day.

About fifteen years ago the " pattern " was growing
small and dying out, but a feis, the second feis in
Ireland [in modern times] was held on Deglan's Sunday,
and thousands and thousands of people came to it, and
there had not been such a " pattern " for fifty years.
I myself have often seen people passing under the stones.

Every second person in the " seana-phoball," and in
the parish of Ardmore also, is called Deglan down to the
present day. Scarcely a month passes that a child is not
christened Deglan. The explanation that the people
give of the name of the parish called " Seana-phoball,"
or Old Parish, is that Deglan had made a parish of it
and that there were Christians there before there was
a parish, or before there were Christians in any other
place in Ireland, and " old phoball" is the same as " old
paróiste " or parish.

[The above story is the folk version of part of the following, which is here translated for the first time from an Irish MS. in my own possession. St. Deglan's church is spoken of in the MS. as still standing, and his miraculous stone as being still preserved there when the account was written. This throws back the account many hundreds of years. I collated my MS. carefully with one written in 1758 [23 M 50], preserved in R.I.A. It has never been printed, but I believe my friend, Father Power, will soon publish the entire life of St. Deglan.]

ST. DEGLAN.

OF HOW TRAMORE GOT ITS NAME.

And the people of the island concealed the ship so that Deglan could not embark on it, for they disliked it greatly that Deglan should inhabit it, for fear they themselves might be banished out of it.

His disciples then said to Deglan, " Father, thou often requirest to come to this place. We pray thee to avoid it, and mayest thou receive from God that the sea should ebb away from the land so that people may go into it with dry feet, for Christ has said that whatever shall be asked of My Father in My name He shall give it you, for it is not easy for thou to inhabit this place or to protect it."

And Deglan said, " This place which was promised me by God and where my burial was promised, how shall I be able to avoid it ? But concerning this thing which ye desire me to do, namely, to inhabit it, I like not to pray against the will of God concerning the taking away from the sea its own natural movement ; howsoever, at your entreaty I shall direct my petition to God, and whatsoever pleases God, let it be done."

Deglan's disciples arose, and they said, " take thy staff as Moses did with the rod, and smite the sea with it, and God shall make manifest His own will to thee in that wise," and his disciples besought him to do that, for they were faithful people. His staff was [accordingly] given into Deglan's hand, and he smote the water with it in the name of the Trinity, and he made the sign of the cross of crucifixion with it on the water, and quickly the sea began to move out of his own place—so quickly that it was scarcely the swift monsters[1] of the sea could keep pace with it by swimming, and it left many of them on the shore high and dry, who were not able to depart with the sea on account of the rapidity with which it moved. And Deglan followed the sea with his crozier in his hand, and his disciples followed him, and there was a cry and a great sounding from the sea and from the monsters departing. And when Deglan reached the place where Tarmuin-na-mara is now, a young child of Deglan's disciples by the name of Mainchin spake, he being terrified at the noises of the sea and at the roaring of the unknown monsters with their mouths open, following the water. " Father," said he, " thou hast displaced the sea enough, for I am afraid of yonder awful monsters." At the word of the child the sea stopped. And Deglan did not like that, and he struck a light blow on his nose, and three drops of blood dropped from him to the ground under Deglan's feet in three places. And Deglan blessed

---

[1] Biastaide luathe na mara.

the nose, and the blood ceased suddenly. And Deglan said, " it is not I who have removed the sea but the power of God, and it would have removed it further had it not been for the words thou spakest." And in the place where those drops of blood fell, three little wells of sweet shining water burst forth from them under the feet of Deglan. And those wells are still there. And they are seldom [without ?] that colour of blood upon them as a remembrance of those miracles. And there is a mile in length and in breadth around them, and the name of it is " the tramore," or " great shore," and good and profitable is the land of Tramore, and there was [built] Deglan's monastery. And the crozier that Deglan had in his hand, when performing that miracle, its name was " Feardhacht Deglan." We shall say something more about its miracles in another place.

Of How Ardmore Got Its Name, and of St. Deglan's Stone.

Deglan proceeded to say mass in a church that lay before him in his way, and a small black stone was sent from heaven through the window of the church to him, and it remained on the altar in his presence. Great joy seized Deglan at beholding it, and he gave praise and glory to God for it. Now his mind was firmly set against ill ways and the unreason of the heathen after the possession of the stone, and he gave that stone to Lunan, son of the King of the Romans, who was in his company, to keep and to carry for him. And the name

of that stone was Bobhur in Ireland,[1] namely Deglan's
" Duibhin " (or little black thing) and it was from its
colour it received that name, for by its colour it was
black, and it revealed [things] by the grace of God,
and Deglan performed many miracles [by it], and it
remains to this day in Deglan's church. . . . . .

. . . .

and on one of these occasions (a visit to Rome) he went
to a holy bishop of the Britons named David, to the
church which is called Cillmhin [Killveen], which is
beside the shore of the sea which divides Britain from
Ireland.   And the bishop received him with honour, and
he was for forty days in his society, with love and joy, and
he used to say mass each day there, and they knit themselves together with bonds of brotherhood and partnership, and [they bound] the people of the place after them.
And on his completing forty days there, they parted with
salutation, and he said farewell to David and gave him
a kiss in token of peace.   And he himself and his disciples
went to the shore of the sea to go into the ship to go to
Ireland.   And that stone I spake of, which was sent to
Deglan from heaven, a monk was carrying it at the time ;
for Deglan was unwilling ever to part with it, and it
used always to be in his company.   And when they came
from the shore into the ship the monk had forgotten it,
[and left it] on a rock which was on the shore.   And until
they had gone about half way over the sea they never
remembered it.   And when they did remember it
Deglan was melancholy, and so was every one else,

---

[1] This passage about Bobhur is not in the R.I.A. copy, only the
part about the Duibhin.

after the gift, which had come down from heaven to Deglan, being forgotten in a place from which they never thought to get it back. Deglan looked above his head to heaven, and clearly prayed to God in his mind. And then he said to his disciples, " lay aside your melancholy, for God who made a gift of that stone from heaven at the first can now send it to us in an unusual ship." Wonderful and splendid it was that the rock without understanding or reason submitted to the Creator contrary to nature, for it swam directly after the ship, with the stone on it, and it was not long until Deglan and his disciples saw the rock after them, and the stone upon it. And when Deglan's people beheld that miracle, they were filled with the love of God and with honour for their master, Deglan. And Deglan spake prophetically : " Let the stone go on in front of you, and follow ye it, for whatsoever harbour it shall arrive at, it is near it that my city shall be, and my house and bishoprick,[1] and it is from that place I shall go to God's heaven, and it is there that my resurrection shall be." And the stone went out past the ship, and ceased the great pace at which it had proceeded up to then, and remained a little in advance of the ship, so that it could be seen from on board the ship, yet in such wise that the ship might not overtake it. And the rock steered for Ireland so that it took harbour in the south, in the Decies, at an island that was at that time called Ard-Innis Caerach, or High Island of the Sheep, and the ship took the same harbour, as Deglan had told them.

---

[1] Mo chathair si agus mo thigheas easbogoidheacht in my MS. " Mo theaghdhais easbogoideachta " 23 M 50. 1758.

Deglan, that holy man, went on shore, and he gave praise and glory and thanks to God because that he had reached the place of his resurrection on that island, where the sheep of the king of the Déise used to be kept usually and herded. And there was a pleasant high hill on it. And one of his disciples said to Deglan on going to the top of that hill " how shall this Ard beag (Little Height) support thy people."

" Beloved son," said Deglan, " say not so. This is no Little Height, but an Ard Mór (Great Height)," and the name has clung to it ever since, namely Ardmore of Deglan.

———

THE LANDING OF ST. DEGLAN AT ARDMORE

ST. PAUL'S VISION;

OR,

THE LAST END OF THE MAN WHO LEADS A BAD LIFE.

PREFACE.

I took the following very curious account from an Irish MS. a couple of hundred years old, which had been thrown away on a loft in a farm house in the County Meath before I secured it. There are other copies of this story in the Royal Irish Academy, and a fragment in the library of University College, Dublin, but mine is the best copy I have met. There is no other version, so far as I know, of St. Paul's Vision that is at all like this. The Vision was at one time well known in Europe. It was at first, according to Tischendorf, probably composed in Greek, and there is a version of it in Syrian and another in Latin. The story is also found in old High German, in Danish, French and Slavonic. The best and longest Latin version is to be found in the Bibliothèque Nationale at Paris, but there is not a word in it, nor in the Greek, nor in the Syrian, of the driving of the soul out of the body, or of the angel Michael's guiding St. Paul to the bedside of the dying man. As it is unlikely that some Irish Gael composed all this out of his own head, I can only surmise that it is a translation of a Latin or Greek original now lost, and that the story now survives through its translation into Irish alone.

We know that the Irish have saved for us several pieces of an apocryphal or mystic character, whose originals are now lost, such as the extraordinary piece called the " Ever-new Tongue," and the " Vision of Tundal."

This story contains a close resemblance to the " Debate between the Body and the Soul," which is usually known as the " Visio Philaberti," ascribed to Walter Mapes, or Map, or else to Walter Grosseteste, bishop of Lincoln, and of which a kind of middle Irish version exists in the " Lea-bhar Breac " and was published by Atkinson in his " Passions and Homilies." Another imperfect version was published by Dottin in the " Revue Celtique," 1903. My MS. from which I have taken this Vision of St. Paul's contains an excellent copy of it also. Almost all the Irish copies ascribe it to Grosseteste.

The longest Latin version of this Vision contains 51 chapters or sections, and deals with St. Paul's account of Paradise and his other wanderings, as well as with the infernal regions.

There is a " Passion of St. Paul " in the Leabhar Breac, or Speckled Book, but there is not a word about this Vision in it. I found an account of St. Paul in another Irish MS., probably taken from some lost source. " A small, miserable-looking person was the apostle Paul. Broad shoulders he had ; a white face with a sedate demeanour. His head small. Pleasant bright eyes he had. Long brows, a projecting (?) nose and a long beard with a little grey hair."

The horrid description of the soul leaving the body with such reluctance has a curious Pagan parallel in an exactly reverse sense in Lucan's Pharsalia, Book vi., 721, in the dreadful account of the sorceress conjuring back a soul into the dead body, and its reluctance to enter it. " Adspicit adstan-tem projecti corporis umbram Exanimes artus, invisaque claustra timentem, Carceris antiqui : pavet ire in pectus apertum, Visceraque, et ruptas letali vulnere fibras. Ah miser extremum qui mortis munus iniquae, Eripitur non posse mori, etc.

The mediæval Irish translator of the Pharsalia revelled in this sorceress episode.

For the original of the following piece, see " Religious Songs of Connacht," vol. II.

THE STORY

THE Apostle Paul, upon a certain time, chanced to be in a city of the name of Smyrna, in the land of Syria. And this is how Paul was, namely, making intercession with God, the all-powerful, to reveal to him something of the pains of hell, so that all the more for receiving that revelation, he might perform the will of God, and give instruction to the congregations. And, as he was beseeching God in this wise, there cometh unto him a youth, and he asketh Paul to go with him, to confirm in his faith a man who was at the point of death. Paul departed along with the youth to the place where was the sick man, and him they found before them struggling with the Death. Now this is the manner wherein the soul parteth from the body—as saith St. Bernard, one of the arch-doctors of the Trinity. He saith that the Death cometh in a cold, unrecognisable, insufferable shape, stabbing the body with spits and arrows. And first it cometh into the outer members, namely the centre of the soles of the feet, and of the palms of the hands, in the veins, and in every other member of the body, until it hunt the noble soul before it out of every member of the body, even as the fisherman routeth the fish under the hollows of the banks (?) to the weedy-place (?) in which the net is set to catch them. Even so doth the Death, routing before it the soul into the heart—the first member of a person to be alive, and the last member to die.

But, howsoever, upon the coming of Paul and of the messenger to the sick man, they perceived how he himself and the Death were struggling with one another, and that the Death was after taking possession of all the body, except that the soul was in the lower chamber of the heart, striving to conceal itself from the Death. But that was in vain for it, for when Death came to the heart, he began ploughing and boring the heart, for he felt certain that it was there the soul was. But when the soul felt its enemy and adversary the Death close to it, it thought to leave the body and to come forth out of the mouth, since it found no dwelling place nor shelter in the body. But it is what it finds before itself there, a frightful fearsome host of black, ugly-coloured devils, and fiery flames full of stench, and a loathsome, insufferable, evil smell coming forth out of their mouths, and each one of them watching with fierceness for the soul to come forth out of the mouth and out of the body, for it was in a state of damnation, without repentance, that this sinner was dying. And when the poor soul beheld this devilish guard in front of it, the soul returned fearful (?) and quaking and cometh into the passage of the nose and thought to come out there. But it beholds the same host before it. It returneth full of weariness and misery and goeth to the eyes, but it is what it findeth there before it—many black, ugly-coloured devils with fiery flames out of their mouths and gullets, and each of them saying, " What is this delay of Death's that he routeth not out to us this damned soul forth from the greedy body in which it is, till we bear it with us to its own abode—a place where there is darkness and eternal pain for ever and ever as its evil deeds have deserved [that were wrought] during the time that it was its own master ? " And on the poor soul's hearing these words it screamed and cried feebly, and wept tearfully, sorrowfully, and with bitter weariness, for it recognised then that it was parted from the eternal life for ever and ever, and it turns back again to the hollows of the ears, where it thought to find a way out, but it is what it finds there before it many loathly worms and evil-shaped terrific serpents of various kinds. When the soul saw that, it returned back to the heart, for it desired to go, as it seemed to it, into hiding, but it found Death before it there, ploughing and boring the heart. Then the soul considered that it had no escape on any side. It despaired of God and of the whole angelic court, and it went aloft to the crown of the head. It goes out and leaves the body and settles on the top of the head. It looks down at that tomb where it had been—namely, the body—and said, " Oh ! all-powerful God ! is it possible that this is the body wherein I was for a brief [space of] happiness ; and if it is, where has gone the blue clear-seeing eye, or the crimson cheek ? 'Tis what I behold in place of the eyes—hollow dry cavities sucked back into the hollow of the skull ; the ruddy handsome cheek now dark and beetle-hued ; the mouth that was to-day red and shapely now closed, not to be opened, livid, hideous, without talk, without speech ; and oh ! all-powerful God ! alas for him who was deceived by the companion at the raising (?) of the body's strength, power, pride, and spirit, which was begotten and which was alive, and whose share of gold and treasures was great ; but I do not see one thing of all that in his pos-session now, nor advantaging nor comforting him at all ; but I see that it is ill he spent the gifts that God gave him, and that on account of this he has damned me for ever."

The body spake, and said : " If it were not for thee these devilish furious hosts would not come to claim me now. For this is how thou wast when thou wast bound to me ; thou wast an active, most powerful spirit, full of understanding and of feeling, and of clear intellect, of nobility and of honour ; thou didst recognise between evil and good ; whilst I was nothing but a fistful of clay, without beauty or strength, or feeling, or sense, or understanding, or power, or guidance, or movement, or sight, or hearing, until thou wast bound to me, and for that reason it is thou who art guilty and not I."

" Thou greedy, carnal, unsubduable worm, all thou sayest is not true, for I was a clean, glorious spirit," said the soul, " who had no necessity for food or clothing or for anything at all, of all that is on the earth, but the joy of holy life, until I was bound to thee. And this is why I was bound to thee, for thee to spend the activity of thy feet, the labour of thy hands, the sight of thy eyes, the hearing of thy ears, the speech of thy mouth, the thoughts of thy heart, and every other gift that God gave thee, so as to do ministering, to make submission, and to perform every other service to glorious God throughout thy period on this world, so that after that I and thou might find the fruit of those good deeds in the enjoyment of eternal glory in the company of God and of the Blessed Virgin Mary, and of all the angelic heavenly court, where cometh everyone who has done good deeds, such as fasting, alms-giving, prayers, acts of friendship to a neighbour, listening willingly to the words of God, and acting accordingly ; and who used not to refuse to relieve the necessity of the poor, and the like. But those are not the things that thou didst, but spending the gifts God gave with gluttony, drunkenness, adultery, pride, arrogance, greed ; with the ruin of thy neighbour's portion ; with lies, noisiness (?) anger, quarrelling, back-biting, folly, pitilessness, injustice, wrath, sloth, envy, lechery, with the spoil of the poor, and with every other sort of sin that the human body thought pleasant ; and lo ! what fruit hast thou for those misdeeds. Dead and feeble are thy limbs which were once active and strong ; closed is the mouth wherewith thou didst use to hold unlawful discourse ; weak is the tongue wherewith thou wast wont to utter obscene barbarous words, giving ill-fame, re-proach, disrespect, shame, contempt, displeasure, and every other sort [of evil] that thy thoughts and intellect could bring to mind. Deaf is the ear that used to listen with pleasure to murmurings, to scandal, to the back-biting of neighbours. Blind and hollow is the eye that used to look with greed, partiality, and malice. There is no fairness nor beauty in the hand on whose fingers the gems used to be. I see them not on thee now. And, more-over, I see not the gold nor the silver nor the various other goods which thou didst get by defrauding, which thou didst rob, which thou gottest from the weak, from the orphan, and from the miserable, with deceptions and ill-will. They are now in the possession of other people, and not one thing of them doing good to thee, but [doing] every evil that is possible to reckon. And, therefore, O greedy, lustful body, most unsubduable worm that God

ever created, it is thou art most guilty and not I," said
the soul.

After the soul uttering those words miserably and
wearily, an evil spirit of that damned host that was waiting
to get the soul into its own possession spake, and said :
" It is a wonder how long Death is without routing this
damned soul to us forth out of the body."

Another devil answered him and spake : " It is not
possible for us to possess it or to take it until Jesus Christ
pass judgment upon it first, according to its actions, bad
and good.   However, its possession for ever is ours ; for
ever, because it was to us it did service and ministry whilst
it was living, and ours is the possession of soul and
body from the day of the last judgment for ever."

After the devils speaking these words, a shining, happy
host of the angels of heaven lowered themselves, with
singing of music, round about the body, and in their
midst a Youth more glorious than the sun.   Many awful,
wide-opened wounds in His skin, and they dripping blood.
The Youth spake to the dead, and asked him how he had
spent the life that he got, or the gifts that God gave him.
The body answered and said: " O Jesus Christ, O Lamb,
Son of God, I am not able to deny it, that it was ill I
spent my time and the gifts that I got ; that Thou didst
suffer passion-pains and death on my behalf, and that
I paid no regard to that, and therefore I am myself
admitting that Thou hast no power (from the true
right of Thy divinity, and from the plentifulness of my
evil deeds, since I did not make repentance of them either
early or late) not to pass judgment damning me now.
And alas ! now I see the wrong, the loss, and the harm,

of the neglect I was guilty of, in putting off repentance, until Thy messenger, the Death, came to me, and, my grief ! I was not prepared for him, and, moreover, I got no respite when he came, until he destroyed me—and that is my account of my life, and indeed it is more evil than it is good."

"Well, then," said the Youth on whom were the wounds, " all that thou hast committed of faults and of evil deeds throughout thy life, if thou wert to make true repentance from thy heart of them, I would make thee as clean as the sun, and I would place thee in the company of the angels and of the saints, enjoying everlasting glory, and the devilish host which is waiting for thee would have no power nor might over thee. But since thou hast not done that, it is necessary to pass judgment upon thee according to thy deeds, bad and good."

Then there came each one of the demon host that was waiting for the poor soul, and a roll of dark black parchment in the hand of each of them, in which was written all that the dead man had done in the service of the devil. On the Saviour Jesus Christ perceiving that, it was what He said, " Take with you this damned soul to hell, to pain it till the day of the general judgment, and from that out ye shall have the body as well as the soul, enduring eternal pains."

Then came the devilish host that was waiting for the soul. They drew the poor soul with fiery crooks, and they made of it a lump of fire, and they were hunting it before them to hell, and it calling and crying out faintly and fearfully.

Paul the Apostle was observing each thing of those, because it was God who had sent His messenger to him, so that he might get a view of the person who led a bad life, at the point of death, according to the prayer he had made. Then, upon the departure of the accursed host and of the soul out of sight, Paul cried aloud, weeping and lamenting, to get a sight of the end that was being brought upon the soul. Then the messenger asked Paul did he desire to get a sight of the pains of that soul and of the other damned souls. " I should so desire," said Paul, " if it were God's will." " Well, then," said the messenger, " I will give thee a sight of them, for I am not a man of this earth, but an angel that God has sent to thee to show thee these things, and I am Michael the Arch-Angel," said he.

After these words the angel brought him to the brink of a valley that was stupendous for depth and fearfulness. Paul beheld, amongst the first things there, a great, dark, frightful river. Blacker than coal was its appearance, and jet black the bubbling terrible water that was in it, so that one puff alone of the venemous wind that used to come out of it would kill all the men and women of the world— were it not for the Spirit of God succouring them it would split stones and trees—and he beheld many loathly worms and snakes, and devils of divers shapes in it, raging, beating, gnawing (?), and bone-cutting one another ; cursing the day in which they were born or were created. And on the other opposite side of the river there was a dark cave in which were many damned souls screaming (?) ; being bound (?) and lashed. And some of them were in this wise, sitting on the fiery hearth of pains ;

many black, ugly-shaped devils serving and administering the insufferable pains to them, such as fiery flames, sharp and hurting (?), and the devils tossing them and turning them (?) with sharp-pointed spits in those flames. And there was a resting-lake (?) of very cold ice, full of venom, into which the damned souls used to leap, seeking cooling and comfort from the sharp goading of the fire. However, no sooner would they go to the lake than they would leap out of it again into the fire, by reason of its cold, and of the sharp venom that was in the water, and here are the words some of them would say :—" O all-powerful God, is there any redemption or help in store for us, or shall we be for ever in these pains, or in what place is Death that he cometh not unto us to put us into nothingness, so that we might find a sleep, on our being dead ? " Another spirit of them answered and said : " O accursed, devilish, damned spirits," said he, " there is no help nor redemption laid out for you for ever and ever, because this is the end your misdeeds deserved whilst ye were in life, with pride, with haughtiness, with gluttony, with inordinate desire, and with every other sort of sin. Ye have spent the gifts that God gave you, namely feeling, beauty, strength, airiness (?), happiness, the sight of the eyes, the hearing of the ears, the speaking of the mouth, the movement of the limbs, and all those [given] to do the service of God. However, what ye have done was to spend them in the service of the devil, and it is he who shall give you your wages in pains, without help or relief, for ever and ever."

" Knowest thou, O Paul," said the angel, " who they are who are pained like this ? "

"I know not," said Paul, "but it is on them are the hardships impossible to count-up or to show-forth."

"There," said the angel, "are the people of haughtiness and pride, who used to be bruising-to-pieces the poor, who gave themselves up to drinking and the evil desires of the world. Yon devils are beating them, and ministering to them eternal pains, and they shall be so for ever and ever, in eric for their misdeeds."

Paul beheld another band upon the fiery hearth of pains, many loathsome beetle-worms and serpents gnawing and bone-cutting each member of them ; some of the worms going into their mouths and their necks and coming out on their ears, and the spirits themselves collecting and drawing those devils and those loathsome reptiles to themselves.

"Knowest thou, O Paul," said the angel, "what people are pained like this ? "

"I know not," said Paul.

"Those," said the angel, "are the people of adultery and disgusting lust ; and in eric for the fair-coloured, gaudy clothes that they used to put upon themselves, both men and women, deceiving one another, those devils are for ever gnawing, overthrowing, and bone-cutting them."

Paul beheld another lot upon the fiery hearth of hell. Great mountains of fire on every side of them, many ill-shaped devils throwing down those mountains upon the very top of them, bruising them together and bitter-urging them for ever.

"Knowest thou, O Paul," said the angel, "what people are pained like this ? "

" I know not," said Paul.

" Those," said the angel, " are the people of greed, the lot who store and gather their neighbours' portion unlawfully, who used not to show mercy or give alms or act with humanity to the poor, and who used to oppress the feeble."

Paul saw another lot of people on the fiery hearth of pains, ever-hideous devils, their eyes straying in their heads, being pained and bitter-tortured, and being tightened with fiery chains.

" Knowest thou, O Paul," said the angel, " what people are pained like this ? "

" I know not," said Paul.

" Those are the people of envy, the lot who used to be tortured and burnt with envy and with jealousy when they used to see their neighbours' goods or possessions, and who would not be satisfied with the gifts that God would give themselves—and in eric for that they shall be tortured in this way for ever."

Paul beheld another band upon the hearth of fiery pains, up to their chins in cold frosty water of the colour of coal. More stinking was that water than a dead carcase after corruption. Many reptiles, swimming before them in that water, they being tortured with famine and with thirst, their mouths opened, crying for food and drink, it set before them, without its being in their power to taste it, for as often as they would make an attempt it used to remove farther from them.

" Knowest thou, O Paul," said the angel, " what people are pained like this ? "

" I know not," said Paul.

" Those are the people of gluttony, the people who never fasted nor abstained nor gave alms nor said prayers, who used to be eating and drinking forbidden food and drink, who used to give to the body its own satisfaction, with drunkenness, gluttony and lust, and never checked the want of the poor."

Paul beheld another band upon the hearth of fiery pains, and this is how that lot were, with fiery flames out of their mouths and gullets. An evil disgusting, insufferable smell upon that flame. Their eyes ghastly wandering, straying in their heads ; they pulling one another and beating one another like fully famished lions.

" Knowest thou, O Paul," said the angel, " what people are pained like that ? "

" I know not," said Paul.

" Those are the people of anger, of disobedience and of despair. They shall be thus for ever and ever."

Paul beheld another lot very cold and dark, upon the hearth of pains, bound with chains upon their narrow beds, bruised and tortured and tightened in bondage by those chains, full of foulness and of evil disgusting smell, and every pain that it is possible to think of.

" What people are those ? " said Paul.

" Those," said the angel, " are the people of sloth who used to remain away from Mass, from sermons, and from the service of God. Through sloth they used to neglect and disregard good deeds, and alas for him who is journeying towards that kingdom," said the angel, " for that is the habitation of the fiery pains and of the misery, the lake of cold, the prison of gall, the cave of darkness, the congregation of curses, the hearth of anger, the ford of snow, the captivity of sloth, the abode of misery, the dungeon of venom, the court of dispute, the war of the damned devils, the lake and the sea that is filled with wrath, with want, with envy, with covetous desire, with jealousy, and with all evil. *Uch hone, uch!* Alas for him who is journeying to it."

Howsoever, the angel showed Paul, at full length and completely, the pains of hell. And, on Paul's beholding all that, with the grace of God, and with the help of the angel, he gave thanks to God for receiving that vision, and he fell to thinking bitterly about the numbers of people on the world who were journeying to those pains. Then the angel led Paul from the clouds of hell until he gave him a sight of the glory of the heaven of God. And, on Paul's beholding that sight, no sorrow of all he had had in his life oppressed him. He beheld the entire glory of the heavenly palace. He beheld our Saviour Jesus Christ in the midst of the angels on His throne, and the Lord gave Paul a gentle, friendly welcome, and told him that it was a short time until he should come to eternal glory. Then the angel took Paul with him from the sight of the glory [of heaven], and left him in the place where he had found him at first, bade him farewell, and departed to heaven.

Paul was throughout his life teaching and preaching to the congregations and to the Gentiles about the glory of the heavens and the pains of hell.

Glory be to the living God !

OSCAR OF THE FLAIL.

PREFACE.

I wrote down the following story from the mouth of John Cunningham of Ballinphuill, Co. Roscommon, on the high road between Frenchpark and Ballaghaderreen, about twenty years ago. Oscar's flail is well known in Irish tradition. The poet O'Kelly, in his series of English curses on Doneraile, alludes to it—

> May Oscar with his fiery flail
> To pieces dash all Doneraile.

Mr. Stephen Gwynn, M.P., found a variant of this story in Donegal and has given a spirited poetic version of it. The story is also known in Waterford. It is probably spread all over the lands occupied by the Gael, and contains elements that are exceedingly old. The very verses about " the humming gnat or the scintilla of a beam of the sun " which I wrote down from the mouth of old John Cunningham in the Co. Roscommon, had been already jotted down in phonetics by Magregor, the Dean of Lismore, in Argyllshire in the year 1512. I printed the whole story with a French translation and introduction in the " Revue Celtique," vol. 13, p. 425, showing how in the Tripartite life of St. Patrick the story of piercing a penitent's foot is told of a son of the King of Munster. But, as his name was doubtless soon forgotten, the story got fathered upon Oisín.

The story had its rise, no doubt, in the sorrow felt by the people when the clerics told them that their beloved Fenians and Oisín and Finn were damned, and the story was probably invented by some clever person to save them from perdition. There are scores of MSS. which contain disputes between

St. Patrick and Oisín, or Ossian as the Scotch call him, on this very subject. See " Religious Songs of Connacht," vol. I., p. 209. For the allusion to Elphin, see the poem which follows.

THE STORY

SAINT PATRICK came to Ireland, and Oisín met him in Elphin and he carrying stones.

> And whatever time it might be that he got the food,
> It would be long again till he would get the drink.

" Oisín," says he, " let me baptize you."

" Oh, what good would that do me ? " says Oisín.

" Oisín," says St. Patrick, " unless you let me baptize you, you will go to hell where the rest of the Fenians are."

" If," says Oisín, " Diarmaid and Goll were alive for us, and the king that was over the Fenians, if they were to go to hell they would bring the devil and his forge up out of it on their back."

" Listen, O gray and senseless Oisín, think upon God, and bow your knee, and let me baptize you."

" Patrick," says Oisín, " for what did God damn all that of people ? "

" For eating the apple of commandment," says St. Patrick.

" If I had known that your God was so narrow-sighted that he damned all that of people for one apple, we would have sent three horses and a mule carrying apples to God's heaven to Him."

" Listen, O gray and senseless Oisín, think upon God, and bow your knee, and let me baptize you.

Oisín fell into a faint, and the clergy thought that he had died. When he woke up out of it, " O Patrick, baptize me," says he—he saw something in his faint, he saw the thing that was before him. The spear was in St. Patrick's hand, and he thrust it into Oisín's foot purposely ; and the ground was red with his share of blood.

" Oh," says St. Patrick to Oisín, " you are greatly cut."

" Oh, isn't that for my baptism ? " says Oisín.

" I hope in God that you are saved," says St. Patrick, " you have undergone baptism and . . . .?"

" Patrick," says Oisín, " would you not be able to take the Fenians out of hell "—he saw them there when he was in his sleep.

" I could not," says St. Patrick, " and any one who is in hell, it is impossible to bring him out of it."

" Patrick," says Oisín, " are you able to take me to the place where Finn and the Fenians of Erin are ? "

" I cannot," says St. Patrick.

> As much as the humming gnat
> Or a scintilla of the beam of the sun,
> Unknown to the great powerful king
> Shall not pass in beneath my shield.

" Can you give them relief from the pain ? " says Oisín.

St. Patrick then asked it as a petition from God to give them a relief from their pain, and he said to Oisín that they had found relief. This is the relief they got from God. Oscar got a flail, and he requested a fresh thong to be put into the flail, and there went a green rush as a thong into it, and he got the full of his palm of green sand,

and he shook the sand on the ground, and as far as the sand reached the devils were not able to follow ; but if they were to come beyond the place where the sand was strewn, Oscar was able to follow *them*, and to beat them with the flail. Oscar and all the Fenians are on this side of the sand, and the devils are on the other side, for St. Patrick got it as a request from God that they should not be able to follow them where the sand was shaken,— and the thong that was in the flail never broke since !

OISIN IN ELPHIN.

PREFACE.

In the story which I have just given it is said that St.
Patrick met Oisin when he was carrying stones in Elphin,
a small village in the County Roscommon, which was once
a great ecclesiastical centre founded by St. Patrick. I
had often heard other people in Roscommon tell about
Oisín's carrying those stones in Elphin, and of St. Patrick
meeting him there, but I always imagined that they had
localised the story because they themselves belonged to the
place. That this is not so, however, and that the story
of the ancient warriors being forced to carry stones in his
old age is old and genuine is proved by Magregor in Argyllshire jotting down a verse 400 years ago in which Ossian
tells how Finn had prophesied to him that he would yet be
carrying stones for the " Tailgin."

> Bea tou schell a tarraing clooch,
> Ma in deyt how in weit wronyth.

> i.e., béiᵭ τú ſeal·aꝃ ταſſⱥⁱⁿꝃ cloċ,
> man [rul] ᵭτéⁱᵭ τu ón ᵭⁱτ ᵭſⱥⁱⁿⱥċ

and the very poem (which I give here, taken from a Belfast
MS.) was written in phonetics by Magregor in far-away
Argyll.

Magregor's first line as read by McLaughlin (Skene's
Book of Lismore) runs " is fadda noch ni nelli fiym," but Dr.
Cameron later on gave a more correct reading " is fadda
not ni nelli finni." It is not to be translated as McLaugh-
lan does, " long are the clouds this night above me," but
" long is to-night in Elphin," ni nelli finni being evidently
to be transliterated as " i n-Ailfinne." This poem may
almost be looked upon as a pendant to the last piece. See
my " Religious Songs of Connacht."

COLD ELPHIN.

Long was last night in cold Elphin,
  More long is to-night on its weary way,
Though yesterday seemed to me long and ill,
  Yet longer still was this dreary day.

And long, for me, is each hour new-born,
  I fall forlorn to grinding grief
For the hunting lands, and the Fenian bands,
  And the long-haired generous Fenian Chief.

I make no music, I find no feast,
  I slay no beast from a bounding steed,
I give no gold, I am poor and old,
  I am cursed and cold without wine or mead.

No more I court, and I hunt no more,
  These were before my strong delight,
I have ceased to slay, and I take no prey,
  —Weary the day and long the night.

No heroes come in their war array,
  No game I play, and no gold I win ;
I swim no stream with my men of might,
  —Long is to-night in cold Elphin.

Would I were gone from this evil earth,
  I am wan with dearth, I am old and thin,
Carrying stones in my own despite,
  —Long is to-night in cold Elphin.

Ask, O Patrick, of God, for grace,
  And tell me what place he will hold me in,
And save my soul from the Ill One's might
  —For long is to-night in cold Elphin.

THE PRIEST WHO WENT TO DO PENANCE.

PREFACE.

This story I wrote down most carefully, word for word, from the telling of Mairtin Ruadh O Giollaruath, near Monivea, Co. Galway. He knew no English. I printed it in my " Sgeuluidhe Gaedhealach," published in Rennes. I know no variant of this story.

THE STORY.

THERE arose some little difference between three sons. A farmer's sons they were. One man of them said that he would leave home and go to an island (*i.e.*, emigrate). Another man of them became a priest, and the eldest brother remained at home.

The young priest never stopped until he went to Athlone to the college there, and he remained there for five years until his term had expired, and he was turned out a professed priest. He got himself ready, then, in the college, and said that he would go home to visit his father and mother.

He bound his books together in his bag, and then he faced for home. There was no mode of conveyance at that time; he had to walk. He walked all through the day until night was coming on. He saw a

light at a distance from him.   He went to it and found
a gentleman's big house.   He came into the yard and
asked for lodgings until the morning.   He got that from
the gentleman and welcome, and the gentleman did not
know what he would do for him, with the regard he had
for him.

The priest was a fine handsome man, and the daughter
of the gentleman took, as you would say, a fancy to him,
when she was bringing his supper—and a fine supper it
was he got.   When they went to sleep then the young
woman went into the room where the priest was.   She
began entreating him to give up the church and to marry
herself.   The gentleman had no daughter but herself,
and she was to have the house and place, all of it, and she
told that to the priest.

Says the priest, " don't tell me your mind," says he ;
" it's no good.   I am wed already to Mary Mother, and
I shall never have any other wife," says he.   She gave
him up then when she saw that it was no good for her,
and she went away.   There was a piece of gold plate in
the house, and when the young priest fell asleep she came
back again into his room, and she put the gold plate
unbeknownst to him into his bag, and out she went again.

When he rose then, in the morning, he was getting
himself ready to be going off again.   It was a Friday,
a fast day, that was in it, but she got a piece of meat
and put it into his pocket, unbeknownst to him.   Now
he had both the meat and the gold plate in his bag, and off
my poor man went, without any meal in the morning.
When he had gone a couple of miles on his road, up she
rose and told her father that the man that he had last

night with him, " it was a bad man he was, that he stole
the gold plate, and that he had meat in his pocket, going
away of him, that she herself saw him eating it as he went
the road that morning." Then the father got ready a
horse and pursued him, and came up with him and got
him taken and brought back again to his own house,
and sent for the peelers.

" I thought," said he, " that it was an honest man
you were, and it's a rogue you are," said he.

He was taken out then and given to the jury to be tried,
and he was found guilty. The father took the gold
plate out of the bag and showed it to the whole jury.
He was sentenced to be hanged then. They said that any
man who did a thing of that sort, he deserved nothing
but to put his head in the noose[1] and hang him.

He was up on the stage then going to be hanged,
when he asked leave to speak in the presence of the people.
That was given him. He stood up, then, and he told all
the people who he himself was, and where he was going
and what he had done ; how he was going home to his
father and mother, and how he came into the gentleman's
house. " I don't know that I did anything bad," said
he, " but the daughter that this gentleman had, she came
in to me, into the room, where I was asleep, and she asked
me to leave the church and to marry herself, and I would
not marry her, and no doubt it was she who put the gold
plate and the fish into my bag," and he went down on his
two knees then, and put up a petition to God to send them
all light that it was not himself who was guilty.

---

[1] Literally, " in the gallows."

" Oh, it was not fish that was in your bag at all but meat," said the daughter.

" It was meat perhaps that *you* put in it, but it was fish that I found in it," says the priest.

When the people heard that, they desired to bring the bag before them, and they found that it was fish in the place of meat that was in it.   They gave judgment then to hang the young woman instead of the priest.

She was put up then in place of him to be hanged, and when she was up on the stage, going to be hanged, " Well, you devil," said she, " I'll have you, in heaven or on earth," and with that she was hanged.

The priest went away after that, drawing on home. When he came home he got, after a while, a chapel and a parish, and he was quiet and satisfied, and everybody in the place had a great respect for him, for he was a fine priest in the parish.   He was like this for a good while, until a day came when he went to visit a great gentleman who was in that place ; just as yourself might come into this garden,[1] or like that, and they were walking outside in the garden, the gentleman and himself.   When he was going up a walk in this garden a lady met him, and when she was passing the priest on the walk, she struck a light little blow of her hand on his cheek.   It was that lady who had been hanged who was in it, but the priest did not recognise her, [seemingly] alive, and thought she was some other fine lady who was there.

She went then into a summer house, and the priest went in after her, and had a little conversation with her,

---

[1] This story was told to me in the garden of Mr. Reddington Roche, at Rye Hill.

and it is likely that she beguiled him with melodious conversation and talk before she went out.   When she
herself and he himself were ready to depart, and when they
were separating from one another, she turned to him and
said, " you ought to recognize me," said she, " I am
the woman that you hanged ; I told you that day that I
would have you yet, and I shall.   I came to you now to
damn you."   With that she vanished out of his sight.

He gave himself up then ; he said that he was damned
for ever.   He was getting no rest, either by day or by
night, with the fear that was on him at her having met
him again.   He said that it was not in his power either
to go back or forward—that he was to be damned for
ever.   That thought was preying on him day and night.

He went away then, and he went to the Bishop, and he
told him the whole story and made his confession to him,
and told him how she met him and tempted him.   Then the
bishop told him that he was damned for ever, and that there
was nothing in the world to save him or able to save him.

" I have no hope at all, so ? " said the priest.

The bishop said to him, " you have no hope at all,
till you get a small load of cambrick needles,"—the
finest needles at all—" and get a ship, and go out to
sea, and according as you go every hundred yards on the
sea you must throw away a needle from you out of the
ship.   Be going then," says he, " for ever," says he,
" until you have thrown away the last of them.   Unless
you are able to gather them up out of the sea and to bring
them all to me back again here, you will be lost for ever."

" Well that's a thing that I never shall do ; it fails
me to do that," said the priest.

He got the ship and the needles and went out to sea. according as he used to go a piece he used to throw a needle from him. He was going until he was very far away from land, and until he had thrown out the last needle. By the time he had thrown away the last needle, his own food was used up, and he had not a thing to eat. He spent three days then, on end, without bite or sup or drink, or means to come by them.

Then on the third day he saw dry land over from him at a distance. " I shall go," said he, " to yon dry land over there, and perhaps we may get something there that we can eat." The man was on the road to be lost. He drew towards the place and walked out upon the dry land. He spent from twelve o'clock in the day walking until it was eight o'clock at night. Then when the night had fallen black, he found himself in a great wood, and he saw a light at a distance from him in the wood, and he drew towards it. There were twelve little girls there before him and they had a good fire, and he asked of them a morsel to eat for God's sake. Something to eat was got ready for him. After that he got a good supper, and when he had the supper eaten he began to talk to them, telling them how he had left home and what it was he had done out of the way, and the penance that had been put on him by the bishop, and how he had to go out to sea and throw the needles from him.

" God help you, poor man," said one of the women, " it was a hard penance that was put upon you."

Says he, " I am afraid that I shall never go home. I have no hope of it. Have you any idea at all for me down from heaven as to where I shall get a man who

will tell me whether I shall save myself from the sins that
I have committed ? "

" I don't know," said a little girl of them, " but we
have mass in this house every day in the year at twelve
o'clock. A priest comes here to read mass for us, and
unless that priest is able to tell it to you there is no use
in your going back for ever."

The poor man was tired then and he went to sleep.
Well now, he was that tired that he never felt to get up,
and never heard the priest in the house reading mass
until the mass was read and priest gone. He awoke then
and asked one of the women had the priest come yet.
She told him that he had and that he had read mass
and was gone again. He was greatly troubled and
sorry then after the priest.

Now with fear lest he might not awake next day, he
brought in a harrow and he lay down on the harrow
in such a way that he would have no means, as he
thought, of getting any repose.

But in spite of all that the sleep preyed on him so much
that he never felt to get up until mass was read and the
priest gone the second day. Now he had two days lost,
and the girls told him that unless he got the priest the
third day he would have to go away from themselves.
He went out then and brought in a bed of briars on which
were thorns to wound his skin, and he lay down on them
without his shirt in the corner, and with all sorts of tor-
ture that he was putting on himself he kept himself awake
throughout the night until the priest came. The priest
read mass, and when he had it read and he going away,
my poor man went up to him and asked him to remain,

that he had a story to tell him, and he told him then the way in which he was, and the penance that was on him, and how he had left home, and how he had thrown the needles behind him into the sea, and all that he had gone through of every kind.

It was a saint who was in the priest who read mass, and when he heard all that the other priest had to tell him, " to-morrow," says the saint to him, " go up to such and such a street that was in the town in that country ; there is a woman there," says he, " selling fish, and the first fish you take hold of bring it with you. Fourpence the woman will want from you for the fish, and here is the fourpence to give her. And when you have the fish bought, open it up, and there is never a needle of all you threw into the sea that is not inside in its stomach. Leave the fish there behind you, everything you want is in its stomach ; bring the needles with you, but leave the fish." The saint went away from him then.

The priest went to that street where the woman was selling fish, as the saint had ordered, and he brought the first fish he took hold of, and opened it up and took out the thing which was in its stomach, and he found the needles there as the saint had said to him. He brought them with him and he left the fish behind him. He turned back until he came to the house again. He spent the night there until morning. He rose next day, and when he had his meal eaten he left his blessing to the women and faced for his own home.

He was travelling then until he came to his own home. When the bishop who had put the penance on him heard that he had come back he went to visit him.

" You have come home ?" said the bishop.

" I have," said he.

" And the needles with you ? " said the bishop.

" Yes," says the priest, " here they are."

" Why then, the sins that are on me," said the bishop, " are greater than those on you."

The bishop had no rest then until he went to the Pope, and he told him that he had put this penance on the priest, " and I had no expectation that he would come back for ever until he was drowned," said he.

" That same penance that you put upon the priest you must put it on yourself now," said the Pope, " and you must make the same journey. The man is holy," said he.

The bishop went away, and embarked upon the same journey, and never came back since.

THE FRIARS OF URLAUR.

PREFACE.

There is scarcely another country in Europe, outside perhaps of a part of Switzerland and the Tyrol, in which there is the same veneration for purity and female chastity as in the Irish-speaking provinces of Ireland. In the pathetic and well-known song which begins " tá mé sínte ar do thuamba, "I am stretched upon thy tomb," the man who was in love with the maiden who had died says :

> The priests and the friars
>   Wear faces of gloom
> At me loving a maiden
>   And she cold in her tomb.
> I would lie on your grave-sod
>   To shield you from rain,
> This the thought of you there, love,
>   Has numbed me with pain.
>
> When my people are thinking
>   That I am asleep,
> It is on your cold grave, love,
>   My vigil I keep.
> With desire I pine
>   And my bosom is torn,
> You were mine, you were mine,
>   From your childhood my storeen.

But the mourner is not left entirely without comfort when he remembers the purity of her who had died :

> You remember the night
>   'Neath the thorn on the wold,
> When the heavens were freezing
>   And all things were cold.
> Now thanks be to Jesus,
>   No tempter came o'er you,
> And your maidenhood's crown
>   Is a beacon before you.

In the story about St. Peter we saw how our Lord is made to say that the old drunkard who had kept a woman from evil had done more good than the friars themselves.

The following story seems to contain the same moral. It shows how it was not in the power of anything except virginity itself to banish the foul and evil spirit which had invaded the peace of the friars. There is a certain humour in the way in which the laziness, drunkenness and carelessness of the piper are portrayed, for by this is thrown into better relief the excellence of the only good deed he had performed.

The monastery of the friars is on the brink of the lake called Urlaur (floor), Orlar on the map. Àr-làr (slaughter-site) suggested in the text, is only folk-etymology. The remains are still to be seen, just inside the borders of the County Roscommon, and on the brink of the Co. Mayo. The monastery was built by Edward Costello and his wife Finuala, a daughter of the O'Conor Donn for the Dominican Friars, and was dedicated to St. Thomas. The Dominicans settled in it about the year 1430. On the dissolution of the monasteries it was granted to Lord Dillon, and it has now, with the rest of his enormous property, been bought by the Congested Districts Board and distributed amongst the tenants. We are told that there was once a town there, but there is now no trace of it. The monastery, being in such a retired spot, was set aside for the reception of novices throughout Connacht. The " pattern " here spoken of, *i.e.*, the gathering held in honour of the " patron " saint, used to take place on the 4th of August, St. Dominick's day. The place is four or five miles from the town of Kilkelly, and Tavran or Towrann, where the piper came from, is a townland between Ballaghaderreen and Lough Errit, not very far from Urlaur. For the original, see " Religious Songs of Connacht."

THE STORY.

In times long ago there was a House of Friars on the brink of Loch Urlaur but there is nothing in it now except the old walls, with the water of the lake beating up against them every day in the year that the wind be's blowing from the south.

Whilst the friars were living in that house there was happiness in Ireland, and many is the youth who got good instructions from the friars in that house, who is now a saint in heaven.

It was the custom of the people of the villages to gather one day in the year to a " pattern," in the place where there used to be fighting and great slaughter when the Firbolgs were in Ireland, but the friars used to be amongst the young people to give them a good example and to keep them from fighting and quarrelling. There used to be pipers, fiddlers, harpers and bards at the pattern, along with trump-players and music-horns ; young and old used to be gathered there, and there used to be songs, music, dancing and sport amongst them.

But there was a change to come and it came heavy. Some evil spirit found out its way to Loch Urlaur. It came at first in the shape of a black boar, with tusks on it as long as a pike, and as sharp as the point of a needle

One day the friars went out to walk on the brink of the lake. There was a chair cut out of the rock about twenty feet from the brink, and what should they see seated in the chair but the big black boar. They did not know what was in it. Some of them said that it was a great water-dog that was in it, but they were not long in doubt about it, for it let a screech out of it that was heard seven miles on each side of it ; it rose up then on its hind feet and was there screeching and dancing for a couple of hours.   Then it leaped into the water, and no sooner did it do that than there rose an awful storm which swept the roof off the friar's house, and off every other house within seven miles of the place. Furious waves rose upon the lake which sent the water twenty feet up into the air.   Then came the lightning and the thunder, and everybody thought that it was the end of the world that was in it. There was such a great darkness that a person could not see his own hand if he were to put it out before him.

The friars went in and fell to saying prayers, but it was not long till they had company.   The great black boar came in, opened its mouth, and cast out of it a litter of bonhams.   These began on the instant running backwards and forwards and screeching as loud as if there were the seven deaths on them with the hunger.   There was fear and astonishment on the friars, and they did not know what they ought to do.   The abbot came forward and desired them to bring him holy water.   They did so, and as soon as he sprinkled a drop of it on the boar and on the bonhams they went out in a blaze of fire, sweeping part of the side-wall with them into the lake. " A thousand thanks to God," said the Father Abbot, " the devil is gone from us."

But my grief ! he did not go far.   When the darkness departed they went to the brink of the lake, and they saw the black boar sitting in the stone chair that was cut out in the rock.

" Get me my curragh," said the Father Abbot, " and I'll banish the thief."

They got him the curragh and holy water, and two of them went into the curragh with him, but as soon as they came near to the black boar he leaped into the water, the storm rose, and the furious waves, and the curragh and the three who were in it were thrown high up upon the land with broken bones.

They sent for a doctor and for the bishop, and when they told the story to the bishop he said, " There is a limb of the devil in the shape of a friar amongst you, but I'll find him out without delay." Then he ordered them all to come forward, and when they came he called out the name of every friar, and according as each answered he was put on one side. But when he called out the name of Friar Lucas he was not to be found. He sent a messenger for him, but could get no account of him. At last the friar they were seeking for came to the door, flung down a cross that he had round his neck, smote his foot on it, and burst into a great laugh, turned on his heel, and into the lake. When he came as far as the chair on the rock he sat on it, whipped off his friar's clothes and flung them out into the water. When he stripped himself they saw that there was hair on him from the sole of his foot to the top of his head, as long as a goat's beard. He was not long alone, the black boar came to him from the bottom of the lake, and they began romping and dancing on the rock.

Then the bishop enquired what place did the rogue come from, and the (father) Superior said that he came a month ago from the north, and that he had a friar's dress

on him when he came, and that he asked no account from
him of what brought him to this place.

" You are too blind to be a Superior," said the bishop,
" since you do not recognise a devil from a friar." While
the bishop was talking the eyes of everyone present were
on him, and they did not feel till the black boar came
behind them and the rogue that had been a friar riding on
him. " Seize the villain, seize him," says the bishop.

" You didn't seize me yourself," says the villain, " when
I was your pet hound, and when you were giving me the
meat that you would not give to the poor people who
were weak with the hunger ; I thank you for it, and I'll
have a hot corner for you when you leave this world."

Some of them were afraid, but more of them made an
attempt to catch the black boar and its rider, but they went
into the lake, sat on the rock, and began screaming so loud
that they made the bishop and the friars deaf, so that they
could not hear one word from one another, and they
remained so during their life, and that is the reason they
were called the " Deaf Friars," and from that day (to this)
the old saying is in the mouth of the people, " You're as
deaf as a friar of Urlaur."

The black boar gave no rest to the friars either by night
or day : he himself, and the rogue of a companion that he
had, were persecuting them in many a way, and neither
they themselves nor the bishop were able to destroy or
banish them.

At last they were determining on giving up the place
altogether, but the bishop said to them to have patience till
he would take counsel with Saint Gerald, the patron saint
of Mayo. The bishop went to the saint and told him the

story from beginning to end. " That sorrowful occur-
rence did not take place in my county," said the saint,
" and I do not wish to have any hand in it." At this
time Saint Gerald was only a higher priest in Tirerrill (?)
but anything he took in hand succeeded with him, for he
was a saint on earth from his youth. He told the bishop
that he would be in Urlaur, at the end of a week, and that
he would make an attempt to banish the evil spirit.

The bishop returned and told the friars what Gerald had
said, and that message gave them great courage. They
spent that week saying prayers, but the end of the week
came, and another week went by, and Saint Gerald did
not come, for " not as is thought does it happen." Gerald
was struck with illness as it was fated for him, and he could
not come.

One night the friars had a dream, and it was not one
man alone who had it, but every man in the house. In the
dream each man saw a woman clothed in white linen, and
she said to them that it was not in the power of any man
living to banish the evil spirit except of a piper named
Donagh O'Grady who is living at Tavraun, a man who did
more good, says she, on this world than all the priests and
friars in the country.

On the morning of the next day, after the matin
prayers, the Superior said, " I was dreaming, friars, last
night about the evil spirit of the lake, and there was a ghost
or an angel present who said to me that it was not in the
power of any man living to banish the evil spirit except
of a piper whose name was Donagh O'Grady who is
living at Tavraun, a man who did more good in this world
than all the priests and friars in the country."

" I had the same dream too," says every man of them.

" It is against our faith to believe in dreams," says the Superior, " but this was more than a dream, I saw an angel beside my bed clothed in white linen."

" Indeed I saw the same thing," says every man of them.

" It was a messenger from God who was in it," said the Superior, and with that he desired two friars to go for the piper. They went to Tavraun to look for him and they found him in a drinking-house half drunk. They asked him to come with them to the Superior of the friars at Urlaur.

" I'll not go one foot out of this place till I get my pay," says the piper. " I was at a wedding last night and I was not paid yet."

" Take our word that you will be paid," said the friars.

" I won't take any man's word ; money down, or I'll stop where I am." There was no use in talk or flattery, they had to return home again without the piper.

They told their story to the Superior, and he gave them money to go back for the piper. They went to Tavraun again, gave the money to the piper and asked him to come with them.

" Wait till I drink another naggin ; I can't play hearty music till I have my enough drunk ? "

" We won't ask you to play music, it's another business we have for you."

O'Grady drank a couple of naggins, put the pipes under his oxter (arm-pit) and said, " I'm ready to go with ye now."

" Leave the pipes behind you," said the friars, " you won't want them."

" I wouldn't leave my pipes behind me if it was to Heaven I was going," says the piper.

When the piper came into the presence of the Superior, the Superior began examining him about the good works he had done during his life.

" I never did any good work during my life that I have any remembrance of," said the piper.

" Did you give away any alms during your life ? " said the Superior.

" Indeed, I remember now, that I did give a tenpenny piece to a daughter of Mary O'Donnell's one night. She was in great want of the tenpenny piece, and she was going to sell herself to get it, when I gave it to her. After a little while she thought about the mortal sin she was going to commit, she gave up the world and its temptations and went into a convent, and people say that she passed a pious life. She died about seven years ago, and I heard that there were angels playing melodious music in the room when she was dying, and it's a pity I wasn't listening to them, for I'd have the tune now ! "

" Well," said the Superior, " there's an evil spirit in the lake outside that's persecuting us day and night, and we had a revelation from an angel who came to us in a dream, that there was not a man alive able to banish the evil spirit but you."

" A male angel or female ? " says the piper.

" It was a woman we saw," says the Superior, " she was dressed in white linen."

" Then I'll bet you five tenpenny pieces that it

was Mary O'Donnell's daughter was in it," says the piper.

" It is not lawful for us to bet," says the Superior, " but if you banish the evil spirit of the lake you will get twenty tenpenny pieces."

" Give me a couple of naggins of good whiskey to give me courage," says the piper.

" There is not a drop of spirits in the house," says the Superior, " you know that we don't taste it at all."

" Unless you give me a drop to drink," says the piper, " go and do the work yourself."

They had to send for a couple of naggins, and when the piper drank it he said that he was ready, and asked them to show him the evil spirit. They went to the brink of the lake, and they told him that the evil spirit used to come on to the rock every time that they struck the bell to announce the " Angel's Welcome " [Angelical Salutation].

" Go and strike it now," says the piper.

The friars went, and began to strike the bell, and it was not long till the black boar and its rider came swimming to the rock. When they got up on the rock the boar let a loud screech, and the rogue began dancing.

The piper looked at them and said, " wait till I give ye music." With that he squeezed on his pipes, and began playing, and on the moment the black boar and its rider leapt into the lake and made for the piper. He was thinking of running away, when a great white dove came out of the sky over the boar and its rider, shot lightning down on top of them and killed them. The waves threw them up on the brink of the lake, and the piper went and told the

Superior and the friars that the evil spirit of the lake and its rider were dead on the shore.

They all came out, and when they saw that their enemies were dead they uttered three shouts for excess of joy. They did not know then what they would do with the corpses. They gave forty tenpenny pieces to the piper and told him to throw the bodies into a hole far from the house. The piper got a lot of tinkers who were going the way and gave them ten tenpenny pieces to throw the corpse into a deep hole in a shaking-scraw a mile from the house of the friars. They took up the corpses, the piper walked out before them playing music, and they never stopped till they cast the bodies into the hole, and the shaking-scraw closed over them and nobody ever saw them since. The " Hole of the Black Boar " is to be seen still. The piper and the tinkers went to the public house, and they were drinking till they were drunk, then they began fighting, and you may be certain that the piper did not come out of Urlaur with a whole skin.

The friars built up the walls and the roof of the house and passed prosperous years in it, until the accursed foreigners came who banished the friars and threw down the greater part of the house to the ground.

The piper died a happy death, and it was the opinion of the people that he went to Heaven, and that it may be so with us all !

DIALOGUE BETWEEN TWO OLD WOMEN.

PREFACE.

This story of the two women I got from Francis O'Connor. He said he heard it from one Mary Casey, a Co. Galway woman, but I don't know from what part of Galway. It is I who am responsible for the dialogue form of it, which I have used instead of putting in an occasional bald " said Mary," " said Sheela " ; but it really was told more in a dramatic then a narrative form, the reciter's voice showing who was speaking. The words I have not interfered with.

I once heard a dialogue not unlike this between two Melicete Indians in Canada who fell to discussing Theology over the camp-fire at night after hunting. One was a Catholic and the other a close replica of Maurya in our dialogue.

The story of Páidin Críona seems familiar to me, but I cannot think where or in what literature I have met it before.

THE STORY.

MAURYA.

A HUNDRED welcomes Sheela, it's a cure for sore eyes to see you ; sit down and rest and tell us your news.

SHEELA.

Musha ! I have no news. It is not news that's troubling me.

MAURYA.

Arrah ! and what's troubling you ? sure you're not ill !

SHEELA.

I'm not ill, thanks be to God and to His blessed mother, but I do be thinking of the four last ends—the Death and the Judgment, and Hell and Heaven, for I know I shan't be much longer in this sorrowful world, and I wouldn't mind if I were leaving it to-morrow.

MAURYA.

No nonsense at all of that sort ever comes into *my* head, and I'm older than you. I'm not tired of this world yet. I have knowledge of this world, and I have no knowledge at all of the other world. Nobody ever came back to tell me about it. I'll be time enough thinking of Death when he comes. And, another thing,—I don't believe that God created anyone to burn him in hell eternally.

SHEELA.

You're going astray Maurya ; were you at mass last Sunday ?

MAURYA.

Indeed and I was not ! I was doing a thing more profit-able. It was taking care of my hens I was, to keep them from laying abroad, or I wouldn't have the price of a grain of tea or sneesheen throughout the week. That *bolgán-béiceach* Father Brian wouldn't give me a penny if it was to keep me from being hanged. He's only a miserable greedy *sanntachán*. I had a little sturk of a pig last Christ-mas and he asked me to sell it to give him a shilling on Christmas Day, and as I didn't do that, he called out my name the Sunday after, in the chapel. He's not satisfied

with good food, and oats for his horse, and gold and silver
in his pocket. As I said often, I don't see any trade as
good as a priest's trade ; see the fine working clothes they
wear, and poor people earning it hard for them.

SHEELA.

I wonder greatly at your talk. Your unbelief is great.
I wonder that you speak so unmannerly about Father
Brian, when if you were dying to-morrow, who would
give you absolution but the same father ?

MAURYA.

Arrah ! Sheela, hold your tongue. Father Brian
wouldn't turn on his heel, either for you or for me, without
pay, even if he knew that it would keep us out of hell.

SHEELA.

The cross of Christ on us !   I never thought that it was
that sort of a woman you were. Did you ever go to
confession ?

MAURYA.

I went the day I was married, but I never bowed my
knee under him before or since.

SHEELA.

You have not much to do now, and you ought to think
about your poor soul.

MAURYA.

That wouldn't keep the hens from laying abroad on me,
and if I were to go to confess to Father Brian, instead of
absolution it's a barging I'd get from him, unless I had a
half-crown on the top of my fingers to give him.

SHEELA.

Father Brian isn't half as bad as you say ; I'm to go to

his house this evening with fresh eggs and a print of butter.
I'll speak to him about you if you give me leave.

MAURYA.

Don't trouble yourself about me, for I'm not going near
Father Brian : when I'll be on my death-bed *he'll* come
to *me*.

SHEELA.

And how do you know that it's not a sudden death
you'd get, and what would happen to you if you were to
get a " death without priest ? "

MAURYA.

And wouldn't I be as well off as the thousands who got
death without e'er a priest.   I haven't much trust in the
priests.   It's sinners that's in them all ; they're like our-
selves, exactly.   My own notion is that there's nothing in
religion but talk.   Did you ever hear mention of Páidín
Críona[1] [wise Patsy].

SHEELA.

I did, often.

MAURYA.

Very well ; did you ever hear his opinion about religion ?

SHEELA.

Indeed, I never did, but tell it to me if you please.

MAURYA.

Musha, then, I will.   There were three officers living in
one house and Paudyeen Críona [Cree-on-a] was servant
to them.   There were no two of them of the same religion,
and there used often to be a dispute amongst them—and
every man of them saying that it was his own religion was

---

[1] Pronounced " Paudyeen Creeŏna."

the best religion. One day a man of them said, "We'll leave it to Wise Paudyeen as to which of us has the best religion." "We're satisfied," said the other two. They called in Paudyeen and a man of them said to him, "Paudyeen, I'm a Catholic, and what will happen to me after my death?"

"I'll tell you that," says Paudyeen. "You'll be put down into the grave, and you'll rise again and go up to the gate of heaven. Peter will come out and will ask you, 'what religion are you of.' You'll tell him, and he'll say, 'Go and sit in that corner amongst the Catholics.'"

"I'm a Protestant," said the second man, "and what'll happen to me after my death?"

"Exactly as the other man. You will be put sitting in the corner of the Protestants!"

"I'm a Hebrew," says the third man, "and what will happen to me after my death?"

"Exactly as the other two; you will be put sitting amongst the Hebrews."

Now there was no one of them better off than the other, as Paudyeen left them, and so the Catholic asked Paudyeen, "Paudyeen, what's your own religion?"

"I have no religion at all," says he.

"And what'll happen to you after your death?"

"I'll tell you that. I shall be put down into the hole, I shall rise again and go up to the gate of heaven. Peter will come and ask me, 'of what religion are you?' I will say that I have no religion at all, and Peter will say then, 'come in, and sit down, or walk about in any place that you have a wish for.'"

Now, Sheela, don't you see that he who had no religion at all was better off than the people who had a religion ! Every one of them was bound to the corner of his own creed, but Paudyeen was able to go in his choice place, and I'll be so too.

SHEELA.

God help you Maurya ; I'm afraid there's a long time before your poor soul in Purgatory.

MAURYA.

Have sense Sheela ; I'll go through Purgatory as quickly as lightning through a gooseberry bush.

SHEELA.

There's no use talking to you or giving you advice. I'll leave you.

When Sheela was going out, Maurya let a screech out of her which was heard for a mile on every side of her. Sheela turned round and she saw Maurya in the midst of a flame of fire. Sheela ran as fast as was in her to Father Brian's house, and returned with him running to Maurya's house. But, my grief ! the house was burned to the ground, and Maurya was burnt with it ; and I am afraid that the [her] poor soul was lost.

THE MINISTER AND THE GOSSOON.

PREFACE.

This curious little piece is another dialogue in the same form as the last.   These are the only two stories, if one may call them stories, which I have found couched in this form. so partly for that reason I give it here.

———

THE STORY

ONE day there was a poor little gossoon on the side of the road, and he taking care of an old sow of a pig, and a litter of bonhams along with her.   A minister came the way, and he riding upon a fine horse, and he said to the gossoon, " Where does this road bring you ? "

GOSSOON.

I'm here for a fortnight, and it never brought me anywhere yet.

MINISTER.

Now, isn't it the wise little boy you are !   Whose are the little pigs ?

GOSSOON.

They're the old sow's.

MINISTER.

I know that, but I'm asking you who is the master of the bonhams.

GOSSOON.

That little black-and-white devil that you see rooting, he's able to beat the whole of them.

MINISTER.

That's not what I'm asking you at all, but who is your own master?

GOSSOON.

My mistress's husband, a man as good as you'd get from here to himself.

MINISTER.

You don't understand me yet. Who is your mistress—perhaps you understand that?

GOSSOON.

I understand you well. She is my master's wife. Everyone knows that.

MINISTER.

You're a wise little boy; and it's as good for me to let you be, but tell me do you know where Patrick O'Donnell is living?

GOSSOON.

Yes, indeed. Follow this road until you come to a boreen on the side of your thumb-hand. Then follow your nose, and if you go astray break the guide.

MINISTER.

Indeed, and you're a ripe (precocious) little lad! What trade will you have when you'll be older?

GOSSOON.

Herding a pig. Don't you see that I'm putting in my term. What is your own trade?

MINISTER.

A good trade. I am showing the people what is the way to heaven.

GOSSOON.

Oh, what a liar !   *You* can't show the way to any place. You don't know the way to Patrick O'Donnell's, a man that everybody—big and little—in this country knows, and I'm certain sure you have no knowledge of the road to heaven.

MINISTER.

I'm beaten. Here's half a crown for you for your cleverness, and when I come again you'll get another

GOSSOON.

Thank you. It's a pity that a fool like you doesn't come the way every day.

THE KEENING OF THE THREE MARYS.

PREFACE.

I got the following poem from a schoolmaster called O'Kearney, near Belmullet, in West Mayo, who told me that he had taken it down from the recitation of an old man in the neighbourhood. I got another version of it afterwards from Michael Mac Ruaidhri of Ballycastle, Co. Mayo, with quite a different " cur-fa " or refrain, namely *ŏch ōch agus ŏch ūch ān* after the first two lines, and *ŏch ŏch ōch ŏn ō* after the next two. Spelt phonetically in English and giving *gh* the guttural value of *ch* in German, and *oa* the same sound as in English *roach* and *oo* the sound of oo in *pool*, it would run—

> Let us go to the mountain
> All early on the morrow,
> Ugh oagh agus ugh oogh awn.
> Hast thou seen my bright darling,
> O Peter, good apostle,
> Ugh ugh agus oagh on ó.

The agus " and " is pronounced nearly as " oggus " The story I have not traced, but it may have come from an Irish version of one of the apocryphal gospels.

THE STORY

> Let us go to the mountain
> All early on the morrow,
> (Ochone! agus ochone, O !)
> " Hast thou seen my bright darling,
> O Peter, good apostle ? "
> (Ochone! agus ochone, O !)

" Aye ! truly O Mother
    Have I seen him lately,
      (Ochone agus ochone, O !)
Caught by his foemen,
    They had bound him straitly,"
      (Ochone agus ochone, O !)

" Judas, as in friendship,
    Shook hands, to disarm him,"
      (Ochone agus ochone, O !)
Oh, Judas ! vile Judas !
    My love did never harm him.
      (Ochone agus ochone, O !)

No child has he injured,
    Not the babe in the cradle,
      (Ochone agus ochone, O !)
Nor angered his mother
    Since his birth in the stable.
      (Ochone agus ochone, O !)

When the demons discovered
    That she was his mother,
      (Ochone agus ochone, O !)
They raised her on their shoulders
    The one with the other ;
      (Ochone agus ochone, O !)

And they cast her down fiercely
    On the stones all forlorn,
      (Ochone agus ochone, O !)
And she lay and she fainted
    With her knees cut and torn,
      (Ochone agus ochone, O !)

" For myself, ye may beat me,
    But, oh, touch not my mother,"
      (Ochone agus ochone, O !)
" Yourself,—we shall beat you,
    But we'll slaughter your mother."
      (Ochone agus ochone, O !)

They dragged him off captive,
    And they left her tears flowing,
      (Ochone agus ochone, O !)
But the Virgin pursued them
    Through the wilderness going,
      (Ochone agus ochone, O !)

" Oh, who is yon woman ?
    Through the waste comes another,"
      (Ochone agus ochone, O !)

" If there comes any woman
        It is surely my mother,"
        (Ochone agus ochone, O !).

" Oh John, care her, keep her,
        Who comes in this fashion,"
        (Ochone agus ochone, O !)
    But Oh, hold her from me
        Till I finish this passion,"
        (Ochone agus ochone, O !)

    When the Virgin had heard him
        And his sorrowful saying,
        (Ochone agus ochone, O !)
    She sprang past his keepers
        To the tree of his slaying,
        (Ochone agus ochone, O !)

" What fine man hangs there
        In the dust and the smother ? "
        (Ochone agus ochone, O !)
" And do you not know him,
        He is *your* son, O Mother."
        (Ochone agus ochone, O !)

" Oh, is that the child whom
        I bore in this bosom,
        (Ochone agus ochone, O !)
    Or is that the child who
        Was Mary's fresh blossom ' !
        (Ochone agus ochone, O !)

    They cast him down from them
        A mass of limbs bleeding,
        (Ochone agus ochone, O !)
" There now he is for you,
        Now go and be keening,"
        (Ochone agus ochone, O !)

    Go call the three Marys
        Till we keene him forlorn,
        (Ochone agus ochone, O !)
    O Mother thy keeners
        Are yet to be born,
        (Ochone agus ochone, O !)

    Thyself shall come with me
        Into Paradise garden,
        (Ochone agus ochone, O !)
    To a fair place in heaven
        At the side of thy darling,
        (Ochone agus ochone, O !)

THE FARMER'S SON AND THE BISHOP.

PREFACE.

The following story is an extract from a much longer piece in prose and verse, which I take from a manuscript in my own possession made by Patrick O Prunty (grand-uncle, I think of Charlotte Brontë), in 1764. It is called "the Counsel of Mac Lava from Aughanamullin to Red Archy, that is Red Shane, son of Bradach, son of Donal the gloomy, son of Shane, son of Torlogh, etc." In a manuscript in the Royal Irish Academy I find it entitled "The Counsel of Mac Lavy from Aughanamullin to his cousin Red Archy Litis on his forsaking his wife to take the yoke of piety on him, that is of Priestifying; or, the 'Priest of the Stick' by Laurence Faneen." In another MS. of mine, written by the well-known scribe Labhrás O Fuartháin from Portlaw in Co. Waterford, in 1786, it is called "The Counsel of Mac Clava from Aughanamullin to Red Archy Mac a Brady."

The poem is entirely satirical, and the gist of it is that the writer advises Archy not to be working like a poor man in dirt and misery, but from himself to earn the reputation of having a little Latin, and to become a *bullaire,* a comic word for bull-promulgator or priest. Any kind of Latin he tells him will do with an uneducated congregation. such as " Parva nec invideo " or " Hanc tua Penelope," or " Tuba mirum spargens sonum " or " ego te teneo, Amen ! " The poet tells his victim that when he is reading he can twist and stifle his voice " like a melodious droning and partly a humming (?) through the nose, and partly the smothering of a cough, and then the wealthy full-ignorant laity amongst the congregation shall say that it is a great pity the short-

ness of breath, the pressure on the chest, and the tightness
round the breast that strikes the blessed, loud-voiced, big-
worded priest at the time of service." He then proceeds
to tell him the following story, in the style of the Irish
romances common in the eighteenth century. For the
original Irish and the poem and notes, see vol. I., p. 180,
" Religious Songs of Connacht."

THE STORY.

O, Cousin Archy, I must now tell you a little allegory
which has a bearing upon your own present case, about a
greedy, fat-boned, stoop-headed, bashful fellow of a son,
that a long-bearded, broad-sided, cow-herd-ful, large-
flock-having Farmer had, who was once on a time residing
by the side of the island and the illustrious Church of
Clonmacnois. And this aforesaid Farmer was accus-
tomed to double his alms to a godly-blessed hermit
who was living close by him, [giving] with excess of
diligence beyond [the rest of] the congregation, in order
that he might have the aid of this hermit in putting
forward that blockhead (?) of a son towards the priesthood.

At last, on the priest of that parish in which they were,
dying, the Farmer promulgates and lays bare to the
hermit the secret conception and intention which he had
stored up for a long time before that, and it was what he
said to him, that he considered, himself, that there was
no person at all who would better suit that congregation
as a parish priest than this son of his own, from the
love of the priesthood which he had.

The Farmer beseeches and begs him—giving him large offerings on the head of it—to go with his son to the presence of the Bishop of Clonmacnois. They set forth all three, side by side, on that journey, the farmer, the hermit, and the farmer's son, together with a great congregation of their friends and cousins, and of the Farmer's acquaintance accompanying him to the strand and harbour of that island of Clonmacnois.

It was then a gentleman who was in the assembly asked the Farmer with prophesying truly-wise words whether he knew if his lad of a son were wise [educated] enough to receive the grade of priesthood on that occasion. He answered that he knew, himself, that he was, without any doubt, because he had been for seven years clerk of salt and water [i.e., acolyte] to the blessed godly Father who departed to heaven from us but now, and moreover, that he was plentiful with his Amens at time of mass or marriage, and that in this respect he had generally too much rather than too little. " Oh, I am satisfied," said the gentleman, turning his back on him, bursting into a fit of laughing.

However, upon the Farmer thus satisfying the gentleman's question, they were all silent, until the hermit's lad the " Shouting Attendant " (?) gave a shout at the beach, asking for a curach and means of transport to row to the island. After that comes to them a broad-wombed, long-timbered boat, with eight loutish, big-biting, lumpish (?), dawdling (?), raw-nosed (?), great-sleeping spalpeens of the parish on the left hand of the Farmer's son. They enjoin on the Farmer with his people to wait on the beach of the harbour until they themselves should come back. This they do.

In the meantime, on the above-mentioned couple going into the bishop's presence, the hermit discloses the reason and meaning of his journey. The bishop consents, at the request of the hermit, to confer the degrees of priesthood on the Farmer's son, and makes some of the clergy who were along with him put scholarly questions to the youth, so that they might have some knowledge of the amount of his learning to give the bishop. However, they found nothing either great or small of any kind of learning whatsoever in him. After that they report to the bishop about the youth's ability.

The bishop is angry at the clergy on hearing their report, and 'twas what he said that it was shame or fright (?) they put on the youth, and he himself calls him with him far apart, to the brink and very margin of the lake, in solitude, so that they came within the view of the Farmer and his people on the opposite side, and he addresses him in Latin with courteous truly-friendly words, and 'twas what he said—

Quid est sacramentum in nomine Domini ?

Qui fecit cœlum et terram, says the fellow.

Numquam accedes ad altare Dei, says the bishop.

Ad Deum qui laetificat juventutem meam, says the lad.

Non fies sacerdos per me in sæcula sæculorum, says the bishop.

Amen, says he.

Then was the bishop excessively enraged against the Farmer's son, and raised his arm with a thick-butted apple-knotted * * * * ? cudgel of a stick, that he had in his right hand, and begins lacing and leathering and whaling the Farmer's son without sparing, so that his blood and inwards ran down to the very ground.

" Ow ! but that's sad, my son's case now," says the Farmer, " and I think myself that every comfort and satisfaction (?) and roasted hen and every bottle that he shall get like a prolute (prelate ?) sitting in his coverlet with kindness from this out, is not to be begrudged him ; for it's hard and pitiably, it's patiently, gently, meekly and humbly my child takes the religious yoke and the grade of priesthood on him this night, and it's not easily it will be forgotten by him to the termination of his career and his life, for it's diligently, piously, firmly, and soundly, the blessed bishop drives it into his memory with swift hand-blows of the large stick."

However, on the bishop's parting from the Farmer's son, the aforesaid spalpeens came up to the young priest and asked his blessing. He lifted up his hands clericlike and piously above their heads, and gave them general absolution, saying *Asperges me Domine hysoppo et mundabor, lavabis me et super nivem dealbabor.*

They carried him with them to the curach after that, and leapt into it, flowingly and high-spiritedly, until they reached land on the other side, and all that were in the island harbour made the same reverence to the Farmer's son, and they asked him where was his bull or charter of priesthood.

He said he had no charter but the bull of the race of stoop-headed Conor Mac. Lopus of Cavan to the Vicarage of Leargan,—the will of the people.

They swore by the God of the elements that he never could have a better charter than that, and they bound themselves by the sun and the moon to defend that parish for him to the end of his term and his life. And they did so.

And now Archy, the story which does not concern a smotàn (?) is good, for it is you that the application of this story concerns, and it is the good advice to you to take the same grade of priesthood, and if blows of a stick be struck on you, it is small damage compared with every comfort and ease that you will get on the head of it, and in addition to every other advice I have given you, here are a couple of little ranns for you which shall be in your memory continually, so that they may be a good help in every pinch that is before you.   *   *   *   *   *   *

SHAUN THE TINKER.

PREFACE.

I wrote down this story carefully from the mouth of Mártain Ruadh O Giollarnáth from near Monivea, Co. Galway. He had no English. The story is a well-known one. It is the basis of Father O'Leary's delightful book "Séadna." It has been examined at great length with much learning and perspicacity by Carl Marstrander in the Miscellany presented to Kuno Meyer, pp. 386 ff., to which I refer the reader.

According to a Donegal story, called " Domhnall O Dochartaigh," taken down and given me by the late Mr. Larminie, Death is the being who is tricked. But, according to a Galway story which I heard, the Tinker had a son whose godfather was Death. He became a doctor and cured everybody at whose feet he saw Death standing. Death gave him leave to do this. Attracted one day by a huge bribe he turned round the bed where the patient lay so that Death, who had been at the patient's head with intent that he should die, was now at the patient's foot, who consequently recovered. After this Death is tricked in much the same way as the Devil in our story.

THE STORY.

THEY were poor, both of them, the man and his wife. The man had no other means in the world except his day's pay, going here and going there, and earning his day's wages from place to place.

The beginning of the harvest was come now, and he went in to the wife and said to her—Elleesh was the wife's name—" Elleesh," says he, " stand up," says he, " and make ready my meal for me until I go to Kildare to-morrow."

Elleesh got ready the meal for him as well as ever she was able, and she washed him and tidied him up and put good clean trousers on him, and himself got ready to be going. And the poor man did go, off he went. He had no provisions going away then, only four shillings to pay his way.

He was going then and journeying until he came to the top of a bridge, and there he met with a stumble and was thrown on one knee. " Oh, musha," says he, " the devil break my neck when I'll pass this way again."

He went on then and he never stopped until he came into Kildare, and he settled with a farmer there and spent four years with him without coming home at all. He never took one penny from the farmer in the course of the four years except as much as put clothing on him. Now at the end of the four years he took it into his head to be going home again.

And this was what he was getting in the year—five pounds. And likely enough, when he took it into his head to be going, that he said to the farmer and to the farmer's wife that he was to be departing in the morning. They gave him his share of money then. Then he made for home, and fifteen pounds was what he had coming home of him. He never spent but five pounds on his clothes all the time he was with the farmer.

He was coming and ever-coming along the road until

he came to a corner where four roads met. A poor man met him and asked alms of him. " God salute you," says he.

" God and Mary salute you," says Shaun.

" In Kildare you were," says he.

" Well, yes," says Shaun.

" You have money so," says he, " and I am asking my alms of you in honour of God and of Mary."

" He gave him alms then—five pounds he gave him. " Now Shaun," says the poor man, when he was going away from him. " I don't like you to go away without giving you [your] earned reward for your five pounds. " What is the thing that you most wish for ? "

" Anything that I desire," says Shaun, " me to have lots of money for it in my pocket. And anything that would be putting trouble on me, me to have leave to shut it up in this bottle which I have in my hand."

" You'll get that," says he.

He was going along then until he came to the corner of four other roads and another poor man met him. " God salute you," says the poor man. " God and Mary salute you." " You were in Kildare," said the poor man. " That's the place I was," says Shaun. " If you are coming back out of Kildare you're not without money, and I am asking my alms of you in honour of God and Mary. " It's short till I have my money spent," says Shaun. " But here," says he, putting the hand in his pocket, " here's five pounds for you."

When he gave it to him, the poor man said, " I don't like you to go away without giving you a reward for your five pounds. What sort of a thing is it that you'd

like best to have?" "Any person that would be
doing anything at all out of the way with me [me
to be able] to put him into my budget and him to
remain there until myself would give him leave to go
away, or until myself would let him out. "You'll have
that to get," says he.

He went away, then, and he was travelling until he
went where four other roads met. There was another
poor man before him there. "This is the third man,"
says Shaun. "God salute you, Tinker Shaun," says he
as soon as Shaun came up with him. "God and Mary
salute you." "You're coming out of Kildare, Shaun,"
says he. "I am, indeed," says Shaun. But he said to
himself, "Isn't it well how every man recognises me and
without me recognising them." "I am asking my alms
of you in honour of God and of Mary if you have any
money with you coming from Kildare." "Oh, musha,
I'll give you that and my blessing. I met another
pair before this and I gave five pounds to each
man of them, and here's five pounds for you." "I
don't like you to go away Shaun without your reward,
and what is the thing you'd have most desire for?"
"Well, then," says Shaun, "when I was at home I had
an apple tree in the garden at the back of the house, and
I used to be troubled with gossoons coming there and
stealing the apples. I should like, since I am going home
again now, that every person except myself who shall lay
his hand on that tree that his hand should stick to it,
and that he should have no power of himself to go away
without leave from me. "You'll get that Shaun," says
he.

He was travelling then until he came to the bridge where he had stumbled as he was going to Kildare the time he was thrown on one knee. Who should be standing on the bridge before him but the Devil. " Who are you ?" says Tinker Shaun. " I am the Devil," says he.

" And what sent you here ? " says Shaun.

" Well," says he, " when you went this way before didn't you say that if you were to go this way again might the Devil break your neck ? "

" I said that," says Shaun.

" Well, I've come before you now that I may break your neck."

" Try if you can," said Shaun. The Devil moved over towards him and was going to kill him, when Shaun said, " In with you into my bag this moment and don't be troubling me." The Devil had to go into the bag because Shaun had that power.

Shaun was going along then, and the Devil in the bag slung over his back. When he came to the next bridge he stood to take a rest and there were two women washing there. " I'll give ye five pounds and give my bag a good dressing with the beetles." They began beating it. " The bag is harder than the Devil himself," say they. " It is the Devil himself that's in it," says Shaun, " and lay on him." They beat it really then until they gave him enough.

He threw it up over his back then and off he went until he came to a forge. He went into the forge. " I'll give you five pounds," says he to the smith, " and strike a good spell on this bag." There were two smiths there and they began leathering the bag. " Why, then," says one of the smiths, " your bag is harder than the Devil himself." " It is the Devil himself that's in it," says Shaun, " and lay on him, ye, and beat him." One of the men put a hole in the bag with the blow he gave it and he looked in on the hole and he saw the Devil's eye at the hole. The poker was in the fire and it red hot The smith stuck it into the hole in such a way that he put it into the Devil's eye, and that's the thing which has left the old Devil half blind ever since.

He raised the bag on his back then, and he was going away when the Devil rose up and burst the bag and departed from him. Shaun came home.

At the end of a quarter of a year when Shaun was at home with the wife the Devil came to him again " You must come with me, Shaun," says he ; " make your soul," says he, " I'll give you death without respite."

" I'll go with you," says Shaun ; " but give me respite until to-morrow until I have everything ready, and I'll go with you then and welcome."

' I won't give you any respite at all ; neither a day nor an hour, you thief."

" I won't ask you for any respite," says Shaun, " only as long as I would be eating a single apple off that tree. Pull me one yourself, and I'll be with you."

The old Devil moved over to the tree, and took hold of a branch to pluck an apple off it and he stuck to the branch, and was not able to loose himself. He remained there on the branch during seven years.

One day that Shaun was in the garden again by himself he was not thinking, but he went gathering a bundle of

kippeens for Elleesh, to make a fire for her, and what was
the branch it should fall to him to cut for Elleesh but the
branch in which the Devil was. The Devil gave a leap
into the air. " Now Shaun," says he, " be ready ;
you will never go either forward nor back. You must
come with me on the spot."

" Well I'll go," says Shaun ; "I'll go with you," says
he ; " but it's a long time we are at odds with one another, and we ought to have a drink together. Elleesh
has a good bottle and come in till we drink a drop of it
before we go." " Why, then, I'll go with you," says the
Devil, as there was the Devil's thirst on him after his being
up in the tree so long. They drank their enough then
inside in Elleesh's hovel, and when the Devil had the
bottle empty he rose up standing, that he might get a grip
of Shaun's throat to choke him. " In with you into the
bottle," says Shaun. " In with you this moment," says
he. " Did you think that you would play on me," says he.
The Devil had to go into the bottle, and he spent seven
years inside the bottle, with Shaun, without being
let out.

Now it fell out that Elleesh had a young son, and there
was a bottle wanting to go for stuff for Elleesh. What
was the bottle they should bring with them but the
bottle in which the Devil was down, and when they took
the cork out of it the Devil went off with himself.

Shaun was gone away looking for gossips for his son.
The Son of God met him.

" God salute you, Shaun," says he.

" God and Mary salute you."

" Where were you going now, Shaun ? " says he.

" I was hunting for gossips for my son," says Shaun.

" Would you give him to me, and I'll stand for him ? "

" Who are you ? " says Tinker Shaun.

" I am the Son of God " says he.

" Well, then, indeed, I won't give him to you," says Shaun, " you give seven times their enough to some people, and you don't give their half enough to other people."

The Son of God departed.

The King of Sunday met him then and they saluted one another.

" Where were you going ? " says the King of Sunday.

" Well, then, I was going hunting for a gossip for my son."

" Will you give him to me ? " says the King of Sunday.

" Who are you ? " says Shaun.

" I am the King of Sunday."

" Indeed, then, I won't give him," says Shaun. " You have only a single day in the week and you're not able to do much good that day itself."

In this way he refused him, and the King of Sunday departed from him.

Who should meet him then and he coming home but the Death. [The Devil was afraid to go near him again, but he sent the Death to meet him.] " Make your soul now Shaun," says he, " I have you."

" Oh, you wouldn't give me death now," says Shaun, " until I baptise my son."

" All right, baptise him," said the Death. " Who will you put to stand for him ? "

" I don't see any person," says Shaun, " better than yourself. It's you who will leave him longest alive," says he.

When he got the son baptised he gave death to Shaun. He would not allow him to be humbugging him.

MARY AND ST. JOSEPH AND THE CHERRY TREE.

PREFACE.

I wrote down this poem from the mouth of Michael Mac Ruaidhri or Rogers, from near Ballycastle, in the Co. Mayo. The last five verses of it, which he had not got, I obtained from Martin O'Callaly (or Caldwell in English) in Erris, in the same county. There is a cherry tree carol in English, and an excellent one in German. The original legend was probably told of a date tree. A fifteenth century Dutch carol retains the date tree. In a legendary life of the Blessed Virgin, quoted by Jewitt in his book "The Nativity in Art and Song," we are told that the Blessed Virgin, during the flight into Egypt, resting in the heat of the noon day, saw a palm loaded with dates and desired them, but they were high up out of reach. Then the child Jesus, who was yet in the arms of Mary and had never spoken, lifted up his voice and said to the palm tree, "bend thy branches O tree, bow down and offer thy fruits to My mother," and immediately the tree bent down its top even to the feet of Mary, and all were nourished with the fruits it bore. And the palm tree remained bent to the earth awaiting that He whom it had obeyed should bid it again to rise. And Jesus said, "Arise, O palm tree ; thou shalt be the companion of the trees which grow in the paradise of my father." And while He was yet speaking behold an angel of the Lord appeared, and taking a branch from the tree he flew through the midst of heaven holding the palm in his hand.

The story has found its way into art. In "A Flight into Egypt," by Martin Schongaur, angels bow the palm tree

and St. Joseph gathers the dates. In a work of Andrea
Solario (Milanese School) St. Joseph is seen giving the fruit
with one hand to the Virgin, and with the other to her
Divine Son.

This poem was at one time known in the Highlands as
well as Ireland, for Carmichael recovered a very poor and
imperfect version of eight verses, which he printed in his
monumental work " Carmina Gadelica," vol. II., p. 162.

A very pretty anonymous sixteenth century German
Christmas hymn appears to allude to our story in the
first verse, which runs as follows :—

> Als Gott der Herr geboren war
>   Da war es kalt,
> Was sieht Maria am Wege stehn
>   Ein Feigenbaum.
> Maria lass du die Feigen noch stehn
> Wir haben noch dreissig Meilen zu gehn.
>   Es wird uns spat.

The word "Als" must here be taken as equivalent to
"Ehe."

———

THE STORY.

> HOLY was good St. Joseph
>   When marrying Mary Mother,
> Surely his lot was happy,
>   Happy beyond all other.

> Refusing red gold laid down,
>   And the crown by David worn,
> With Mary to be abiding
>   And guiding her steps forlorn.

> One day when the twain were talking,
>   And walking through gardens early,
> Where cherries were redly growing,
>   And blossoms were blowing rarely,

> Mary the fruit desired,
>   For faint and tired she panted,
> At the scent on the breezes' wing
>   Of the fruit that the King had planted.

Then spake to Joseph, the Virgin,
    All weary and faint and low,
" O pull me yon smiling cherries
    That fair on the tree do grow,

" For feeble I am, and weary,
    And my steps are but faint and slow,
And the works of the King of the graces
    I feel within me grow."

Then out spake the good St. Joseph,
    And stoutly indeed spake he,
" I shall not pluck thee one cherry,
    Who art unfaithful to me.

" Let him come fetch thee the cherries,
    Who is dearer than I to thee,"
Then Jesus, hearing St. Joseph,
    Thus spake to the stately tree.

" Bend low in her gracious presence,
    Stoop down to herself, O tree,
That My mother herself may pluck thee,
    And take thy burden from thee."

Then the great tree lowered her branches
    At hearing the high command,
And she plucked the fruit that it offered,
    Herself with her gentle hand.

Loud shouted the good St. Joseph,
    He cast himself on the ground,
" Go home and forgive me, Mary,
    To Jerusalem I am bound ;
I must go to the holy city,
    And confess my sin profound."

Then out spake the gentle Mary,
    She spake with a gentle voice,
" I shall not go home, O Joseph,
    But I bid thee at heart rejoice,
For the King of Heaven shall pardon
    The sin that was not of choice."

THE STUDENT WHO LEFT COLLEGE.

PREFACE.

The following curious story has parallels in many countries.
It is probably founded upon the verse in II. Peter iii. 8.
" Quia unus dies apud Dominum sicut mille anni et mille
anni sicut unus dies "—" for a thousand years are with the
Lord as one day, and one day as a thousand years." It
need not, however, be founded upon any Christian concep-
tion, for the purely Pagan story of Oisín or Ossian in the
" Land of the Ever-Young " was known all over Ireland.
Oisín thought he had spent only a short time in the Happy
Other-World, but when he returned to Ireland he found
he had been away for 300 years, and every one he knew had
died.

The reciter had forgotten what the name of the monastery
was, but I believe it to have been the ancient abbey and
school at Killarney, now in ruins. I have heard that the
things told in this story, or one similar to it, were supposed
to have happened there.

The river with water as red as blood reminds us of Thomas
of Ercildoune's experience when rapt away into faërie by
the queen.

> O, they rode on, and farther on
>   And they waded through rivers above the knee,
> And they saw neither sun or moon
>   But they heard the roaring of the sea.

> It was mirk, mirk night, there was nae stern light
>   And they waded through red blude to the knee,
> For a' the blude that's shed on earth
>   Runs through the springs of that country.

Hence it was small wonder that the student thought that
the musicians belonged to the Fairy-Host.

The fact that while in the other world he ate nothing, is pure Pagan tradition, for as is well known from many stories, classical and other, whoso eats or drinks of other-world food is precluded from returning to this life. Proserpine would not eat in Pluto's realm or she must have remained there. The six pomegranate seeds she swallowed cost her six months' stay there.

For the text of this story, see " Religious Songs of Connacht," vol. II., p. 122.

THE STORY.

THERE came a number of young people from the County of Galway, to a great college, to learn and gain instruction, so as to become priests. I often heard the name of this college from my mother, but I do not remember it. It was not Maynooth. There was a man of these of the name of Patrick O'Flynn. He was the son of a rich farmer. His father and his mother desired to make a priest of him. He was a nice, gentle lad. He used not to go dancing with the other boys in the evening, but it was his habit to go out with the grey-light of day, and he used to be walking by himself up and down under the shadow of the great trees that were round about the college, and he used to remain there thinking and meditating by himself, until some person would come to bring him into his room.

One evening, in the month of May, he went out, as was his custom, and he was taking his walk under the trees when he heard a melodious music. There came a darkness or a sort of blindness over his eyes, and when he found his sight again he beheld a great high wall on every side of him, and out in front of him a shining road. The musicians were on the road, and they playing melodiously, and he heard a voice saying, " *Come with us to the land of delight and rest.*" He looked back and beheld a great high wall behind him and on each side of him, and he was not able to return back again across the wall, although he desired to return. He went forward then after the music. He did not know how long he walked, but the great high wall kept ever on each side of him and behind him.

He was going and ever-going, until they came to a great river, and water in it as red as blood. Wonder came upon him then, and great fear. But the musicians walked across the river without wetting their feet, and Patrick O'Flynn followed them without wetting his own. He thought at first that the musicians belonged to the Fairy-Host, and next he thought that he had died and that it was a group of angels that were in it, taking him to heaven.

The walls fell away from them then, on each side, and they came to a great wide plain. They were going then, and ever-going, until they came to a fine castle that was in the midst of the plain. The musicians went in, but Patrick O'Flynn remained outside. It was not long until the chief of the musicians came out to him and brought him into a handsome chamber. He spoke not a word, and Patrick O'Flynn never heard one word spoken so long as he remained there.

There was no night in that place, but the light of day throughout. He never ate and he never drank a single thing there, and he never saw anyone eating or drinking, and the music never ceased. Every half-hour, as he thought, he used to hear a bell, as it were a church-bell, being rung, but he never beheld the bell, and he was unable to see it in any place.

When the musicians used to go out upon the plain before the castle, there used to come a tribe of every sort of bird in the heavens, playing the most melodious music that ear ever heard. It was often Patrick O'Flynn said to himself, " It is certain that I am in heaven, but is it not curious that I have no remembrance of sickness, nor of death, nor of judgment, and that I have not seen God nor His Blessed Mother, as is promised to us ? "

Patrick O'Flynn did not know how long he was in that delightful place. He thought that he had been in it only for a short little time, but he was in it for a hundred years and one.

One day the musicians were out in the field and he was listening to them, when the chief came to him. He brought him out and put him behind the musicians. They departed on their way, and they made neither stop nor stay until they came to the river that was as red as blood. They went across that, without wetting their foot-soles, and went forward until they came to the field near the college where they found him at the first. Then they departed out of his sight like a mist.

He looked round him, and recognised the college, but he thought that the trees were higher and that there was some change in the college itself. He went in, then, but he did not recognise a single person whom he met, and not a person recognised him.

The principal of the college came to him, and said to him, " Where are you from, son, or what is your name ? "

" I am Patrick O'Flynn from the County of Galway," said he.

" How long are you here ? " said the principal.

" I am here since the first day of March," said he.

" I think that you are out of your senses," said the principal, " there is no person of your name in the college, and there has not been for twenty years, for I am more than twenty years here."

" Though you were in it since you were born, yet I am here since last March, and I can show you my room and my books."

With that he went up the stairs, and the principal after him. He went into his room and looked round him, and said, " This is my room, but that is not my furniture, and those are not my books that are in it." He saw an old bible upon the table and he opened it, and said : " This is my bible, my mother gave it to me when I was coming here ; and, see, my name is written in it."

The principal looked at the bible, and there, as sure as God is in heaven, was the name of Patrick O'Flynn written in it, and the day of the month that he left home.

Now there was great trouble of mind on the principal, and he did not know what he should do. He sent for the masters and the professors and told them the story.

" By my word," said an old priest that was in it, " I heard talk when I was young, of a student who went away out of this college, and there was no account of him since, whether living or dead. The people searched the river and the bog holes, but there was no account to be had of him, and they never got the body."

The principal called to them then and bade them

bring him a great book in which the name of every person was written who had come to that college since it was founded. He looked through the book, and see ! Patrick O'Flynn's name was in it, and the day of the month that he came, and this [note] was written opposite to his name, that the same Patrick O'Flynn had departed on such a day, and that nobody knew what had become of him. Now it was exactly one hundred and one years from the day he went until the day he came back in that fashion.

" This is a wonderful, and a very wonderful story," said the principal, " but, do you wait here quietly my son," said he, " and I shall write to the bishop." He did that, and he got an account from the bishop to keep the man until he should come himself.

At the end of a week after that the bishop came and sent for Patrick O'Flynn. There was nobody present except the two. " Now, son," said the bishop, " go on your knees and make a confession." Then he made an act of contrition, and the bishop gave him absolution. Immediately there came a fainting and a heavy sleep over him, and he was, as it were, for three days and three nights a dead person. When he came to himself the bishop and priests were round about him. He rose up, shook himself, and told them his story, as I have it told, and he put excessive wonder upon every man of them. " Now," said he, " here I am alive and safe, and do as ye please."

The bishop and the priests took counsel together. " It is a saintly man you are," said the bishop then, " and we shall give you holy orders on the spot."

They made a priest of him then, and no sooner were holy orders given him than he fell dead upon the altar, and they all heard at the same time the most melodious music that ear ever listened to, above them in the sky, and they all said that it was the angels who were in it, carrying the soul of Father O'Flynn up to heaven with them.

THE HELP OF GOD IN THE ROAD.

PREFACE.

This story was written down by my friend, C. M. Hodgson, from the mouth of one of his brother tenants, James Mac Donough, near Oughterard, in Connemara. Mac Donough called it " Conal, King of the Cats." In a Kerry version of this story it is a poor scholar and a thief who make the bet as to whether honesty or roguery is the best for a man to follow. The people they meet give it in favour of the thief. The poor scholar loses everything, eventually his two eyes. His going under the tombstone is properly motivated by saying that he meant to die there and would then be buried and have a tombstone. The rest of the story is pretty much the same as ours. My friend, the late Patrick O'Leary, found a story called the " Three Crows," something like this, where the crows talk as the cats do in our story, and where they end by picking out the two bad men's eyes, but there is no bet made, the man is simply robbed and blinded for no particular reason.

THE STORY

THERE were two merchants travelling along the road. One of them said to the other that the help of God was in the road. The other said it was not.

" How shall we find that out ? "

" We'll leave it to the judgment of the first man we will meet."

It was short they went till they met a man. They asked him was the help of God in the road. He told them that it was not. Whatever the bet was that they had made about it, he [i.e., the man who said that the help of God was in the road] had to pay.

Well, they walked along for another while, and this man said that he would not give it up [or admit], that the help of God was not in the road.

" What bet will you make now ? " says the other man.

" I've nothing left now except my eye, but I'll bet it with you," says he.

" Well, leave the decision to the first man who shall meet us."

The next man they met said the same as the first man, that the help of God was not in the road.

The other man did nothing but put his finger into the eye and pluck it out.

[Yet the man said] " I'll bet the other eye with you that the help of God is in the road, and let it be left to the judgment of the next man who shall meet us."

It was short they went [had gone] when a man met them. They asked him was the help of God in the road. The man said that it was not.

He plucked the other eye out of him then.

" Now," said he [the blind man], " take me with you and leave me in the church."

He took him with him and left him in under a flagstone in the church.

At that time the cats used to be collecting in gatherings. [They collected in that same church that night]. When they were all gathered together, Conall, the king of the cats, said that himself would tell a story if it were not that he was afraid that some one would be listening.

" Let us get up and search," said some of the cats. They searched through the churchyard and they found no one.

" It is a year from to-night that I went in to the king's daughter.   I rubbed my tale to her mouth, and her father is perished looking for a cure [for her].   There are twelve cats in her stomach."

" Is there anything at all to cure her ? " says one of the cats.

" There is," said Conall ; " if she were to get a drop of the water that is in the well here, it would cure her. If one of those [twelve cats inside her] were to get away they could kill all the kingdom."

" Is there anything else of cure in the well ? "

" There is," said Conall ; " if any one were blind, and he to put a drop of that water on his eyes he would get his sight."

When they had gone away then in the morning, and were departed, the man that was listening to them rose up from [under] the flag.   There was a herd or shepherd going by.   He came to this man who was blind and spoke to him.

" Well, now," says the blind man, " is there any well here ? "

" There is," says the herd.

" Leave me at the brink of the well."

He left him there.

He just put down his hand and splashed a drop of the

water in on his two eyes ; and he had his sight then as well as ever he had.

" Well now," says he to the herd, " would you be so kind as to give me a bottle ? "

" I will," says the herd.

He filled the bottle with the water of the well and off he went. He was travelling until he came to the king's house. He asked to let him in.

The man who was on guard said that he would not let him in, that the king's daughter was sick and ill.

He sent for the king. He told him [by the messenger] that there was a man at the gate who would cure his daughter.

The king came out, and told the gate keeper to let in the man.

When he came in the king took him back into the chamber where his daughter was. When he looked at her [he saw that] she was as big as a horse

" Now," said he to the king, " send for your men at arms, bring them in here."

When the men at arms were inside, he closed the door outside. He told them, anything that she should throw out, they must cut the head off it.

He gave her a drop of the water that was in the bottle to drink. The moment she drank it she threw from her a live cat out of her stomach. The head was cut off it before it reached the ground. They did the same with the twelve cats that she threw out of her stomach. She rose up then as sound and as well as ever she was.

The merchant was about to go away then, but the king

would not allow him to depart.   He said that he must marry his daughter.

[They were married and happy.]

They were one day going in their coach, and they saw the merchant who had made the bet that the help of God was not in the road.   He spoke to him, and the merchant asked him where did he get all his riches.

" I got it in the place where you left me, in the church."

He [the other merchant] went away then at night, and he went in under the same flag, and it happened to the cats that they came together that night.   When they were all assembled together.   " Tell a story, O Conall, king of the cats," said one of them.

" I would tell a story," said he, " but I told one this very night last year, and a man was listening to me, and he cured the king's daughter with a bottle of the water that was in the well."

" We'll rise up [and look] " said the cat ; " there won't be anyone listening to you to-night."

They rose up and they searched until they came to the place where the man was under the flag.   They pulled him out and tore him asunder.

That is how it happened to him on account of the bet he had made that the help of God was not in the road.

THE MINISTER'S SON.

PREFACE.

Perhaps no people ever gave such free rein to the imagination with regard to the infernal regions as did the Irish. It began with St. Fursa, whose story was known to Christendom through Bede, and Adamnan's Vision [he died about 704] is known over Europe. The last to let himself go in this way was Keating. See the amazing alliterative description in his " Three Shafts of Death," Leabhar III. alt 10.

It is curious to find a Mayo peasant reproducing a little of this racial characteristic in the present poem. I often heard of this piece and made many attempts to get it, interviewing several people who I was told had got it, but I failed to get more than a few lines. My friend, John Mac Neill, wrote down for me the present version word for word from the recitation of Michael Mac Ruaidhri, but it is obviously only fragmentary. It is full (in the original, both prose and verse) of curious words and forms, and the periphrasis the " Virgin's Garb " for the scapular is curious.

For the original, see " Religious Songs of Connacht," vol. II., p. 134.

THE STORY.

There was a Roman Catholic girl at service in a minister's house, and she was wearing the Virgin Mary's garb (*i.e.*, a scapular). She once was getting ready to go to Mass, and when she was washing herself she took the garb off her, and laid it on one side. The minister's son came in, and he began rummaging (?) backwards and forwards through the room, and he met the garb. He caught it up in his hand and observed it closely. He put it round his neck, and when the girl turned about she saw the garb on the minister's son, and she got very furious. She gave a step forward and she tore the garb off his neck. She began railing at him and abusing him. She told him that it was not right nor fitting for a man of his religion to lay hold of that garb in his hand, seeing that he had a hatred and a loathing of the glorious Virgin, " and," says she to him, " since it has happened that you have laid hold of the blessed garb, unless you fast next Friday in eric for your sin, one sight of the country of the heavens you shall never see."

Grief and great unhappiness came over the minister's son at the abuse the girl gave him, and he told her that he would fast the Friday.

It was well, and it was not ill. When the minister's son went to sleep that night he got a fit of sickness, and he was very bad in the morning, and he told his mother that he would not let anyone next nor near him except the servant girl, and that he hoped that he would not be long in the fit of sickness.

There was nobody attending him but the girl, because he had a full determination to fast through the Friday. He knew very well that if his mother were coming into the room he would have to eat some food from her, and that is the reason he would not let his mother in.

When the Friday came he never tasted bit nor sup throughout the day.

On the morning of Saturday his mother asked the girl how he was getting on. The girl said that he was going on nicely [literally, " coming to land "]. But when the girl went in at the hour of twelve o'clock in the day he was a corpse, and there came a great dispiritedness [literally, " much-drowning "] over the girl, and she began crying. She went out and told his mother that he was dead.

The story went from mouth to mouth, and one person said to another that it was the girl who had killed him; and they did not know what awful death they would give her.

There was a heap of turf over against the kitchen, and they tied the girl with a chain, fastened in an iron staple that was at the gable of the house, and as soon as ever they would have the body buried they were to put oil and grease on the turf, and give it fire, to burn and to roast the girl.

On Monday morning when they went into the room to put the corpse into the coffin, the minister's son was there alive and alert, in his bed; and he told them the vision that he had seen.

He saw, he said, the fires of Purgatory, the mastiffs of Hell, and the great Devil, Judas, and he told them that it was the glorious Virgin who saved him, and who got him his pardon. She asked it of a request of her One-Son to put him into the world again to teach the people, and she got that request for him; and if it had not been that he had worn the garb of the Virgin [though] only for a moment, when he was on earth, he would not have seen one sight of the country of the heavens for ever; but it was that which saved him from the lowest depths of hell.

He spent [after that] seven years in the world teaching people, and telling them the right religion, and all his family turned Catholics, and it was the minister's son who composed the dán or poem.

___

THE DÁN OF THE MINISTER'S SON.

The body, it lies in the sleep of the dead,
And the candles above it are burning red ;
The old women sit, all silent and dreaming,
But the young woman's cheeks with tears are streaming.

Oh, listen, listen, and hear the story
Of what are the sins that shut out from glory.
Promises, lies, penurious hoarding,
How troubled, how cursed, how damned the story !

But it was there that I saw the wonder !
Three great piles of fire,
And the least fire it rose in a spire
Like fifteen tons of turf on fire,
Or a burning mountain, higher and higher.

It was not long until I saw
The three great mastiffs,
Their gullets opened,
And they a-burning
Like great wax candles
In a mountain hollow,
Waiting for my poor soul
To tear and to swallow,
To bring down to hell's foulness
In anguish to wallow.

I was taken to the gates of hell,
And the hair was burnt off my forehead,
And a sieve of holes was put through my middle ;
It was then it stood to me, that night I fasted,
And wore the garb of the Blessed Virgin,
Or my flesh and my blood had been burned to a puff of ashes.

It was then the jury of the twelve sat on me,
Their evil will than their good will was stronger,
And all that I did since my days of childhood
Was writ upon paper in black and white there ;
One paper in my hand, on the ground another,
To conceal a crime I had no power.

On turning round of me towards the right-hand side,
I beheld the noble, blessed Justice
Beneath his bright mantle,
And he asked of me, with soft, blessed words,
" Where was I living when I was on the earth,
And whether I were not the poor soul who had to go to the
      bar."

On turning round of me, towards the left-hand side,
I beheld the Great Devil that got the bribe,
Going to fall upon me from above [*literally, " on the top of my
      branches or limbs,"*]
And it was then that the thirst grew upon my poor soul !
And, oh ! God ! oh ! it was no wonder !

I looked up and beheld the Blessed Virgin,
I asked a request of her —— to save me from the foul devils.
She lowered herself down actively, quickly,
She laid herself upon her polished smooth knee
And asked a request of her One-Son and her child,
To put me in the top of the branches, or in the fold of a stone,
Or under the ground where the weasel goes,
Or on the north side where the snow blows,
Or in the same body again to teach the people,
—And the blessing of God to the mouth that tells it.

THE OLD WOMAN OF BEARE

PREFACE.

The Old Woman of Beare may, perhaps, have been an historical personage. Kuno Meyer has printed a touching poem (of the 11th century as he thinks) ascribed to her. " It is the lament of an old hetaira who contrasts the privations and sufferings of her old age with the pleasures of her youth when she had been the delight of kings." The ancient prose preface runs, " The Old Woman of Beare, Digdi was her name. Of Corcaguiny she was, *i.e.,* of the Ui Maic Iair-chonchinn. Of them also was Brigit, daughter of Iustan, and Liadain, the wife of Cuirither,[1] and Uallach, daughter of Muinegan.[2] Saint Finan had left them a charter that they should never be without an illustrious woman of their race. . . . . She hadseven periods of youth, one after another, so that every man who had lived with her came to die of old age, so that her grandsons and great-grandsons were tribes and races." Legends about her are common all over Ireland, and even verses are ascribed to her. There is another story about her in O Fotharta's " Siamsa an Gheimhridh," p. 116. She was either a real character, an early Ninon de l'Enclos, or else a mythic personage euphemized by the romancists.

There is a short legend about her under the title of Mór ní Odhrain, written down in County Donegal by, I think, Mr. Lloyd, in which O'Donnell comes to visit her, and counts the bones of 500 beeves, one of which she had killed every year. Mr. Timony found the same story in Blacksod

---

[1] A poetess and the heroine of the tale, " The Meeting of Liadain and Cuirither," published by Kuno Meyer.
[2] A poetess who died in 932.

Bay, only she was there called "Aine an chnuic." She is said in one version to have resided in "Teach Mor," "the house furthest west in Ireland," which Mr. Lloyd identified with Tivore on the Dingle promontory, and in a southern version which I also give she is called The Old Woman of Dingle.

The vision told here as having been seen by the Old Woman is extremely like a story in the "Dialogus Miraculorum of Caesarius of Heisterbach, Dist. xii., cap. 20, quoted by Landau in his "Quellen des Dekameron," and again by Lee in "The Decameron, its Sources and Analogues." It runs as follows:—

"The leman of a priest before her death had made for herself shoes with thick soles, saying ' bury me in them for I shall want them.' The night of her death a knight was riding down the street in the bright moonlight, accompanied by his attendants, when they heard a woman screaming for help. It was this woman in her shift, and with the new shoes on her feet, fleeing from a hunter. One could hear the terrible sound of his horn and the yelping of his hounds. The knight seized the woman by her hanging tresses, wound them round his left arm, and drew his sword to protect her. The woman, however, cried out, "Let me go, let me go, he is coming." As the knight, however, would not let her go, she tore herself away from him, and in so doing left her locks wound round his arm ; the hunter then caught her up, threw her across his horse and rode away with her. On the knight returning home he related what he had seen and was not believed until they opened the woman's grave and found that her hair was missing."

This is obviously the same story as that in our text, with the incidents of the knight and the hair omitted.

It contains, however, (1) the woman and her particular sin ; (2) the fleeing before the hounds ; (3) the pursuing huntsman ; though in peculiarly Irish fashion, it is mercifully left uncertain as to whether she was overtaken or not.

The 8th novel of the 5th day of the Decameron seems to have been drawn from some cognate source. The hero perceives " correndo verso il luogo dove egli era una

bellissima giovane ignuda—piagnendo e gridando forte
mercè. E oltre a questo le vide a fianchi due grandissimi
e fieri mastini." This is the soul of a dead woman with
hell-hounds pursuing her. The very word "mastini"
being the same as in the Irish story.

In the second incident that happened to the Cailleach
there appears to be a reminiscence of Sindbad the sailor.
But the story of the four herds who lifted the bier which
all the men at the funeral had been unable to move, is
told somewhat differently at p. 36 of Michael Timony's
"Sgéalta gearra so-léighte an iarthair." It is there put
into the mouth of "Aine an chnuic," Aine of the hill,
who may be the same as the "Old Woman of Beare,"
and the four herds, the coffin—and a rider on a black horse
who accompanied them—all disappeared in the side
of a rock which opened to receive them and closed after
them. "Aine" of "Cnoc Aine," or "Aine's hill," was
the queen of the Limerick Fairies, but I hardly think that
it is she who has got into the Mayo folk, tale.

There is a proverb in Connacht which says, speaking of
the oldest lives in the world, " the life of the yew tree, the
life of the eagle,[1] and the life of the Old Woman of Beare."

See Kuno Meyer's edition of the song of the Old Woman
of Beare in " Otia Merseiana " and " O Fotharta's Siamsa
an Gheimhridh," p. 116, see also " The Vision of Mac
Conglinne," p. 132, and my " Sgeuluidhe Gaedhealach."

The following story I wrote down very carefully word
for word, about fifteen years ago, from the telling of Michael
Mac Ruaidhri, of Ballycastle, Co. Mayo.

THE STORY.

THERE was an old woman in it, and long ago it was,
and if we had been there that time we would not be here
now ; we would have a new story or an old story, and

---

[1] See the story " The Adventures of Leithin."

that would not be more likely than to be without any story at all.

The hag was very old, and she herself did not know her own age, nor did anybody else. There was a friar and his boy journeying one day, and they came in to the house of the Old Woman of Beare.

" God save you," said the friar.

" The same man save yourself," said the hag ; " you're welcome,[1] sit down at the fire and warm yourself.''

The friar sat down, and when he had well finished warming himself he began to talk and discourse with the old hag.

" If it's no harm of me to ask it of you, I'd like to know your age, because I know you are very old " [said the friar].

" It is no harm at all to ask me," said the hag ; " I'll answer you as well as I can. There is never a year since I came to age that I used not to kill a beef, and throw the bones of the beef up on the loft which is above your head. If you wish to know my age you can send your boy up on the loft and count the bones.

True was the tale. The friar sent the boy up on the loft and the boy began counting the bones, and with all the bones that were on the loft he had no room on the loft itself to count them, and he told the friar that he would have to throw the bones down on the floor—that there was no room on the loft.

" Down with them," said the friar, " and I'll keep count of them from below."

The boy began throwing them down from above and the

---

[1] Literally. ' He (*i.e.*, God) is your life " ; the equivalent of " hail ! " " welcome."

friar began writing down [the number], until he was about tired out, and he asked the boy had he them nearly counted, and the boy answered the friar down from the loft that he had not even one corner of the loft emptied yet.

" If that's the way of it, come down out of the loft and throw the bones up again," said the friar

The boy came down, and he threw up the bones, and [so] the friar was [just] as wise coming in as he was going out.

" Though I don't know your age," said the friar to the hag, " I know that you haven't lived up to this time without seeing marvellous things in the course of your life, and the greatest marvel that you ever saw—tell it to me, if you please."

" I saw one marvel which made me wonder greatly," said the hag.

" Recount it to me," said the Friar, " if you please."

" I myself and my girl were out one day, milking the cows, and it was a fine, lovely day, and I was just after milking one of the cows, and when I raised my head I looked round towards my left hand, and I saw a great blackness coming over my head in the air. " Make haste," says myself to the girl, " until we milk the cows smartly, or we'll be wet and drowned before we reach home, with the rain." I was on the pinch[1] of my life and so was my girl, to have the cows milked before we'd get the shower, for I thought myself that it was a shower that was coming, but on my raising my head again I looked

---

[1] Literally, " the boiling of the angles-between-the-fingers was on me."

round me and beheld a woman coming as white as the
swan that is on the brink of the waves. She went past
me like a blast of wind, and the wind that was before her
she was overtaking it, and the wind that was behind her,
it could not come up with her. It was not long till I saw
after the woman two mastiffs, and two yards of their tongue
twisted round their necks, and balls of fire out of their
mouths, and I wondered greatly at that. And after the
dogs I beheld a black coach and a team of horses drawing
it, and there were balls of fire on every side out of the
coach, and as the coach was going past me the beasts
stood and something that was in the coach uttered from
it an unmeaning sound, and I was terrified, and faintness
came over me, and when I came back out of the faint I
heard the voice in the coach again, asking me had I seen
anything going past me since I came there ; and I told him
as I am telling you, and I asked him who he was himself,
or what was the meaning of the woman and the mastiffs
which went by me.

" I am the Devil, and those are two mastiffs which I
sent after that soul."

" And is it any harm for me to ask," says I, " what
is the crime the woman did when she was in the
world ? "

" That is a woman," said the Devil, " who brought
scandal upon a priest, and she died in a state of deadly
sin, and she did not repent of it, and unless the mastiffs
come up with her before she comes to the gates of Heaven
the glorious Virgin will come and will ask a request of her
only Son to grant the woman forgiveness for her sins,
and the Virgin will obtain pardon for her, and I'll be out

of her. But if the mastiffs come up with her before she goes to Heaven she is mine."

The great Devil drove on his beasts, and went out of my sight, and myself and my girl came home, and I was heavy, and tired and sad at remembering the vision which I saw, and I was greatly astonished at that wonder, and I lay in my bed for three days, and the fourth day I arose very done up and feeble, and not without cause, since any woman who would see the wonder that I saw, she would be grey a hundred years before her term of life[1] was expired.

" Did you ever see any other marvel in your time ? " says the friar to the hag.

" A week after leaving my bed I got a letter telling me that one of my friends was dead, and that I would have to go to the funeral. I proceeded to the funeral, and on my going into the corpse-house the body was in the coffin, and the coffin was laid down on the bier, and four men went under the bier that they might carry the coffin, and they weren't able to even stir[2] the bier off the ground. And another four men came, and they were not able to move it off the ground. They were coming, man after man, until twelve came, and went under the bier, and they weren't able to lift it.

" I spoke myself, and I asked the people who were at the funeral what sort of trade had this man when he was in the world, and it was told me that it was a herd he was. And I asked of the people who were there was there any other herd at the funeral. Then there came four men

---

[1] Literally, " before her age being spent."   [2] Literally, " give it wind."

that nobody at all who was at the funeral had any knowledge or recognition of, and they told me that they were
four herds, and they went under the bier and they lifted
it as you would lift a handful of chaff, and off they went
as quick and sharp as ever they could lift a foot. Good
powers of walking they had, and a fine long step I had
myself, and I cut out after them, and not a mother's son
knew what the place was to which they were departing
with the body, and we were going and ever going until
the night and the day were parting from one another,
until the night was coming black dark dreadful, until the
grey horse was going under the shadow of the docking
and until the docking was going fleeing before him.[1]

> The roots going under the ground,
> The leaves going into the air,
> The grey horse a-fleeing apace,
> And I left lonely there.

" On looking round me, there wasn't one of all the
funeral behind me, except two others. The other people
were done up, and they were not able to come half way,
some of them fainted and some of them died. Going
forward two steps more in front of me I was within in a
dark wood wet and cold, and the ground opened, and I
was swallowed down into a black dark hole without a
mother's son or a father's daughter[2] next nor near me,
without a man to be had to keen me or to lay me out ; so
that I threw myself on my two knees, and I was there
throughout four days sending my prayer up to God to

---

[1] The fairies ride their little grey horses, and stable them at night
under the leaves of the copóg or dock-leaf, or docking. But if they
arrive too late and night has fallen, then the copóg has folded her
leaves and will not shelter them.
[2] Literally, " man's daughter."

take me out of that speedily and quickly. And with the fourth day there came a little hole like the eye of a needle on one corner of the abode where I was ; and I was a-praying always and the hole was a-growing in size day by day, and on the seventh day it increased to such a size that I got out through it. I took to my heels[1] then when I got my feet with me on the outside [of the hole] going home. The distance which I walked in one single day following the coffin, I spent five weeks coming back the same road, and don't you see yourself now that I got cause to be withered, old, aged, grey, and my life to be shortening through those two perils in which I was."

" You're a fine, hardy old woman all the time," said the friar.

---

[1] Literally, " I gave to the soles." Many people still say in speaking English, " I gave to the butts." The Irish word means butt as well as sole.

THE OLD HAG OF DINGLE.

PREFACE.

It is quite obvious that this story from south-west Kerry represents in a feebler manner the same tradition as the story which we have just given from north Mayo, about the Old Woman of Beare. Note that in the Mayo story the appearance of the woman was also prefaced by the blackness of a shower. It is to the Old Woman of Beare that the answer is ascribed in Connacht in which she gives the reason for her longevity, only it is differently worded there.

I never carried the dirt of one puddle beyond another (?)
I never ate food, but when I would be hungry.
I never went to sleep but when I would be sleepy.
I never threw out the dirty water until I had taken in the clean.

This Kerry version of the story was written down by Séamus Shean Ua Connaill, of Sgoil Chill Roilig, and published in " The Lochrann, Mi Eanair agus Feabhra," 1911. In Donegal the reasons given are :—

I never ate a morsel till I'd be hungry,
I never drank a drop till I'd be thirsty.
I never sat at the fire without being working.
If I had not work of my own to do I got it from somebody else."

———

THE STORY.

THERE was a woman in Dingle long ago. She lived 300 years and more. Her name was the Old Hag of Dingle. The story spread throughout Ireland that she had lived for 300 years, and many people used to come to see her.

The Emperor of France and the Earl of Kerry and many other kings and princes came journeying to her, and they asked her what age she was. She told them that she was 300 years and more. They asked her what it was in her opinion which gave her so long a life, beyond any one else.

She told them that she did not know that, except that her little finger and the palm of her hand never saw the air, and that she never remained in her bed but as long as she would be sleepy, and that she never ate meat except when she would be hungry.

She would not herself give any other account of the reason for her long life except that. They said to her that they were sure that she had seen many a marvel, seeing that she had lived all that time.

She said that she never saw anything that she could marvel at particularly, except one day [said she] that gentlemen were here and wanted to go out to the Skelligs, and they got a crew. There was a young priest who was here along with them. They went off and a boat with them. A very fine day it was.

She told them that when they were half way to the Skelligs, the men saw the shower[1] coming along the sea from the north-west, and the weather growing cold. Fear came upon them and they said to face the boat for the land, but the priest told them to keep up their courage, and that there would be no land now, and that perhaps with the

---

[1] Note the Irish idiom—the definite for the indefinite article.

help of God there was no danger of them. The shower was coming on, and the priest said that he himself saw a woman in the shower, and a very great fear came upon them then ; but when the shower was coming [down] on them they all saw her, and her face in the shower, against the wind. When she was making for them the priest moved over to the stern of the boat, he took to him his stole and put it round his neck. He said :

" What have you done that has damned you ? "

" I killed an unbaptized child," said she.

" That did not damn you," said the priest.

" I killed two," said she.

" That also did not damn you," said he.

" I killed three," said she.

" Ah ! that damned you," said he. He drew to him his book. He did a little reading on her. She turned her back then. He gave her that much advantage. They went off then and the weather cleared for them, and they went on their way to the Skelligs. They went all over the Skelligs and they came home.

" I saw that, and that was the greatest wonder I ever saw," said she.

THE POEM OF THE TOR.

PREFACE.

I have heard more than one poem in which occurs a dialogue between a living person and the soul of a dead man. I got the following from Mr. John Kearney, a schoolmaster, at Belmullet, Co. Mayo. The poem is well known round Belmullet, but I have a suspicion that this version of it is not complete. I have not been able, however, to secure a fuller one. It is locally known as the Dán or Poem of the Tor. This Tor is a rock in the sea some twelve miles from land. There is a lighthouse upon it now, but of course that was not so when the poem took shape, and no more lonesome place than it for a soul dreeing its weird could be conceived. The soul was put to do penance on this solitary rock. With the verse about the soul parting from the body under rain under wind, compare the fine North of England wake-dirge with the refrain—

> Fire and sleet and candle light,
> And Christ receive thy saule.

I have come across other allusions in Irish unpublished literature, prayers, etc., to the South being the side of the good angels and the North the side of the bad ones.

> On the side of the north black walls of fire,
> On the side of the south the people of Christ.

The "geilt" which the interlocutor supposes that the ghost may be, is a person who goes wild in madness, and such a one was supposed to have the power of levitation, and to be able to raise himself in the air and fly. See the extraordinary story of Suibhne Geilt, vol. xii. of the Irish Texts Society. See my "Religious Songs of Connacht," vol. i., p. 270.

THE STORY.

[THE MAN.]

O fellow yonder on the mountain
Who art being tortured at the Tor,
[I put] a question on thee in the name ot Jesus,
Art thou a man of this world or a *geilt* ?

[THE SOUL.]

Since the question is put in the name of Jesus,
Indeed I shall answer it for thee :
I am not a person of this world, nor a *geilt*,
But a poor soul who has left this world,
And who never went to God's heaven since.

[THE MAN.]

[I put] a question to thee again
Without doing thee harm :
How long since thou didst leave this world,
Or art thou there ever since ?

[THE SOUL.]

Twenty years last Sunday
The soul parted with the [evil]-inclined body,
Under rain, under wind ;
And if it were not for the blessing of the poor on the world,
I would be hundreds of years more there.
When I was upon the world
I was happy and airy,
And I desired to draw profit to myself,
But I am [now] in great tribulation, paying for that.
When I used to go to Sunday Mass
It was not mercy I used to ask for my soul,
But jesting and joking with young men,
And the body of my Christ before me.
When I would arrive home again
It was not of the voice of the priest I would be thinking,
But of the fine great possessions
I left behind me at home.
Good was my haggard and my large house ;
And my brightness (?) to go out to the gathering,
Riding on a young steed,
Banquet and feast before me.
I set no store by my soul,
Until I saw the prowess of Death assembling :
On the side of the north, black walls of fire
On the side of the south the people of Christ
Gathering amongst the angels,
The Glorious Virgin hastening them.

" I do not know," says Peter,
" Does Christ recognize him ? "
" I do not know," said Christ,
" Bitter alas ! I do not recognize him."

Then spake the Glorious Virgin,
And lowered herself on her white knees,
" O my son, was it not for thee were prepared
The heaps of embers
To burn thy noble body ?"

O Mother, helpful, glorious,
If it be thy will to take him to heaven,
I let him with thee,
And surely one thousand years at the Tor were better for
    you
Than one single hour in foul hell.

———————

COLUMCILLE AND HIS BROTHER DOBHRAN.

PREFACE.

This very interesting story of Columcille's brother, Dobhran, is common amongst Highlanders, but I have found no trace of it in Ireland, nor any mention of a Dobhran. This particular version was written down by the late Rev. Father Allan MacDonald, of Eriskay, who collected a great deal of the folk-lore of that island. The same story was told to me, but somewhat differently, by a Canadian priest from Sydney, Nova Scotia, one of the Clan MacAdam (really Mac Eudhmoinn) and the sixth in descent from the first refugee of his name who fled to Canada after Culloden. He said he had often heard the story, and that Dobhran when he climbed to the edge of the grave uttered three sentences, but two of them he had forgotten, the third was "cha n'eil an iorron chomh dona agus a tháthar ag rádh," (*sic*.) *i.e.*, "Hell is not as bad as people say." It was then Columcille cried out, "úir, úir air Dobhran." "Clay, clay on Dobhran's mouth before he says any more!"[1]

Here follow some stories from Irish sources about Columcille himself. His life was written at considerable length by Adamnan, one of his successors in the Abbacy of Iona, who was born only twenty-seven years after Columcille's death, and has come down to us in the actual manuscript written by a man who died in 713 ; to that we know a good deal about the saint. There exist five other lives of him. According to the Leabhar Breac he died of self-imposed abstinence.

---

[1] See Celtic Review, vol. V., p. 107.

COLUMCILLE'S FASTING.

Colum's angel, whose name was Axal (a name derived from " Auxilium ") requested him to " take virginity around him," but he refused " unless a reward therefor " be given to him. " What reward seekest thou," said the angel. " I declare," said Columcille, " it is not one reward but four." " Mention them," said the angel. " I will," said Columcille, " namely, A death in Repentance, A death from Hunger, and death in Youth[1]—for hideous are bodies through old age." " Even more shall be given thee," said the angel, " for thou shalt be chief prophet of heaven and earth."

And that was fulfilled. He went into pilgrimage, and he was young when he died, and of hunger he perished, but it was wilful hunger.

And this is the cause of that hunger of his. Once it came to pass as he was going round the graveyard in Iona that he saw an old woman cutting nettles to make pottage thereof. " Why art thou doing that, poor woman ? " said Columcille. " O dear father," quoth she, " I have one cow and she has not calved yet, and I am expecting it, and this is what has served me for a long time back."

Columcille then determines that pottage of nettles should be the thing that should most serve him thenceforth for ever, and said, " Since it is because of her expecting the one uncertain cow that she is in this great hunger, meet were [the same] for us though great be the hunger wherein we shall abide expecting God. For better and certain is what we expect, the eternal kingdom." And he said to his servant, " Pottage of nettles give thou to me every night without butter, without a sip therewith."

" It shall be done," said the cook. And he bores the mixing stick of the pottage so that it became a pipe, and he used to pour the milk into that pipe and mix it all through

---

[1] See Stokes' Calendar of Oengus, p. xcix. The fourth request is not mentioned, nor yet in O'Donnell's Life, where the story is much better told. See " Zeitschrift für Celt. Philologie," vol. IV. p. 278.

the pottage. Then the church folk notice this, namely, the cleric's goodly shape, and they talk of it among themselves. This is made known to Columcille, and then he said, "May they who take your place be always murmuring!"

"Well!" quoth he to the servant, "what do you put for me into the pottage every day?" "Thou thyself are witness" said the man, "but unless it comes out of the stick with which the pottage is mixed, I know of nothing else therein save pottage only."

Then the secret is revealed to the cleric and he said, "Prosperity and good-deed for ever to thy successor," said he. And this is fulfilled.

It was then, too, that Boethine told him the remarkable vision he had, namely, three chairs seen by him in heaven; to wit, a chair of gold, and a chair of silver, and a chair of glass. "[The meaning of] that is manifest," said Columcille, "the chair of gold is Ciaran[1] son of the carpenter, for his generosity and hospitality; the chair of silver is thou thyself, O Boethine, because of the purity and lustre of thy devotion; the chair of glass is I myself, for, though my devotion is delightful, I am fleshly and I am often frail!" As a certain poet said—

> Colum, fair formed, powerful,
> Face red, broad, radiant,
> Body white, fame without deceit,
> Hair curling, eye grey, luminous.

St. Patrick prophesied the coming of Columcille, according to the great Life of Columcille, written by Manus O'Donnell, at Lifford, in the year 1532, of which more than one contemporary vellum copy exists.[2]

St. Patrick Prophesies Concerning Columcille.[3]

Once upon a time, as Patrick was finding labour and great inconvenience in converting the men of Ireland and their

---

[1] For Ciaran, see the story of the Eagle Léithin.

[2] The Bodleian copy consists of 120 pages of vellum, each leaf measuring 17 by 11½ inches.

[3] See Zeitschrift für Celt. Phil. vol. III. p. 534, translated by Dr. Henebry.

women to the faith, he was sorry that he did not know how
they would be off for faith and for piety after his own time,
or how would God prosper them, seeing all the labour he
was getting from them.   And he used to pray to God
earnestly to give him knowledge of that.

Then an angel came to him and addressed him, saying
that it was according to the vision to be revealed to him
in his sleep the coming night, that Ireland would be, as
regards the faith during his own life, and after him for
evermore.   And this is the vision that was given him [the
next night].

He saw all Ireland red on fire, and the flame which rose
from it went up into the further aerial spaces, and afterwards
he saw that fire being quenched, only big hills remained on
fire, far apart from one another ; and then again he saw how
even the hills went out, except something like lamps or
candles which remained alight in the place of each hill.   He
saw again even those go out, and only embers or sparks
with a gloom upon them remaining ; however, these smoul-
dered in a few places far scattered throughout Ireland.

The same angel came to him and told him that those were
the conditions through which Ireland should pass after him.
Upon hearing that, Patrick wept bitterly, and spoke with a
great voice and said : " O God of all power, dost Thou
desire to damn and to withdraw Thy mercy from the people
to whom Thou didst send me to bring a knowledge of
Thyself.   Though I am unworthy that Thou shouldst
hear me, O Lord, calm Thy anger in their regard, and
receive the people of this island of Ireland into Thy own
mercy."

And on his finishing these words, the angel spoke in a
pacifying tone, and said, " Look to the north of thee," said
he, " and thou shalt behold the change of God's right hand."
Patrick did as the angel bade him, for he looked to the north,
and he beheld a light arising there, not great at first, then
waxing and tearing the darkness asunder, so that all Ireland
was lighted by it as by the first flame, and he saw it go
through the same stages afterwards.

And the angel explained the meaning of that vision to
Patrick, saying that Ireland would be alight with faith and

piety during his own time, but that darkness would come over that light at his death.   However, there would be good people here and there in Ireland after him, as were the far-sundered hills on fire ; but when those good people died there would come people not so good in their stead, like the lamps and candles of which we have spoken already, and that the faith would be sustained by them only as the embers that were in gloom and mist, until the son of eternal light should come, namely Columcille. And although little at first, in coming into the world, nevertheless he would sow and preach the word of God and increase the faith, so that Ireland should blaze up in his time as it did in the time of Patrick ; and that it would never blaze in the same way again, although there would be good pious people after him.   And that the Church of Ireland would go into decay at the end of time after that, so that there would be, there, of faith and piety, only a semblance of the embers, or little sparks covered with gloom and darkness of which we have spoken already.

THE STORY.

COLUMCILLE began to build on Iona. He gathered together a great host of people. But all that he used to build in the day, it used to be thrown down at night. That drove him to set people to keep a watch on Iona. Every morning those men [whom he had set to watch] used to be dead at the foot of Iona.   He did not continue long to set people to watch there, but since he himself was a holy man he went and remained watching Iona to try if he could see or find out what was going wrong with it.   He was keeping to it and from it, and they were saying that it was on the scaur of the crag near the sea that she was, I did not see her.

He saw a *Biast* coming off the shore and one half of it

was a fish and the other half in the likeness of a woman. She was old, with scales. When she shook herself she set Iona and the land a-quaking. There went from her a tinkling sound as it were earthenware pigs (jars) a-shaking. Columcille went down to meet her and spoke to her, and asked her did she know what was killing the people whom he was setting to watch Iona in the night. She said she did. " What was happening to them ? " said he. She said, " Nothing but the fear that seized them at her appearance ; that when she was a-coming to land the heart was leaping out of its cockles[1] with them."

" Do you know," said he, " what is throwing down Iona that I am building ? "

" I do," said she, " Iona will be for ever falling so, O holy Columcille. It is not I who am throwing it down, but still it is being thrown down." [2]

" Do you know now any means by which I can make Iona go forward ? "

" I do," said she. " O holy Columcille, to-morrow you shall question all the people that you have at work to find out what man will consent to offer himself alive [to be buried] under the ground, and his soul shall be saved if he consents to do that, and people shall never see me here afterwards. Iona shall go forward without any doubt."

On the morrow he put the question to the great host of people, " Was there any one of them at all who would consent to offer himself alive on condition that his soul should be saved in heaven ? "

---

[1] The " cockles of the heart " is a common expression in Anglo-Irish. It is taken from the Irish, cochall, meaning really a cowl.
[2] Thathar ag a leagadh. The autonomous form in Scotch Gaelic.

There was not one man of them willing to go into the grave although he was told that his soul would be saved by the decree of God. She [the *Biast*] had told him too that the grave had to be seven times as deep as the man's length.

Poor Dobhran, his brother, was on the outskirts of the crowd. He came over and stood behind his brother, Columcille, and said that he was quite willing to be offered up alive under the ground on condition that Iona might be built up by his holy brother Columcille, and he gave credence to Columcille that his soul would be saved by the decree of God.

Said Columcille, "Although I have no other brother but poor Dobhran, I am pleased that he has offered himself to go to the grave, and that the *Biast* shall not be seen coming any more to the shore for ever."

The grave was made seven times the height of the man in depth. When Dobhran saw the grave he turned to Columcille and asked him as a favour to put a roof over the grave and to leave him there standing so long as it might please God to leave him alive.

He got his request—to be put down alive into the grave. He was left there.

Columcille came and began to work at Iona [again], and he was twenty days working, and Iona was going forward wondrously. He was pleased that his work was succeeding.

At the end of twenty days when everything was con-jectured to be going on well, he said it were right to look what end had come to poor Dobhran, and [bade] open the grave.

Dobhran was walking on the floor of the grave [when

the roof was taken off].   When Dobhran saw that the grave
was opened and when he heard all the world round it,
he gave an expert leap out of it to the mouth of the grave
and he put up his two hands on high on the mouth of the
grave.   He supported himself on the [edge of the] grave
[by his hands.]   There was a big smooth meadow
going up from Iona and much rushes on it.   All the
rushes that Dobhran's eyes lit upon grew red, and that
little red top is on the rushes ever.

Columcille cried out and he on the far side, " Clay !
clay on Dobhran's eyes ! before he see any more of the
world and of sin ! "

They threw in the clay upon him then and returned to
their work.   And nothing any more went against Columcille until he had Iona finished.

BRUADAR AND SMITH AND GLINN.

A CURSE

PREFACE.

This extraordinary piece of cursing cannot properly be called folk-lore. It is purely pagan in spirit, though the poet has called upon the Deity under all the appellations by which he was known to the Gaels, as King of Sunday (see the story of Shaun the Tinker), the One Son, the King of the Angels, the King of Luan (Monday or Judgment day), the King of Brightness, the Son of the Virgin, etc. I know nothing certain about the circumstances which gave rise to this amazing effusion. It cannot be very old, however, since the last verse mentions the " black peeler." Possibly it was composed not more than seventy years ago. The poet has cleverly interwoven the names of his three enemies in all sorts of different collocations. I give the piece as of interest though not actual folk-lore. It was first published in Iris-leabhar na Gaedhilge by Father Dinneen. For the original and other curses of the same nature, see "Religious Songs of Connacht," vol. II., p. 274.

THE STORY

Bruadar and Smith and Glinn,
    Amen, dear God, I pray,
May they lie low in waves of woe,
    And tortures slow each day !
                    Amen !

Bruadar and Smith and Glinn
    Helpless and cold, I pray,
Amen ! I pray, O King,
    To see them pine away.
                    Amen !

Bruadar and Smith and Glinn
  May flails of sorrow flay !
Cause for lamenting, snares and cares
  Be theirs by night and day !
                    Amen !

Blindness come down on Smith,
  Palsy on Bruadar come,
Amen, O King of Brightness ! Smite
  Glinn in his members numb,
                    Amen !

Smith in the pangs of pain,
  Stumbling on Bruadar's path,
King of the Elements, Oh, Amen !
  Let loose on Glinn Thy wrath.
                    Amen !

For Bruadar gape the grave,
  Up-shovel for Smith the mould,
Amen, O King of the Sunday ! Leave
  Glinn in the devil's hold.
                    Amen !

Terrors on Bruadar rain,
  And pain upon pain on Glinn,
Amen, O King of the Stars ! and Smith
  May the devil be linking him.
                    Amen !

Glinn in a shaking ague,
  Cancer on Bruadar's tongue,
Amen, O King of the Heavens ! and Smith
  For ever stricken dumb.
                    Amen !

Thirst but no drink for Glinn,
  Smith in a cloud of grief,
Amen ! O King of the Saints ! and rout
  Bruadar without relief.
                    Amen !

Smith without child or heir,
  And Bruadar bare of store,
Amen, O King of the Friday ! Tear
  For Glinn his black heart's core.
                    Amen.

Bruadar with nerveless limbs,
  Hemp strangling Glinn's last breath,
Amen, O King of the World's Light !
  And Smith in grips with death.
                    Amen !

Glinn stiffening for the tomb,
  Smith wasting to decay,
Amen, O King of the Thunder's gloom !
  And Bruadar sick alway.
                    Amen

Smith like a sieve of holes,
  Bruadar with throat decay,
Amen, O King of the Orders ! Glinn
  A buck-show every day.
                    Amen !

Hell-hounds to hunt for Smith,
  Glinn led to hang on high,
Amen, O King of the Judgment Day !
  And Bruadar rotting by.
                    Amen !

Curses on Glinn, I cry,
  My curse on Bruadar be,
Amen, O King of the Heaven's high !
  Let Smith in bondage be.
                    Amen !

Showers of want and blame,
  Reproach, and shame of face,
Smite them all three, and smite again,
  Amen, O King of Grace !
                    Amen !

Melt, may the three, away,
  Bruadar and Smith and Glinn,
Fall in a swift and sure decay
  And lose, but never win.
                    Amen !

May pangs pass through thee Smith,
  (Let the wind not take my prayer),
May I see before the year is out
  Thy heart's blood flowing there.
                    Amen !

Leave Smith no place nor land,
  Let Bruadar wander wide,
May the Devil stand at Glinn's right hand,
  And Glinn to him be tied.
                    Amen !

All ill from every airt
  Come down upon the three,
And blast them ere the year be out
  In rout and misery.
                    Amen !

Glinn let misfortune bruise,
  Bruadar lose blood and brains,
Amen, O Jesus ! hear my voice,
  Let Smith be bent in chains.
                    Amen !

I accuse both Glinn and Bruadar,
  And Smith I accuse to God,
May a breach and a gap be upon the three,
  And the Lord's avenging rod.
                    Amen !

Each one of the wicked three
  Who raised against me their hand,
May fire from heaven come down and slay
  This day their perjured band,
                    Amen !

May none of their race survive,
  May God destroy them all,
Each curse of the psalms in the holy books
  Of the prophets upon them fall !
                    Amen !

Blight skull, and ear, and skin,
  And hearing, and voice, and sight,
Amen ! before the year be out,
  Blight, Son of the Virgin, blight !
                    Amen !

May my curses hot and red
  And all I have said this day,
Strike the Black Peeler too,
  Amen, dear God, I pray !
                    Amen !

P

FRIAR BRIAN.

PREFACE.

This story was written down, word for word, and given me by my friend Mr. C. M. Hodgson, from the telling of James Mac Donagh, one of his brother tenants, near Oughterard, Co. Galway. It is obvious that the story is only a fragment, and very obscure, but it is worth preserving if only for the sake of Friar Brian's striking answer to the Devil, which would come home with particular force to all who have ever bought or sold at an Irish fair; the acceptance of " earnest " money is the clinching of the bargain, behind which you cannot go. If you receive " earnest " in the morning you may not sell again, no matter how much higher a price may have been offered you before evening. I have heard another story about Friar Brian.

THE STORY

THERE was a young man in it long ago, and long ago it was, and he had a great love for card-playing and drinking whiskey. He came short [at last] of money, and he did not know what he would do without money.

A man met him, and he going home in the night. " I often see you going home this road," said the man to him.

" There's no help for it now," says he ; " I have no money."

" Now," says the man, " I'll give you money every time you'll want it, if you will give to me written with your own blood [a writing to say] that you are mine such and such a year, at the end of one and twenty years."

It was the Devil who was in it in the shape of a man.

He gave it to him written with his share of blood that he would be his at the end of one and twenty years.

He had money then every time ever he wanted it until the one and twenty years were almost out, and then fear began coming on him. He went to the priest and he told it [all] to him. " I could not do any good for you," says the priest. " You must go to such and such a man who is going into Ellasthrum (?) He has so much of the Devil's influence (?) that he does be able to change round the castle door any time the wind is blowing [too hard] on it."

He went to this man and he told him his story. " I wouldn't be able to do you any good," says he, " you must go to Friar Brian."

He went to Friar Brian and told him his story. The one and twenty years were all but up by this time. " Here is a stick for you," said Friar Brian, " and cut a ring [with the stick] round about the place where you'll stand. He [the Devil] won't be able to come inside the place which you'll cut out with this stick. And do you be arguing with him, and I'll be watching you both," says he. " Tell him that there must be some judgment [passed] on the case before you depart [to go away] with him."

" Very well," says the man.

When the appointed hour came the man was standing in the place he said. The Devil came to him. He told the man that the time was up and that he had to come along.

The man began to say that the time was not up. He cut a ring round about himself with the stick which Friar Brian had given him. " Well, then," says the man, says he [at last], " we'll leave it to the judgment of the first person who shall come past us."

" I am satisfied," says the Diabhac.[1]

Friar Brian came to the place where they were. " What is it all about from the beginning ? " says Friar Brian. The Diabhac told him that he had this man bought for one and twenty years, and that he had to come with him to-day ; " it is left to you to judge the case."

" Now," says Friar Brian, says he, " if you were to go to a fair to buy a cow or a horse, and if you gave earnest money for it, wouldn't you say that it was more just for you to have it than for the man who would come in the evening and who would buy it without paying any earnest money for it ? "

" I say," says the Diabhac, " that the man who paid earnest money for it first, ought to get it."

" And now," says Friar Brian, " the Son of God paid earnest for this man before you bought him."

The Diabhac had to go away then.

Friar Brian asked then what would be done to him now when he had not got the man.

---

[1] Diabhac, pronounced in Connaught, d'youc; a homonym for the more direct diabhal—devil, as " deil " in English.

' I shall be put into the chamber which is for Friar Brian," said the Diabhac. [1]

" And now," said Friar Brian to the man whom he had saved, " I saved you now," says he, " and do you save me."

" What will I be able to do for you to save you ? "

" Get the axe," says Friar Brian to him, " take the head off me," says he, " and cut me up then as fine as tobacco." [2]

He did that, and Friar Brian repented then, and he was saved.

He suffered himself to be cut as fine as tobacco on account of all he had ever done out of the way. There now, that was the end of Friar Brian.

---

[1] The meaning seems to be, that the devil who lost his quarry would suffer the same punishment as was reserved for Friar Brian.

[2] Compare the story of the Tobacco Prayer, p. 244.

HOW THE FIRST CAT WAS CREATED.

PREFACE.

I got the following story from my friend Dr. Conor Maguire, of Claremorris. It explains how the first cat and first mouse were created. I heard many such stories explaining the origin of this thing or the other from the Red Indians in Canada, but, of course, none of them had anything to say to Christianity. It is impossible to tell the age of this legend, but it may be taken for granted that such themes were common in Pagan times just as they are amongst the Red Men to-day, and it may well be that this story in its origin is older than Christianity itself, and that a saint may have taken the place of an enchanter when the people became Christians. I think it is pretty certain that this story originally concerned only the flour—the food of man—and the mice—the enemy of the flour—and the cat—the enemy of the mice; and that the mention of the sow and her litter is a late and stupid interpolation.

THE STORY.

ONE day Mary and her Son were travelling the road, and they heavy and tired, and it chanced that they went past the door of a house in which there was a lock of wheat being winnowed. The Blessed Virgin went in, and she asked an alms of wheat, and the woman of the house refused her.

" Go in again to her," said the Son, " and ask her for it in the name of God."

She went, and the woman refused her again.

" Go in to her again," said He, " and ask her to give you leave to put your hand into the pail of water, and to thrust it down into the heap of wheat, and to take away with you all that shall cling to your hand."

She went, and the woman gave her leave to do that. When she came out to our Saviour, He said to her, " Do not let one grain of that go astray, for it is worth much and much."

When they had gone a bit from the house they looked back, and saw a flock of demons coming towards the house, and the Virgin Mary was frightened lest they might do harm to the woman. " Let there be no anxiety on you," said Jesus to her ; " since it has chanced that she has given you all that of alms, they shall get no victory over her."

They travelled on, then, until they reached as far as a place where a man named Martin had a mill. " Go in," said our Saviour to His mother, "since it has chanced that the mill is working, and ask them to grind that little grain-*een* for you."

She went. " O musha, it's not worth while for me," said the boy who was attending the querns, " to put that little *lockeen* a-grinding for you." Martin heard them talking and said to the lout, " Oh, then, do it for the creature, perhaps she wants it badly," said he. He did it, and he gave her all the flour that came from it.

They travelled on then, and they were not gone any distance until the mill was full of flour as white as snow. When Martin perceived this great miracle he understood well that it was the Son of God and His Mother who chanced that way. He ran out and followed them, at his best, and he made across the fields until he came up with them, and there was that much haste on him in going through a scunce of hawthorns that a spike of the haw-thorn met his breast and wounded him greatly. There was that much zeal in him that he did not feel the pain, but clapt his hand over it, and never stopped until he came up with them. When our Saviour beheld the wound upon poor Martin, He laid His hand upon it, and it was closed, and healed upon the spot. He said to Martin then that he was a fitting man in the presence of God; "and go home now," said He, " and place a fistful of the flour under a dish, and do not stir it until morning."

When Martin went home he did that, and he put the dish, mouth under, and the fistful of flour beneath it.

The servant girl was watching him, and thought that maybe it would be a good thing if she were to set a dish for herself in the same way, and signs on her, she set it.

On the morning of the next day Martin lifted his dish, and what should run out from under it but a fine sow and a big litter of bonhams with her. The girl lifted her own dish, and there ran out a big mouse and a clutch of young mouselets with her. They ran here and there, and Martin at once thought that they were not good, and he plucked a big mitten off his hand and flung it at the young mice, but as soon as it touched the ground it changed into a cat, and the cat began to kill the young mice. That was the beginning of cats. Martin was a saint from that time forward, but I do not know which of the saints he was of all who were called Martin.

GOD SPARE YOU YOUR HEALTH.

PREFACE.

There is an Anglo-Irish proverb to the effect that " fine words butter no parsnips," and an Irish one runs " Ní bheathuigheann na briathra na bráithre," " words don't feed friars." This story is also told in other parts of the country about a cobbler. I have translated this version of it from the Lochrann " Márta agus Abrán, 1912," written down by " Giolla na lice."

THE STORY.

THERE was a smith in Skibbereen long ago, long before the foreigners nested there, and people used to be coming to him who did not please him too well. When he would do some little turn of work for them in the forge they used only have a " God spare you your health " for him. It's a very nice prayer, " God spare you your health," but when the smith used to go out to buy bread he used not to get it without money. Prayers, no matter how good, would not do the business for him. He used often to be half mad with them, but he used not to say anything. He was so vexed with that work one day that he took a hound he had from his house into his forge, and he tied it there with a wisp of hay under it. " Yes," said he, " we will soon see whether the prayers of these poor people will feed my hound."

The first person who came and had nothing but a "God spare you the health" in place of payment. "Right," said the smith, " let my hound have that."

Other people came to the forge, and they without any payment for the poor smith but that same fine prayer, and according as the smith used to get the prayers he used to bestow them on the hound. He used to give it no other food or drink. The prayers were the hound's food, but they made poor meat for him, for the smith found him dead in the morning after his being dependent on the feeding of the prayers.

A man came to the forge that day and he had a couple of hinges and a couple of reaping hooks, that were not too strong, to be fixed. The smith did the work, and the man was thinking of going, " God spare you the health," said he. Instead of the answer " Amen ! Lord ! and you likewise " ; what the smith did was to take the man by the shoulder. " Look over in the corner," said he ; " my hound is dead, and if prayers could feed it, it ought to be fat and strong. I have given every prayer I got this while back to that hound there, but they have not done the business for it. And it's harder to feed a man than a hound. Do you understand, my good man ? "

He did apparently, for he put his hand in his pocket. " What's the cost ? " said he.

It was short until all the neighbours heard talk of the death of that hound of the smith's, and much oftener from that out used their tune to be, " What's the cost, Dermot ? " than " God spare you your health."

TEIG O'KANE (TADHG O CÁTHÁIN) AND THE CORPSE.

PREFACE.

This story of Teig (in the ballad "Tomaus" O'Cahan or O'Kane) and the corpse, was told to me nearly thirty years ago by an old man from near Fenagh in the County Leitrim, whom I met paying his rent to a relative of mine in the town of Mohill. He must have been one of the last Irish speakers in that district. There does not appear to be a trace of Irish left there now. I did not write down the story from his lips, but wrote it out afterwards from memory. I took down the ballad, however, from his recitation so far as he had it; and I afterwards came across a written version of it in the handwriting of Nicholas O'Kearney, of the County Louth. The ballad as written by him coincides pretty closely with my version, but breaks off apparently in the middle, as though O'Kearney had not time to finish the rest of it. The first twenty-three verses are from O'Kearney's version, the rest are from mine. O'Kearney remarks in English at the top of the page: "The following fragment is one of our wild fairy adventures versified . . . . the fragment is preserved on account of the singular wildness of the air."

The only other Irish poem nearly in the same metre which I know of is a poem by Cormac Dall, or Cormac Common, which my friend Dr. Maguire, of Claremorris, took down the other day from the recitation of an old man.

It is on Halloweve night that one is especially liable to

adventures like those of Tomaus O'Cahan, but it is well known that all gamblers coming home at night are exposed to such perils.

THE STORY.

THERE was once a grown-up lad in the County Leitrim, and he was strong and lively, and the son of a rich farmer. His father had plenty of money, and he did not spare it on the son. Accordingly, when the boy grew up he liked sport better than work, and, as his father had no other children, he loved this one so much that he allowed him to do in everything just as it pleased himself. He was very extravagant, and he used to scatter the gold money as another person would scatter the white. He was seldom to be found at home, but if there was a fair, or a race, or a gathering within ten miles of him, you were dead certain to find him there. And he seldom spent a night in his father's house, but he used to be always out rambling, and, like Shawn Bwee long ago, there was

" grádh gach cailín i mbrollach a léine,"

" the love of every girl in the breast of his shirt," and it's many's the kiss he got and he gave, for he was very handsome, and there wasn't a girl in the country but would fall in love with him, only for him to fasten his two eyes on her, and it was for that someone made this rann on him—

" Feuch an rógaire 'g iarraidh póige,
    Ni h-iongantas mór é a bheith mar atá
Ag leanamhaint a gcómhnuidhe d'arnán na graineoige
    Anuas 's aníos 's nna chodladh 'sa lá."

.e.— " Look at the rogue, it's for kisses he's rambling,
    It isn't much wonder, for that was his way ;
He's like an old hedgehog, at night he'll be scrambling
    From this place to that, but he'll sleep in the day."

At last he became very wild and unruly. He wasn't to be seen day nor night in his father's house, but always rambling or going on his kailee (night-visit) from place to place and from house to house, so that the old people used to shake their heads and say to one another, " it's easy seen what will happen to the land when the old man dies ; his son will run through it in a year, and it won't stand him that long itself."

He used to be always gambling and card-playing and drinking, but his father never minded his bad habits, and never punished him. But it happened one day that the old man was told that the son had ruined the character of a girl in the neighbourhood, and he was greatly angry, and he called the son to him, and said to him, quietly and sensibly—" Avic," says he, " you know I loved you greatly up to this, and I never stopped you from doing your choice thing whatever it was, and I kept plenty of money with you, and I always hoped to leave you the house and land and all I had, after myself would be gone ; but I heard a story of you to-day that has disgusted me with you. I cannot tell you the grief that I felt when I heard such a thing of you, and I tell you now plainly that unless you marry that girl I'll leave house and land and everything to my brother's son. I never could leave it to anyone who would make so bad a use of it as you do yourself, deceiving women and coaxing girls. Settle with yourself now whether you'll marry that girl and get my land as a fortune with her, or refuse to marry her and give up all that was coming to you ; and tell me in the morning which of the two things you have chosen."

" Och ! murdher sheery ! father, you wouldn't say

that to me, and I such a good son as I am. Who told you I wouldn't marry the girl ? " says he.

But the father was gone, and the lad knew well enough that he would keep his word too ; and he was greatly troubled in his mind, for as quiet and as kind as the father was, he never went back of a word that he had once said, and there wasn't another man in the country who was harder to bend that he was.

The boy did not know rightly what to do. He was in love with the girl indeed, and he hoped to marry her some time or other, but he would much sooner have remained another while as he was, and follow on at his old tricks— drinking, sporting, and playing cards ; and, along with that, he was angry that his father should order him to marry and should threaten him if he did not do it.

" Isn't my father a great fool," says he to himself. " I was ready enough, and only too anxious, to marry Mary ; and now since he threatened me, faith I've a great mind to let it go another while."

His mind was so much excited that he remained between two notions as to what he should do. He walked out into the night at last to cool his heated blood, and went on to the road. He lit a pipe, and as the night was fine he walked and walked on, until the quick pace made him begin to forget his trouble. The night was bright and the moon half full. There was not a breath of wind blowing, and the air was calm and mild. He walked on for nearly three hours, when he suddenly remembered that it was late in the night, and time for him to turn. " Musha ! I think I forgot myself," says he ; " it must be near twelve o'clock now."

The word was hardly out of his mouth when he heard the sound of many voices and the trampling of feet on the road before him. " I don't know who can be out so late at night as this, and on such a lonely road," said he to himself.

He stood listening and he heard the voices of many people talking through other, but he could not understand what they were saying. " Oh, wirra ! " says he, " I'm afraid. It's not Irish or English they have ; it can't be they're Frenchmen ! " He went on a couple of yards further, and he saw well enough by the light of the moon a band of little people coming towards him, and they were carrying something big and heavy with them. " Oh, murdher ! " says he to himself, "sure it can't be that they're the good people that's in it ! " Every rib of hair that was on his head stood up, and there fell a shaking on his bones, for he saw that they were coming to him fast.

He looked at them again, and perceived that there were about twenty little men in it, and there was not a man at all of them higher than about three feet or three feet and a half, and some of them were grey, and seemed very old. He looked again, but he could not make out what was the heavy thing they were carrying until they came up to him, and then they all stood round about him. They threw the heavy thing down on the road, and he saw on the spot that it was a dead body.

He became as cold as the Death, and there was not a drop of blood running in his veins when an old little grey man*een* came up to him and said, " Isn't it lucky we met you, Teig O'Kane ? "

Poor Teig could not bring out a word at all, nor open

his lips, if he were to get the world for it, and so he gave no answer.

"Teig O'Kane," said the little grey man again, "isn't it timely you met us ? "

Teig could not answer him.

"Teig O'Kane," says he, "the third time, isn't it lucky and timely that we met you ? "

But Teig remained silent, for he was afraid to return an answer, and his tongue was as if it was tied to the roof of his mouth.

The little grey man turned to his companions, and there was joy in his bright little eye. "And now," says he, "Teig O'Kane hasn't a word, we can do with him what we please. Teig, Teig," says he, "you're living a bad life, and we can make a slave of you now, and you cannot withstand us, for there's no use in trying to go against us. Lift that corpse."

Teig was so frightened that he was only able to utter the two words, "I won't;" for as frightened as he was, he was obstinate and stiff, the same as ever.

"Teig O'Kane won't lift the corpse," said the little man*een*, with a wicked little laugh, for all the world like the breaking of a lock of dry kippeens, and with a little harsh voice like the striking of a cracked bell. "Teig O'Kane won't lift the corpse—make him lift it ; " and before the word was out of his mouth they had all gathered round poor Teig, and they all talking and laughing through other.

Teig tried to run from them, but they followed him, and a man of them stretched out his foot before him as he ran, so that Teig was thrown in a heap on the road. Then before he could rise up, the fairies caught him, some by the hands and some by the feet, and they held him tight, in a way that he could not stir, with his face against the ground. Six or seven of them raised the body then, and pulled it over to him, and left it down on his back. The breast of the corpse was squeezed against Teig's back and shoulders, and the arms of the corpse were thrown around Teig's neck. Then they stood back from him a couple of yards, and let him get up. He rose, foaming at the mouth and cursing, and he shook himself, thinking to throw the corpse off his back. But his fear and his wonder were great when he found that the two arms had a tight hold round his own neck, and that the two legs were squeezing his hips firmly, and that, however strongly he tried, he could not throw it off, any more than a horse can throw off its saddle. He was terribly frightened then, and he thought he was lost. "Ochone! for ever," said he to himself, " it's the bad life I'm leading that has given the good people this power over me I promise to God and Mary, Peter and Paul, Patrick and Bridget, that I'll mend my ways for as long as I have to live, if I come clear out of this danger—and I'll marry the girl."

The little grey man came up to him again, and said he to him, " Now, Teigeen," says he, " you didn't lift the body when I told you to lift it, and see how you were made to lift it ; perhaps when I tell you to bury it you won't bury it until you're made to bury it ! "

" Anything at all that I can do for your honour," said Teig, " I'll do it," for he was getting sense already, and if it had not been for the great fear that was on him, he never would have let that civil word slip out of his mouth.

The little man laughed a sort of laugh again. " You're getting quiet now, Teig," says he. " I'll go bail but you'll be quiet enough before I'm done with you. Listen to me now, Teig O'Kane, and if you don't obey me in all I'm telling you to do, you'll repent it. You must carry with you this corpse that is on your back to Teampoll-Démuis, and you must bring it into the church with you, and make a grave for it in the very middle of the church, and you must raise up the flags and put them down again the very same way, and you must carry the clay out of the church and leave the place as it was when you came, so that no one could know that there had been anything changed. But that's not all. Maybe that the body won't be allowed to be buried in that church ; perhaps some other man has the bed, and, if so, it's likely he won't share it with this one. If you don't get leave to bury it in Teampoll-Démuis, you must carry it to Carrick-fhad-vic-Oruis, and bury it in the churchyard there ; and if you don't get it into that place, take it with you to Team-poll-Ronáin ; and if that churchyard is closed on you, take it to Imlogue-Fhada; and if you're not able to bury it there, you've no more to do than to take it to Kill-Breedya, and you can bury it there without hindrance. I cannot tell you what one of those churches is the one where you will have leave to bury that corpse under the clay, but I know that it will be allowed you to bury him at some church or other of them. If you do this work rightly, we will be thankful to you, and you will have no cause to grieve ; but if you are slow or lazy, believe me we shall take satisfaction of you."

When the grey little man had done speaking, his com-

rades laughed and clapped their hands together. " Glic !
Glic ! Hwee ! Hwee ! " they all cried ; " go on, go on,
you have eight hours before you till daybreak, and if you
haven't this man buried before the sun rises, you're lost."
They struck a fist and a foot behind on him, and drove him
on in the road. He was obliged to walk, and to walk fast,
for they gave him no rest.

He thought himself that there was not a wet path, or a
dirty boreen, or a crooked contrary road in the whole
county that he had not walked that night. The night was
at times very dark, and whenever there would come a cloud
across the moon he could see nothing, and then he used
often to fall. Sometimes he was hurt, and sometimes he
escaped, but he was obliged always to rise on the moment
and to hurry on. Sometimes the moon would break out
clearly, and then he would look behind him and see the
little people following at his back. And he heard them
speaking amongst themselves, talking and crying out, and
screaming like a flock of sea-gulls ; and if he was to save
his soul he never understood as much as one word of what
they were saying.

He did not know how far he had walked, when at last
one of them cried out to him, " Stop here ! " He stood,
and they all gathered round him.

" Do you see those withered trees over there ? " says the
old boy to him again. " Teampoll-Démuis is among
those trees, and you must go in there by yourself, for we
cannot follow you or go with you. We must remain here.
Go on boldly."

Teig looked from him, and he saw a high wall that was in
places half broken down, and an old grey church on the

inside of the wall, and about a dozen withered old trees scattered here and there round it. There was neither leaf nor twig on any of them, but their bare crooked branches were stretched out like the arms of an angry man when he threatens. He had no help for it, but was obliged to go forward. He was a couple of hundred yards from the church, but he walked on, and never looked behind him until he came to the gate of the churchyard. The old gate was thrown down, and he had no difficulty in entering. He turned then to see if any of the little people were following him, but there came a cloud over the moon, and the night became so dark that he could see nothing. He went into the churchyard, and he walked up the old grassy pathway leading to the church. When he reached the door, he found it locked. The door was large and strong, and he did not know what to do. At last he drew out his knife with difficulty, and stuck it in the wood to try if it were not rotten, but it was not.

" Now," said he to himself, " I have no more to do ; the door is shut, and I can't open it."

Before the words were rightly shaped in his own mind, a voice in his ear said to him, " Search for the key on the top of the door, or on the wall."

He started. " Who is that speaking to me ? " he cried, turning round ; but he saw no one. The voice said in his ear again, " Search for the key on the top of the door, or on the wall."

" What's that ? " said he, and the sweat running from his forehead ; " who spoke to me ? "

" It's I, the corpse, that spoke to you ! " said the voice.

" Can you talk ? " said Teig.

" Now and again," said the corpse.

Teig searched for the key, and he found it on the top of the wall. He was too much frightened to say any more, but he opened the door wide, and as quickly as he could, and he went in, with the corpse on his back. It was as dark as pitch inside, and poor Teig began to shake and tremble.

" Light the candle," said the corpse.

Teig put his hand in his pocket, as well as he was able, and drew out a flint and steel. He struck a spark out of it, and lit a burnt rag he had in his pocket. He blew it until it made a flame, and he looked round him. The church was very ancient, and part of the wall was broken down. The windows were blown in or cracked, and the timber of the seats was rotten. There were six or seven old iron candlesticks left there still, and in one of these candlesticks Teig found the stump of an old candle, and he lit it. He was still looking round him on the strange and horrid place in which he found himself, when the cold corpse whispered in his ear, " Bury me now, bury me now ; there is a spade and turn the ground." Teig looked from him, and he saw a spade lying beside the altar. He took it up, and he placed the blade under a flag that was in the middle of the aisle, and leaning all his weight on the handle of the spade, he raised it. When the first flag was raised it was not hard to raise the others near it, and he moved three or four of them out of their places. The clay that was under them was soft and easy to dig, but he had not thrown up more than three or four shovelfuls, when he felt the iron touch something soft like flesh. He threw up three or four more shovelfuls from around

it, and then he saw that it was another body that was
buried in the same place.

"I am afraid I'll never be allowed to bury the two
bodies in the same hole," said Teig, in his own mind.
"You corpse, there on my back," says he, "will you be
satisfied if I bury you down here?" But the corpse
never answered him a word.

"That's a good sign," said Teig to himself. "Maybe
he's getting quiet," and he thrust the spade down in the
earth again. Perhaps he hurt the flesh of the other body,
for the dead man that was buried there stood up in the
grave, and shouted an awful shout. "Hoo! hoo!!
hoo!!! Go! go!! go!!! or you're a dead, dead,
dead man!" And then he fell back in the grave again.
Teig said afterwards, that of all the wonderful things
he saw that night, that was the most awful to him. His
hair stood upright on his head like the bristles of a pig,
the cold sweat ran off his face, and then came a tremor
over all his bones, until he thought that he must fall.

But after a while he became bolder, when he saw that
the second corpse remained lying quietly there, and he
threw in the clay on it again, and he smoothed it overhead,
and he laid down the flags carefully as they had been
before. "It can't be that he'll rise up any more," said
he.

He went down the aisle a little further, and drew near
to the door, and began raising the flags again, looking for
another bed for the corpse on his back. He took up three
or four flags and put them aside, and then he dug the clay.
He was not long digging until he laid bare an old woman
without a thread upon her but her shirt. She was more

lively than the first corpse, for he had scarcely taken any of the clay away from about her, when she sat up and began to cry, " Ho, you bodach (clown) ! Ha, you bodach ! Where has he been that he got no bed ? "

Poor Teig drew back, and when she found that she was getting no answer, she closed her eyes gently, lost her vigour, and fell back quietly and slowly under the clay. Teig did to her as he had done to the man—he threw the clay back on her, and left the flags down overhead.

He began digging again near the door, but before he had thrown up more than a couple of shovelfuls, he noticed a man's hand laid bare by the spade. " By my soul, I'll go no further, then," said he to himself ; " what use is it for me ? " And he threw the clay in again on it, and settled the flags as they had been before.

He left the church then, and his heart was heavy enough, but he shut the door and locked it, and left the key where he found it. He sat down on a tombstone that was near the door, and began thinking. He was in great doubt what he should do. He laid his face between his two hands, and cried for grief and fatigue, since he was dead certain at this time that he never would come home alive. He made another attempt to loosen the hands of the corpse that were squeezed round his neck, but they were as tight as if they were clamped ; and the more he tried to loosen them, the tighter they squeezed him. He was going to sit down once more, when the cold, horrid lips of the dead man said to him, " Carrick-fhad-vic-Oruis," and he remembered the command of the good people to bring the corpse with him to that place if he should be unable to bury it where he had been

He rose up and looked about him. " I don't know the way," he said.

As soon as he had uttered the words, the corpse stretched out suddenly its left hand that had been tightened round his neck, and kept it pointing out, showing, him the road he ought to follow. Teig went in the direction that the fingers were stretched, and passed out of the churchyard. He found himself on an old rutty, stony road, and he stood still again, not knowing where to turn. The corpse stretched out its bony hand a second time, and pointed out to him another road—not the road by which he had come when approaching the old church. Teig followed that road, and whenever he came to a path or road meeting it, the corpse always stretched out its hand and pointed with its fingers, showing him the way he was to take.

Many was the cross-road he turned down, and many was the crooked boreen he walked, until he saw from him an old burying-ground at last, beside the road, but there was neither church nor chapel nor any other building in it. The corpse squeezed him tightly, and he stood. " Bury me, bury me in the burying-ground," said the voice.

Teig drew over towards the old burying-place, and he was not more than about twenty yards from it, when, raising his eyes, he saw hundreds and hundreds of ghosts— men, women, and children—sitting on the top of the wall round about, or standing on the inside of it, or running backwards and forwards, and pointing at him, while he could see their mouths opening and shutting as if they were speaking, though he heard no word, nor any sound amongst them at all.

He was afraid to go forward, so he stood where he was, and the moment he stood, all the ghosts became quiet, and ceased moving. Then Teig understood that it was trying to keep him from going in that they were. He walked a couple of yards forwards, and immediately the whole crowd rushed together towards the spot to which he was moving, and they stood so thickly together that it seemed to him that he never could break through them, even though he had a mind to try. But he had no mind to try it. He went back broken and disspirited, and when he had gone a couple of hundred yards from the burying-ground, he stood again, for he did not know what way he was to go. He heard the voice of the corpse in his ear, saying "Teampoll-Ronáin," and the skinny hand was stretched out again, pointing him out the road.

As tired as he was, he had to walk, and the road was neither short nor even. The night was darker than ever, and it was difficult to make his way. Many was the toss he got, and many a bruise they left on his body. At last he saw Teampoll-Ronáin from him in the distance, standing in the middle of the burying-ground. He moved over towards it, and thought he was all right and safe, when he saw no ghosts nor anything else on the wall, and he thought he would never be hindered now from leaving his load off him at last. He moved over to the gate, but as he was passing in, he tripped on the threshold. Before he could recover himself, something that he could not see seized him by the neck, by the hands, and by the feet, and bruised him, and shook him up, and choked him, until he was nearly dead ; and at last he was lifted up, and carried more than a hundred yards from that place, and then thrown down in an old dyke, with the corpse still clinging to him.

He rose up, bruised and sore, but feared to go near the place again, for he had seen nothing the time he was thrown down and carried away

" You, corpse up on my back," said he, " shall I go over again to the churchyard ? "—but the corpse never answered him. " That's a sign you don't wish me to try it again," said Teig.

He was now in great doubt as to what he ought to do, when the corpse spoke in his ear, and said " Imlogue-Fhada."

" Oh, murder ! " said Teig, " must I bring you there ? If you keep me long walking like this, I tell you I'll fall under you."

He went on, however, in the direction the corpse pointed out to him. He could not have told, himself, how long he had been going, when the dead man behind suddenly squeezed him, and said, " There ! "

Teig looked from him, and he saw a little low wall, that was so broken down in places that it was no wall at all. It was in a great wide field, in from the road ; and only for three or four great stones at the corners, that were more like rocks than stones, there was nothing to show that there was either graveyard or burying-ground there.

" Is this Imlogue-Fhada ? Shall I bury you here ? " said Teig.

" Yes," said the voice.

" But I see no grave or gravestone, only this pile of stones," said Teig.

The corpse did not answer, but stretched out its long

fleshless hand, to show Teig the direction in which he was
to go. Teig went on accordingly, but he was greatly terrified, for he remembered what had happened to him at the
last place. He went on, " with his heart in his mouth,"
as he said himself afterwards ; but when he came to within
fifteen or twenty yards of the little low square wall, there
broke out a flash of lightning, bright yellow and red, with
blue streaks in it, and went round about the wall in one
course, and it swept by as fast as the swallow in the clouds,
and the longer Teig remained looking at it the faster it
went, till at last it became like a bright ring of flame round
the old graveyard, which no one could pass without being
burnt by it. Teig never saw, from the time he was born,
and never saw afterwards, so wonderful or so splendid a
sight as that was. Round went the flame, white and
yellow and blue sparks leaping out from it as it went, and
although at first it had been no more than a thin, narrow
line, it increased slowly until it was at last a great broad
band, and it was continually getting broader and higher,
and throwing out more brilliant sparks, till there was
never a colour on the ridge of the earth that was not to be
seen in that fire ; and lightning never shone and flame
never flamed that was so shining and so bright as
that.

Teig was amazed ; he was half dead with fatigue, and he
had no courage left to approach the wall. There fell a
mist over his eyes, and there came a soorawn in his head,
and he was obliged to sit down upon a great stone to
recover himself. He could see nothing but the light, and
he could hear nothing but the whirr of it as it shot round
the paddock faster than a flash of lightning.

As he sat there on the stone, the voice whispered once
more in his ear, " Kill-Breedya " ; and the dead man
squeezed him so tightly that he cried out. He rose again,
sick, tired, and trembling, and went forwards as he was
directed. The wind was cold, and the road was bad, and
the load upon his back was heavy, and the night was dark,
and he himself was nearly worn out, and if he had had
very much farther to go he must have fallen dead under
his burden.

At last the corpse stretched out its hand, and said to
him, " Bury me there."

" This is the last burying-place," said Teig in his own
mind ; " and the little grey man said I'd be allowed to
bury him in some of them, so it must be this ; it can't
be but they'll let him in here."

The first faint streak of the ring of day was appearing in
the east, and the clouds were beginning to catch fire, but it
was darker than ever, for the moon was set, and there were
no stars.

" Make haste, make haste ! " said the corpse ; and Teig
hurried forward as well as he could to the graveyard, which
was a little place on a bare hill, with only a few graves in it.
He walked boldly in through the open gate, and nothing
touched him, nor did he either hear or see anything. He
came to the middle of the ground, and then stood up and
looked round him for a spade or shovel to make a grave.
As he was turning round and searching, he suddenly perceived what startled him greatly—a newly-dug grave right
before him. He moved over to it, and looked down, and
there at the bottom he saw a black coffin. He clambered
down into the hole and lifted the lid, and found that (as he

thought it would be) the coffin was empty. He had hardly mounted up out of the hole, and was standing on the brink, when the corpse, which had clung to him for more than eight hours, suddenly relaxed its hold of his neck, and loosened its shins from round his hips, and sank down with a plop into the open coffin.

Teig fell down on his two knees at the brink of the grave, and gave thanks to God. He made no delay then, but pressed down the coffin lid in its place, and threw in the clay over it with his two hands ; and when the grave was filled up, he stamped and leaped on it with his feet, until it was firm and hard, and then he left the place.

The sun was fast rising as he finished his work, and the first thing he did was to return to the road, and look out for a house to rest himself in. He found an inn at last, and lay down upon a bed there, and slept till night. Then he rose up and ate a little, and fell asleep again till morning. When he awoke in the morning he hired a horse and rode home. He was more than twenty-six miles from home where he was, and he had come all that way with the dead body on his back in one night.

All the people at his own home thought that he must have left the country, and they rejoiced greatly when they saw him come back. Everyone began asking him where he had been, but he would not tell anyone except his father.

He was a changed man from that day. He never drank too much ; he never lost his money over cards ; and especially he would not take the world and be out late by himself of a dark night.

He was not a fortnight at home until he married Mary,
the girl he had been in love with ; and it's at their wedding
the sport was, and it's he was the happy man from that day
forward, and it's all I wish that we may be as happy as
he was.

———

TOMAUS O CAHAN AND THE GHOST.

Come hear my walking, my midnight walking,
  A cause of dread, and a cause of dread,
With that corpse of faierie could get no stretching
  Amongst the dead men, amongst the dead.

[THE CORPSE SPEAKS.]
" Raise my dead body with no rejoicing
  And a beef I'll give thee, a beef I'll give,

[TOMAUS ANSWERS.]
" If I should settle on that condition
  Where is the beef, and where is the beef ? "

[THE CORPSE SPEAKS.]
" It's old Shaun Bingham and Shaun Oge Bingham
  My sureties be, my sureties be,
In the crooked letter I wrote a ticket
  To Bél-in-Assan beside the sea."

" You will get a heaplet beneath the midden
  So green and gloomy, green and gloomy,
Then take it with thee for thy provision
  Beneath thy armpit—against thy journey."

The corpse was raised on Tomaus his back,
  In the ways of night, in the ways of night,
Through roads that were narrow and hard and crooked,
  By the pale moonlight, by the pale moonlight.

And long was the route, and the cross-track journey,
  Through miry bogs and through dripping glooms,
Westward to Lugh-moy-more-na-mrauher[1]
  Of the grass green tombs, of the grass green tombs.

[THE CORPSE SPEAKS.]

" At thy right hand is a spade for digging,
  Behind the door post it will be found,
With a strong thrust, thrust ; with a thrust not timid,
  And turn the ground, and turn the ground."

[TOMAUS SPEAKS.]

" At my right hand did I find the spade,
  'Twas behind the door there, behind the door,
And a strong thrust downward I quickly made
  Through the earthen floor, through the earthen floor."

" I struck it strongly, I drove it down,
  Through the upper earth, through the upper earth,
Till I broke the thigh of the English clown,
  Who was sleeping there in his clay cold berth."

" ' A thousand pililloos,' cries the trooper,
  ' Where is my pistol that I may slay ? '
Cries Mary O'Reilly, Lord Guido's wife,
  ' Come clear the way there, come clear the way ! ' "

[THE CORPSE SPEAKS.]

" Oro ! oh Tomaus ! oro ! oh Tomaus !
  Do not leave me here I beseech of thee,
I've a mother's relative's son in Craggan
  And it's buried there I shall have to be."

On Tomaus his back was the body hoisted,
  In the ways of night, in the ways of night,
Through roads that were crooked and rough and narrow
  By the pale moonlight, by the pale moonlight.

---

[1] = great Louth of the Friars.

" Going down of a race and in great disorder,
    To the Craggan More, to the Craggan More,
I found a spade at my right hand lying
    Behind the door there, behind the door."

" I found a spade at my right hand laid,
    Behind the door there, behind the door,
Two thrusts that were heavy and strong I made
    Through the earthen floor, through the earthen floor "

" 'Til I broke the hip bone of Watson Harford
    Was beneath the ground and he raised a clamour,
' Hubbubboo,' cried the Gowa Dhu
    ' Where is my hammer, where is my hammer.' "

[THE CORPSE SPEAKS.]

" Oro ! oh Tomaus ; uch, uch, uch, oh !
    Do not leave me here I beseech of thee,
For my father's brother's son is in Derry
    And it's buried there I shall have to be."

" On reaching the place all spent and lonely
    And I despairing, and I despairing,
The gates were all strongly barred before me
    But I smote upon them with sudden daring."

" Said the Mayor of the place, in his grave clothes rising,
    In his winding sheet from his clay bed taken,
' Why knock so hard, each to his part ;
    Come dead awaken, come dead awaken.' "

" Bodies and coffins came pouring upwards
    From the ground beneath in the pale moonlight,
And they ranged themselves in a raging rabble
    On the bare wall's height, on the bare wall's height."

"' A hundred pililloos ! ' cried they all,
    ' What is the matter, where are we hurried ? ' "

[TOMAUS ANSWERS.]

" It is one of your friends who has died and here
  Is the place where he says that he must be buried.
For his kindred are here and it's well they are,
  Then take him from me, and good's my riddance."

[THE GHOST ASKS.]

" Who of his people is buried here
  To claim admittance, claim admittance? "

[TOMAUS ANSWERS.]

" I know not myself of what tribe my man is
  On the ridge of earth if I'm not a liar,
There's a stir and a voice in him, ask himself,
  Of himself inquire, himself inquire."

The corpse was raised on Tomaus his back,
  Than a gad more tight, than a gad more tight,
Till he took a skreep to the Teampoll-Démuis,
  And he found it fastened that weary night.

[THE CORPSE SPEAKS.]

" Search for the key, you will find it lying
  Behind the door, or upon the wall."

He searched for the key and he found and opened
  And wide and silent and dark was all.

[THE CORPSE SPEAKS AGAIN.]

" Oro, oh, Tomaus ! Oro, oh, Tomaus !
  Oh, bury me quick out of sight and sound,
See yonder the spade forenenst you lying,
  And turn the ground, and turn the ground."

He took the spade in his hand, and quickly
  He turned the ground so black and bare,
Till he broke the bones of an English bodach
  Who had long been there, who had long been there.

" Blood and owns, you broke my bones,"
   That man kept crying with teeth that chatter,
And then spoke Smiler, the wife of Simon,
   " What is the matter ?   What is the matter ? "

" Where was he, or where did he pass his life,
   That he's got no bed where he now may go ? "

[TOMAUS ANSWERS.]

" He's there before you who knows it best.
   You must ask him yourself, for I do not know."

Then Feeny arose and he took some snuff
   And he seized an alpeen and gripped it tight,
And there was the slashing and noise and smashing
   Till the morning light, till the morning light.

The Corpse was raised on Tomaus his back,
   Like a tightened gad, like a tightened gad,
And he brought it up, and he brought it down,
   And the way was long and the way was bad.

To Carrick-vic-oruis and Teampoll-Ronáin
   And Imlogue-Fhada the corpse was hurried,
But in Kill-Vreedya the skreep was over
   The corpse was buried, the corpse was buried.

A STICK AND A STONE ON IT,
AND BAD LUCK ON IT !

PRAYER AFTER TOBACCO.

PREFACE.

There is at times a certain connection between the use of tobacco and the solemn presence of the dead. Both snuff and tobacco for smoking are handed round at wakes. Pipes and tobacco are, in fact, the principal portion of the equipment of the corp-house. To the present moment when one accepts a pinch of snuff it is customary to say in Irish, " the blessing of God be with the souls of your dead." I have heard this a hundred times. But I never heard the tobacco prayer except once or twice from very old people; and, in spite of this story, I don't believe that it was ever in any way usual to say a prayer over tobacco except perhaps in some isolated parts of the country. All I can say is that I have never heard it said spontaneously. This story was written down word for word for me by my friend Mr. John Mac Neill from the recitation of Michael Mac Rury or Rogers, from Ballycastle, in the County Mayo. The tobacco prayer[1] translated, runs as follows :—

Eighteen fulls of the churchyard of Patrick, of the mantle[2] of Brigit, of the tomb of Christ, of the palace of Rome, of the church of God, be with thy soul (and with the soul of him above whose head was this tobacco),[3] and with the souls of the dead in Purgatory all together.

> May not more numerous be
> The grains of sand by the sea,
> Or the blades of grass on the lea,
> Or the drops of dew on the tree,
> Than the blessings upon thy soul
> And the souls of the dead with thee,
> And my soul when the life shall flee.

It is for God to give shelter, light, and the glory of the heavens to the souls of the dead of Purgatory.

---

[1] For the original, see my "Religious Songs of Connacht," vol. II. p. 66.

[2] The Mantle of Brigit is a common expression. Even in Scotland " St. Bride and her brat [mantle] " is a well-known saying.

[3] This obviously shows that the prayer was intended to be said at wakes.

The story was evidently invented with the didactic intention of encouraging the use of prayer, and of inculcating the truth that just as we ought to be thankful to God for our meals, so ought we to be thankful to Him for our tobacco, and for all the good things of life.

THE STORY.

THERE was a woman in it long ago, and she had an only son. When he came to age she sent him to college, and made a priest of him. After his coming from the college he was a short little while at home ; and he was one day walking out in the garden when there came a saint [in the air] over his head, and spoke down to him, and told the priest that he himself and all who belonged to him were damned on account of his mother.

The priest asked him what was the crime his mother had committed, and the saint told him that she was smoking tobacco for twelve years and had never said the tobacco prayer all that time

" Bad enough ! " says the priest, " is there anything at all down from heaven to set that right ? " says the priest.

" There's nothing but one thing alone," says he, " and this is it. When you go in to your mother tell her as I have told it to you. And unless she shall be prepared to suffer the death that I'll tell you, not a sight of the country of heaven will your mother or anyone of her family see for ever."

" What death is it ? " said the priest to him.

" She must let you," says he, " carve every bit off her body as fine as sneeshin."

The priest went into the house and a heavy load on his heart. He sat upon a chair and there was a great grief to be seen in his face. His mother asked him what was on him, and what had happened to him since he went out.

" Ah, there's nothing on me but a little weariness," says he, " kindle the pipe for me mother," says he, " I'd like to get a blast of tobacco."

" I'll kindle it and welcome," says she, " I thought avourneen," says she, " that you were not using tobacco."

" Ah, maybe a whiff would take this weariness off me," said he.

True was the story. She put a coal in the pipe, and after smoking enough of the pipe herself she handed it to the priest, but she never said the prayer. And that was the reason the priest had told her to kindle the pipe, hoping that she would say the prayer, but she did not.

" Poor enough ! " said the priest in his own mind.

The priest told her then as the saint had told him, and she threw herself on her two knees praying God and shedding tears, and, said she, " a hundred welcomes to the graces of God, and if it is the death that God has promised me, I am satisfied to suffer it ; go out now my son," says she, " and when I'll be ready for you to get to your work I'll call you in."

The priest went out, fervently reading and praying to God.

The mother washed and cleaned herself. She got sheets and sharp knives ready for the work, and when she had everything prepared she called the priest to come in. And as the priest turned round on his foot, the brightness came over his head again, and it said to him that all his family had found forgiveness for their sins, on account of the earnest repentance that his mother was after making, and the awful death that she was fully satisfied to suffer.

The priest came into the house, and a great joy in his heart, and his mother was stretched on the length of her back on the table, and sheets under her and over her, and her two hands stretched out from her, and she praying to God, and two sharp knives by her side; and, says the priest to her, " Rise up, mother," says he, " I have got forgiveness from the King of the graces, for our sins, and I beseech you now from this day out, do not forget to diligently offer up the tobacco prayer every time you use it."

And true was the story. There was never a time from that day till the day that the priest's mother went into the clay that she did not earnestly offer up the prayer to God and to the glorious Virgin.

And the old people throughout the country [added the reciter, talking of West Mayo] are offering up that same prayer daily, and they shall do so as long as a word of our Irish language shall remain alive on the green island of the saints.

THE BUÍDEACH, THE TINKER, AND THE BLACK DONKEY.

PREFACE.

I got this story from O'Connor, who himself got it from a man of the name of Peter Srehane, who lived near Castlebar, Co. Mayo.

It is a melange of many curious beliefs, metempsychosis, "St. Patrick's Purgatory" (so well known over Europe in the middle ages), the purse of Fortunatus, fairy gold changing to pebbles, etc. I printed this story with a French translation in my "Sgeuluidhe Gaedhealach." It is the 23rd story in that volume.

THE STORY.

In times long ago there was a poor widow living near Castlebar, in the County Mayo. She had an only son, and he never grew one inch from the time he was five years old, and the people called him Buídeach[1] as a nick-name.

One day when the Buideach was about fifteen years of age his mother went to Castlebar. She was not gone more than an hour when there came a big Tinker, and a

---

[1] Or better, Buighdeach, pronounced Bweed-yach, i.e., Bweed-ya with a guttural ch (as in loch) at the end.

Black Donkey with him, to the door, and "Are you in, woman of the house ? " said the tinker.

" She is not," said the Buideach, " and she told me not to let anyone in until she'd come home herself."

The Tinker walked in, and when he looked at the Buideach he said, " Indeed you're a nice boy to keep anyone at all out, you could not keep out a turkey cock."

The Buideach rose of a leap and gave the big Tinker a fist between the two eyes and pitched him out on the top of his head, under the feet of the Black Donkey.

The Tinker rose up in a rage and made an attempt to get hold of the Buideach, but he gave him another fist at the butt of the ear and threw him out again under the feet of the Black Donkey.

The donkey began to bray pitifully, and when the Buideach went out to see [why], the Tinker was dead. " You have killed my master," said the Black Donkey, " and indeed I am not sorry for it, he often gave me a heavy beating without cause."

The Buideach was astonished when he heard the Black Donkey speaking, and he said, " You are not a proper donkey."

" Indeed, I have only been an ass for seven years. My story is a pitiful one. I was the son of a gentleman."

" Musha, then, I would like to hear your story," said the Buideach.

" Come in, then, to the end of the house. Cover up the Tinker in the dunghill, and I will tell you my story."

The Buideach drew the dead man over to the dunghill and covered him up. The Black Donkey walked into the house and said, " I was the son of a gentleman, but I was a bad son, and I died under a heavy load of deadly sins on my poor soul ; and I would be burning in hell now were it not for the Virgin Mary. I used to say a little prayer in honour of her every night, and when I went into the presence of the Great Judge I was sentenced to hell until His mother spoke to the Judge and He changed his sentence, and there was made of me a Black Donkey, and I was given to the Tinker for the space of seven years, until he should die a worldly [or corporeal] death. The Tinker was a limb of the devil, and it was I who gave you strength to kill him ; but you are not done with him yet. He will come to life again at the end of seven days, and if you are there before him he will kill you as sure as you are alive."

" I never left this townland since I was born," said the Buideach, " and I would not like to desert my mother."

" Would it not be better for you to leave your mother than to lose your life in a state of mortal sin and be for ever burning in hell ? "

" I don't know any place where I could go into hiding," said the Buideach ; " but since it has turned out that it was you who put strength into my hand to kill the Tinker, perhaps you would direct me to some place where I could be safe from him."

" Did you ever hear talk of Lough Derg ? "

" Indeed, I did," said the Buideach ; " my grandmother was once on a pilgrimage there, but I don't know where it is."

" I will bring you there to-morrow night. There is a monastery underground on the island, and an old friar in it who sees the Virgin Mary every Saturday. Tell him

your case and take his advice in every single thing. He
will put you to penance, but penance on this world is
better than the pains of hell for ever. You know where
the little dún¹ is, which is at the back of the old castle.
If you are in the dún about three hours after nightfall
I shall be there before you and bring you to Lough Derg.

"I shall be there if I'm alive," said the Buideach ;
"but is there any fear of me that the Tinker will get up
before that time ? "

"There is no fear," said the Black Donkey, "unless
you tell somebody that you killed him. If you tell anything about him he will get up and he will slay yourself
and your mother."

"By my soul, then, I'll be silent about him," said the
Buideach.

That evening when the Buideach's mother came home
she asked him did anybody come to the house since
she went away.

"I did not see anyone," said he, "but an old pedlar
with a bag, and he got nothing from me."

"I see the track of the shoe of a horse or a donkey
outside the door, and it was not there in the morning
when I was going out," said she.

"It was Páidin Éamoinn the fool, who was riding
Big Mary O'Brien's ass," said the Buideach.

The Buideach never slept a wink all that night but
thinking of the Tinker and the Black Donkey. The next
day he was in great anxiety. His mother observed that
and asked him what was on him.

---

¹ Literally, "fort," pronounced like "dhoon." Usually a half-
levelled earthen rampart.

" There's not a feather on me," says he.

That night when the mother was asleep the Buideach stole out and never stopped until he came to the little dún ; the Black Donkey was there before him and said, " Are you ready ? "

" I am," said the Buideach, " but I am grieved that I did not get my mother's blessing ; she will be very anxious until I come back again."

" Indeed she will not be anxious at all, because there is another Buideach at your mother's side at home, so like you that she won't know that it is not yourself that's in it ; but I'll bring him away with me before you come back."

" I am very much obliged to you and I am ready to go with you now," said he.

" Leap up on my back ; there is a long journey before us," said the Donkey.

The Buideach leapt on his back, and the moment he did so he heard thunder and saw great lightning. There came down a big cloud which closed around the black ass and its rider. The Buideach lost the sight of his eyes, and a heavy sleep fell upon him, and when he awoke he was on an island in Lough Derg, standing in the presence of the ancient friar.

The friar began to talk to him, and said, "What brought you here, my son ? "

" Well, then, indeed, I don't rightly know," said the Buideach.

" I will know soon," said the friar ; " come with me."

He followed the old friar down under the earth, until

they came to a little chamber that was cut in the rock. " Now," said the friar, " go down on your knees and make your confession and do not conceal any crime."

The Buideach went down on his knees and told everything that happened to him concerning the Tinker and the Black Donkey.

The friar then put him under penance for seven days and seven nights, without food or drink, walking on his bare knees amongst the rocks and sharp stones. He went through the penance, and by the seventh day there was not a morsel of skin or flesh on his knees, and he was like a shadow with the hunger. When he had the penance finished the old friar came and said, " It's time for you to be going home."

" I have no knowledge of the way or of how to go back," said the Buideach.

" Your friend the Black Donkey will bring you back," said the friar. " He will be here to-night ; and when you go home spend your life piously and do not tell to anyone except to your father-confessor that yo were here."

" Tell me, father, is there any danger of me from the Tinker ? "

" There is not," said the friar ; " he is an ass [himself now] with a tinker from the province of Munster, and he will be in that shape for one and twenty years, and after that he will go to eternal rest. Depart now to your chamber. You will hear a little bell after the darkness of night [has fallen], and as soon as you shall hear it, go up on to the island, and the Black Donkey will be there

before you, and he will bring you home ; my blessing
with you."

The Buideach went to his room, and as soon as he heard
the bell he went up to the island and his friend the Black
Donkey was waiting for him.

" Jump up on my back, Buideach, I have not a moment
to lose," said the donkey.

He did so, and on the spot he heard the thunder and
saw the lightning. A great cloud came down and en-
veloped the Black Donkey and its rider. Heavy sleep fell
upon the Buideach, and when he awoke he found himself
in the little dún at home standing in the presence of the
Black Donkey.

" Go home now to your mother. The other Buideach
is gone from her side ; she is in deep sleep and she
won't feel you going in."

" Is there any fear of me from the Tinker ? " said he.

" Did not the blessed friar tell you that there is not,"
said the Black Donkey. " I will protect you. Put your
hand in my left ear, and you will get there a purse which
will, never be empty during your life. Be good to poor
people and to widows and to orphans, and you will have
a long life and a happy death, and heaven at the
end."

The Buideach went home and went to sleep, and the
mother never had had a notion that the other Buideach
was not her own son.

At the end of a week after this the Buideach said to his
mother, " Is not this a fair day in Castlebar ? "

" Yes, indeed," said she,

" Well then, you ought to go there and buy a cow,"
says he.

" Don't be humbugging your mother or you'll have no
luck," says she.

" Upon my word I am not humbugging," said he.
" God sent a purse my way, and there is more than the
price of a cow in it."

" Perhaps you did not get it honestly ; tell me where
did you find it ? "

" I'll tell you nothing about it, except that I found it
honestly, and if you have any doubt about my word, let
the thing be."

Women are nearly always given to covetousness, and
she was not free from it.

" Give me the price of the cow."

He handed her twenty pieces of gold. " You'll get a
good cow for all that money," said he.

" I will," said she, " but I'd like to have the price of a
pig."

" Do not be greedy, mother," said he ; " you won't
get any more this time."

The mother went to the fair and she bought a milch
cow, and some clothes for the Buideach, and when he
got her gone he went to the parish priest and said that
he would like to make confession. He told the priest
then everything that happened to him from the time he
met the Tinker and the Black Donkey.

" Indeed, you are a good boy," said the priest, "give me
some of the gold."

The Buideach, gave him twenty pieces, but he was not
satisfied with that, and he asked for the price of a horse.

"I did not think that a priest would be covetous," said he, " but I see now that they are as covetous as women. Here are twenty more pieces for you ; are you satisfied now ? "

" I am, and I am not," said the priest. " Since you have a purse which will never be empty as long as you live, you should be able to give me as much as would set up a fine church in place of the miserable one which we have in the parish now."

" Get workmen and masons, and begin the church, and I'll give you the workmen's wages from week to week," said the Buideach.

" I'd sooner have it now," said the priest. " A thousand pieces will do the work, and if you give them to me now I'll put up the church."

The Buideach gave him one thousand pieces of gold out of the purse, and the purse was none the lighter for it.

The Buideach came home and his mother was there before him, with a fine milch cow and new clothes for himself. " Indeed, that's a good cow," said he ; " we can give the poor people some milk every morning."

" Indeed they must wait until I churn, and I'll give them the buttermilk—until I buy a pig."

" It's the new milk you'll give the poor people," said the Buideach, " we can buy butter."

" I think you have lost your senses," says the mother. " You'll want the little share of riches which God sent you before I'm a year in the grave."

" How do you know but that I might not be in the grave before you ? " said he ; " but at all events God will send me my enough."

When they were talking there came a poor woman,

and three children to the door and asked for alms in the honour of God and Mary.

" I have nothing for ye this time," said the widow.

" Don't say that, mother," said the Buideach. " I have alms to give in the name of God and His mother Mary." With that he went out and gave a gold piece to the poor woman, and said to his mother, " Milk the cow and give those poor children a drink."

" I will not," said the mother.

" Then I'll do it myself," said he.

He got the vessel, milked the cow, and gave lots of new milk to the poor children and to the woman. When they were gone away the mother said to him, " Your purse will be soon empty."

" I have no fear of that," said he ; " it's God who sent it to me, and I'll make a good use of it," says he.

" Have your own way,"[1] said she ; " but you'll be sorry for it yet."

The next day lots of people came to the Buideach asking for alms, and he never let them go away from him empty-[handed]. The name and fame of the Buideach went through the country like lightning and men said that he was in partnership with the good people [*i.e.* fairies]. But others said that it was the devil who was giving him the gold, and they made a complaint against him to the parish priest. But the priest said that the Buideach was a decent good boy, and that it was God who gave him the means, and that he was making good use of them.

The Buideach went on well now, and he began growing until he was almost six feet high.

----

[1] Literally, " do you our will."

His mother died and he fell in love with a pretty girl, and he was not long until they were married.

He had not a day's luck from that time forward. His wife got to know that he had a wonderful purse and nothing could satisfy her but she must get it. He refused her often, but she was giving him no rest, day or night, until she got the purse from him at last. Then, when she got it, she had no respect for it. She went to Castlebar to buy silks and satins, but when she opened the purse in place of gold pieces being in it there was nothing but pieces of pebbles. She came back and great anger on her ; and said, " Isn't it a nice fool you made of me giving me a purse filled with little stones instead of the purse with the gold in it."

" I gave you the right purse," said he ; " I have no second one."

He seized the purse and opened it, and as sure as I'm telling it to you, there was nothing in it but little bits of pebbles.

There was an awful grief upon the Buideach, and it was not long until he was mad, tearing his hair, and beating his head against the wall.

The priest was sent for but he could get neither sense nor reason out of the Buideach. He tore off his clothes and went naked and mad through the country.

About a week after that the neighbours found the poor Buideach dead at the foot of a bush in the little dún.

That old bush is growing in the dún yet, and the people call it the " Buideach's Bush," but [as for himself] it is certain that he went to heaven.

THE GREAT WORM OF THE SHANNON

PREFACE.

This curious conception of the greatest river in Ireland owing its origin to the struggles of a great worm or serpent is new to me. I got it from Pronisias O'Conor, who was in the workhouse in Athlone at the time, and he got it himself from a man called George Curtin from near Urlaur [1] on the borders of Mayo and Roscommon, who had also been in the workhouse. Unfortunately, after writing it down, I lost the first half of the story, which was the most interesting, and I have had to supply a brief summary of it in brackets, so far as my very imperfect recollection of it goes. I have quite forgotten the incidents which led up to the druids' prophecy and the Worm's hearing about it.

THE STORY.

[THE druid foretold that a man was coming to Ireland who would banish all the snakes, dragons and serpents. The great Ollpheist, or worm, or serpent, was at this time in the pool near the Arigna mountains, from which the Shannon partly takes its rise. It heard of this prophecy and was greatly concerned about its future. It determined to leave Ireland and make his way to the sea before the man came who should have the power to kill or banish serpents. The man the druid had prophesied about was Saint Patrick.

---

[1] For this place, see the story of the " Friars of Urlaur."

The story describes the desperate efforts of the great
worm to make a waterway for itself by cutting away
the hole in which it was enclosed. It was its efforts to
escape which made the river Shannon. At every pro-
minent part of the Shannon its adventures are related.
As it went on its way, working a channel for itself by which
to swim out to the sea, it used to commit the most terrible
depredations on cattle and sheep, and destroy the country
wherever it happened to be The adventures of the worm
at Jamestown, Athleague, Lanesborough and other places
are described. Near Athleague the people, led by a
drunken piper called O'Rourke, made head against it, but
it swallowed the piper at one gulp. The noise of the
pipes was too much for it and it threw him up again, after
a time, but it lost several days work at the river. After
getting rid of the piper who had so troubled its inside
it began to work hard to make up for the time it had lost[1]]
for it was greatly afraid of the good and powerful man
who was to come.

After a week or so O'Rourke was blind drunk again,
and he faced for the place where the Great Worm had
been before, but by this time it had worked its passage
far away from that place. The piper, however, walked
into the river, and everyone thought that he was drowned,
but one of the enchanted eels was left in the hole and the
eel put O'Rourke under enchantment too, and it was
not long until they heard him playing music in the hole.
But he never came up on land since. Only every morning
and evening they used to be listening to him playing
music in the hole, and from that day to this there is no

[1] Here begins the half which I did not lose.

other name on that same spot but the Piper's Hole. And everybody in Athlone knows the Piper's Hole as well to-day as the people who were alive a thousand years ago knew it.

The Great Worm went on very well until it came to the place which is now Lough Ree. There was a great tribe of venemous serpents there and they attacked it. Some went in front of it, others came behind it, others came on each side of it. They fought for seven nights[1] and seven days ; they made the hard ground soft and the soft ground hard. They sent stones and great rocks flying more than half a mile up in the air. Floods of blood were running as plentiful as the water itself, and indeed people thought that it was the end of the world that was in it. The battle went on for a month without any signs of victory on one side or the other, and the people of the villages round about were in great fear ; but as the old saying puts it, every battle has an end. When the most of the serpents were dead they asked the Great Worm for peace. He granted that and both sides were rejoiced. The Great Worm was wounded and bruised and in much pain.

After that great battle the Worm had to take a rest, and that gave great ease to the people of the villages, because it ate neither cow nor sheep nor pig for the space of three months, but it ate up all the serpents that it had killed in the fighting. It never left so much as a bit of bone behind it, and the people began to think that it would never claim its food off them any more. But so soon as it set to work again they had to supply it with

---

[1] The night is usually put before the day in Irish.

cows, sheep, and pigs once more, because it thought that this was its [lawful] wages for cutting out the river for them. And everyone knows that the river did much good for the country on each side of it; and only for the Great Worm there would have been no river.

The Worm worked hard and went on well until it came to the place which is now Lough Derg. The venemous serpents were collected before it in that place and they gave it battle. If hundreds attacked it in Lough Ree thousands attacked it in Lough Derg, and the first battle was only sport in comparison to this one. They attacked before, behind, and on every side, and some of them made holes under its belly so that they might be able to thrust it through in that place, and such a cutting and scalping and tearing and killing there had never been in the world before, and it's likely that there won't be again. They made the dry earth wet, the wet earth dry, and they sent stones and great rocks flying into the air quick as lightning, and God help the man one of them would fall on, it was a warrant of death for him. They fought for a month without appearance of victory on either side, and during all that time the lake was red (dearg) with blood, and the old people say that this is the reason it was called Loch Dearg or Derg. After a month of fighting the Worm gained the battle. It rose of one leap in the air, and came down on top of the serpents, making a mash of them, and those that were not killed went off over the country.

The Worm was torn and wounded and in great pain after this hard battle, and had to take a long rest. But it never went in pursuit of food from the people of the villages, because it ate its enough of the serpents every day until the last of them was eaten by it

As soon as its wounds were closed and it had rested, it began working again, and nothing wonderful happened to it until it came to the place where the city of Limerick is to-day. In that place there was a great troop of enchanted heroes near the spot where the Treaty Stone is now. The warriors threatened it and told it not to come any further, but it challenged them to battle. They attacked it with battle-axes and great clubs, and they were cutting it and beating it throughout the day until they thought it was dead. Then they went away. But as soon as the sun went down it came to itself again and it was as strong as it was at the commencement of the battle. It came up on land and went to the castle of the enchanted warriors. They were asleep, and it threw down the castle on top of them and killed every mother's son of them. Then it returned to go in face of its work.

It went on well after leaving Limerick, for there was nothing to hinder it. For that reason it made the river wider in that place than in any other. But as soon as it got out into the sea a great whale met it and it had to fight a hard battle, and was nearly beaten, when a sea-maiden came and helped it and they killed the whale.

The sea-maiden and the Great Worm went on side by side until they came to a village on the coast, where there were about three score of men in boats fishing. The Great Worm was very hungry and began swallowing them down greedily, men and boats and all, until the sea-maiden spoke and said that it was a shame. That angered it and it attacked her, but she was too clever for it. She drew out a golden comb with venom in it, and thrust it into the Worm's eye and blinded it out and out. Then said the Worm to her, " I would sooner be dead than alive ; put a hole in my stomach with your scissors." She did that and it died in a moment.

The water was ebbing, and when it had gone out the Great Worm was left dead on the sand. The people of the villages round about came ; they opened the worm, and every mother's son that he had swallowed they found alive and in a heavy sleep at the bottom of their boats. The bones of the Great Worm remained on the shore of Bantry Bay until the fishermen made oars out of them. If my story is not true, there is no water in the sea and no river Shannon in Ireland.

THE POOR WIDOW AND GRANIA OÏ.

PREFACE.

This story I got from Pronisias O'Conor when he was in the workhouse in Athlone, and he had it from one Rose Grennan or in Irish, Róise nic Ghrianain, from a parish near Athlone.

This story is chiefly remarkable for the introduction of Grainne Oigh, which seems to mean Grania the virgin. But who was Grainne ? My narrator could tell me nothing about her. She occurs in the story of " William of the Tree " in my " Beside the Fire," and Alfred Nutt has an interesting note on her at p. 194, but it throws no light upon the subject. There, as here, she appears as a beneficent being, very pious, powerful and mysterious, and able to work miracles. The town of Moate, in Co. Westmeath, is called in Irish the Moat of Grainne Óg, who is said to have been a Munster princess, very good and very wise, and there seems to have been some body of legend connected with her, alluded to by Caesar Otway in his " Tour in Connaught," p. 55. See also Joyce's " Names of Places," vol. I, p. 270. Whether Grainne Óg and Grainne Oigh are the same person seems doubtful, but I should think it very probable, and the appellation of " Oigh " may have tended to some confusion with Muire Oigh. Except in these two stories, one from O'Conor and the other from a man named Blake, near Ballinrobe, I have never met or heard or read of any allusion to this being. But the town of Athlone, being half in Westmeath, the county with which Grainne Óg is associated, and the very old woman who told this story being from the borders of that county, would suggest that there was some connection between the mysterious being and the princess from whom Moate is said to have got its name.

THE STORY.

LONG, long ago there was a poor Widow living in the County Clare, and she had seven children, and the eldest was only ten years old.   It was a Christmas night that was in it, and she had not a morsel to give them to eat, and since she hadn't, she prayed God to take them to Himself.

It was not long after her prayer until the door opened and Grania Oï[1] walked in and two young women after her, carrying a big dish filled with fine food.   They were all clad in raiment as white as mountain snow.   The Widow welcomed the ladies, and she said, " Perhaps ye would give some relief to a poor family that is fasting all the day."

" God has sent us in answer to your prayer to give you relief at the present time, and to ask if you are ready and submissive to part with the whole of your family."

" I am not," said the Widow.

" Did you not pray to God to take them to Himself a short while ago ? "

" Indeed, I don't know," said she, " I was half mad at seeing them fasting, but if God has a place for myself along with my family I am obedient and ready to go."

Then Grania Oï laid down the dish upon the table and said to the Widow, " Eat that, yourself and your family,

---

[1] In Irish " Grainne Oigh," pronounced like " Grania O-ee."

and when it's eaten I'll come again." Then they went out and it was not long till the Widow and her family began eating, and when they were satisfied, still the food on the dish was no less than when they began to take from it.

They were eating at that dish and it never emptied until the evening before Good Friday. That evening the Widow and her family were without bite or sup and they were hoping for Grania Oï and the two young women. But when the darkness of the night was falling a tall thin man walked in. He was dressed in a gentleman's garb. The Widow gave him a chair, and asked him to sit down and take a rest.

" I have no time to sit down," said he, " I have lots of business to do. You yourself and your family are without bite or sup."

" We are," said she, " but I hope for succour soon."

" Have no hope in the promise of a woman of beauty or you will be deceived. The woman who gave you the dish is participator with the fairies, she is trying to get your family from you ; but pay her no attention."

There was great fear on the poor Widow, and she said, " It was a messenger from God who brought us the dish."

" Believe me they were fairies who brought you the dish and that it was fairy food that was in it," said the thin man, " and if you accept another dish from her, yourself and your family will be in Knock Ma[1] amongst the fairies ; have you ever heard of that place ? "

---

[1]Cnoc Meadha, generally called in English " Castlehacket," a hill to the west of Tuam, Co. Galway, reputed to be the head-quarters of all the Tuatha de Danann and shee-folk of Connacht. There dwell Finvara and Nuala, king and queen of the fairies of that province. Many stories are told about it.

" Indeed I have," said she ; " but we shall have no more to do with the fairies.   I and my family would sooner die of the hunger than accept a bite or sup from her again."

" But don't you know that she has power over you on account of all the fairy food you yourself and your family have eaten this four months, and now unless ye take my advice ye shall be lost."

" Thank you," said the Widow, " it is a friend who would give me good advice."

Now it was the Devil who was talking to the Widow ; He had come to put temptation on her.   " Well," said he, " you have holy water in the house."

" I have," said she.

" I can tell you that it is fairy water, and that there is no virtue in it.   Go now and throw it in the fire."   The woman did so.   But no sooner did she do so than there arose a blue flame, and the house was filled with smoke of the same colour.   When the smoke cleared away he said, " Well, one part of the fairies' power is gone.   You have a cross, throw it in the fire, and they will have no power over you at all.   And then as soon as you are free from them I will give yourself and your family a means of livelihood, and, better than that, yourself and your family shall have great riches if you do as I shall tell you."

" I don't like to burn my cross, it was my mother who gave it to me," said the Widow.

Then he pulled out a purse filled with gold and silver, and said, " I had this purse to give you if you had accepted my advice, and not that alone, but yourself and your family would have had a long life."

Great greed for riches came upon the poor Widow, and

she said. " I ask your pardon, noble sir, I am submissive to you in every thing.   I myself and my family are under your control."

At that he handed her the purse and said : " Throw the cross into the fire."   She did so, but instead of its burning there began a stream of blood to come from it.   " Ha! ha ! " said he, " look at the fairy blood.   Here !   put your name to this paper.   I must give my master an account that I have given you the purse and that you are freed from the Shee-folk, and under my control."

The poor woman put her hand to the pen and made her mark, because she did not know how to write or read, and she did not know what was in the paper.   He held the paper on the moment to the fire till it was dry, and he went out leaving the cross in the fire and blood running from it.   As soon as he was gone the Widow took up the cross.   The blood ceased and there was no sign of burning upon it.   She was greatly astonished and did not know what she would do.

While she was thinking of the wonderful things that had happened she heard a voice calling her.   When she went to the door she saw Grania Oï and two maidens carrying a great dish filled with food.

" We don't want any fairy food," said the Widow. " We have plenty of gold and silver.   Go to Knock Ma, and don't come near us any more."

Grania Oï thought that the Widow had lost her senses, and she said : " In God's name have sense, and in Christ's name come here till I talk with you."   She did not wish to come, but some power drew her forward until she stood in front of Grania Oï, and she shaking from head to foot.

" What happened to you since I was here before, and where did you get the gold and the silver ? "

" A princely [a generous] man came to me this evening, and said that you were a fairy woman, and that you were giving myself and my family fairy food in order to get us into your power. He told me to throw the holy water into the fire, and when I did that there rose a blue flame out of it, and the house was filled with smoke of the same colour. When the smoke cleared away he said, " One part of the fairies' power is gone. You have a cross, throw it into the fire and they won't have any power at all over you ; and when you're freed from them I'll give yourself and your family a means of livelihood, and better than that, you and your family will have great riches. I told him that I did not like to burn my cross, that it was my mother who gave it to me, but he said, ' I had this purse for you if you had taken my advice, and not only that, but that I and my family would have a long life.' Greed for riches came over me, and I begged his pardon, saying that I would be submissive to him in everything, and that I and my family were under his control. With that he handed me the purse and said, ' Throw the cross into the fire.' I did so, but in place of burning, a stream of blood began to flow out of it. He laughed and said that it was fairy blood that was in it. Then he gave me a paper to put my name to, because he had an account to give his master that he had given me the purse—and that I was free from the Shee.[1] I cannot write or read, but I made a mark with the pen. When

---

[1] This is the Irish word translated by " fairy," in Irish " *sidhe* " : a common diminutive is *sidheög* " shee-ogue."

he went away I took up the cross and it was not burnt."

"I put the cross of Christ between myself and you, accursed woman. You have sold your soul and the souls of your family to the devil for the sake of gold and silver, and now you are lost for ever, and you have shed the blood of Christ before the day of His crucifixion. Go to your parish priest as soon as you can and tell him every-thing, and how it happened, and tell him that it was Grania Oï who sent you to him. If you yourself are lost your family is not lost for there is no deadly sin upon them."

The Widow went into the house and took out the purse, and asked, "What shall I do with this gold and silver ? "

"Throw it into the fire and say at the same time, ' I renounce the devil and all his works.' "

As soon as she threw the purse into the fire and said the words, the Devil came into her presence and said, "You cannot renounce me. You are mine in spite of priest, bishop, or pope. I have the bargain under your [own] hand."

"In the name of Jesus go away from me," said the Widow ; and when he heard that name he was obliged to go.

The Widow went to the priest and told him the story. "I am afraid," said he, "that you are lost ; but at all events I'll write to the bishop about you. Go home now and begin doing penance. I'll send for you when I get an answer from the bishop."

When she came home she found the family eating out of a great dish which Grania Oï had left with them ; but the eldest of them said to her not to put her hand in the dish, that this was the lady's order, but that when she should be in want of food they would give it to her.

At the end of a week the priest sent for her, and said that he had got an answer from the bishop to say that he would not be able to have any hand in the case until he would get an order from the Pope ; but he bade her to make repentance day and night.

At the end of a month after this the priest sent for her again, and said, " I have a letter from the Pope to say that there is only one way to save you.   Put off your shoes and go on a pilgrimage to Lough Derg.   Don't sleep the second night in any house, and only eat one meal in the twenty-four hours, make the journey of the cross seven times in the day and seven times in the night for seven days. Take no bread with you, and neither gold nor silver, but ask alms in the name of God, and when you come back again I shall tell you what it is proper for you to do. Here is a piece of the true cross to keep the Devil from you.   Go now in the name of God."

When the widow came home Grania Oï was before her at the door, and asked what the priest had said to her. She told her everything that she had to do.   " Go without delay," said Grania Oï, " and I'll take care of your family until you come back."

The Widow went away.   She endured thirst and hunger, cold and bitter hardship.   But she did everything as the Pope had ordered.   At the end of three months she came back and it was scarcely her own family recognised her, she was so withered and thin.

It was not long until the priest came and said, " You have a pilgrimage to make to Croagh Patrick, and you must walk on your knees from the foot to the top of the Reek,[1] and no doubt you will see a messenger from God on the top of the Reek, and you will obtain knowledge from him. Go, now, or perhaps you would be late." The Widow departed, although her feet were cut and the blood coming from them. She went on her knees at the foot of the Reek, and she was two days and two nights going to the top of it. When she sat down a faintness came over her and she fell into a sleep.

When she awoke Grania Oï was by her side. She handed her a paper and said, " Look ! is that the paper you put your hand to when you sold yourself and your family ?"

" I see that it is," said the poor Widow. " I give a thousand thanks and laudations to God that I am saved."

When she came home the priest came and said Mass in the house. The Widow went to confession. She herself and her seven children received the body of Christ from the priest, and at the end of half an hour she herself and her family were dead, and there is no doubt but that they all went to heaven, and that we may go to the same place !

---

[1] Croagh Patrick or Reek Patrick is one of the highest mountains in Connacht. It is 2,510 feet high and difficult to climb. St Patrick is reputed to have driven all the serpents in Ireland into the sea down its slopes. It has always been a noted pilgrimage.

THE GAMBLER OF THE BRANCH.

PREFACE.

This is a story which used to be common in West Roscommon and East Mayo. I often heard it when I was young.
The following version was written down and given me by
my friend Mr. John Rogers [Seághan O Ruaidhri]
about five miles away from the place where I used to be told
the same story. He published it in 1900 in " Irishleabhar
na Gaedhilge." There is another story also about a
gambler who played cards with the devil.

THE STORY.

LONG ago there used to be a king over every kind
of trade and special society and it was the " Gambler of
the Branch " [1] who was king over all the gamblers and
players, and he was so skilful that nobody on the face of
the earth could win a match against him in playing cards
or any other game.

At last, and on account of this, he grew lonesome and
dissatisfied, and he said that since he was not able to get
a game with a man of this world that he would go to try
it in the other world. He went off, walking away, and he

---

[1] " To bear alway the branch," is the Irish expression for having
first place, or in English, carrying off the palm.

never stopped of that journey until he came to the great doors of hell, and knocked stoutly at them. " Who is there ? " said the porter.

" I am ; I the Gambler of the Branch from the upper world," said he, " and I am seeking to play a game of cards with the Arch-demon."

The Arch-demon came, and he said, " What stake have you to play for with me, for I only play for people's souls ?"

" I'll play my own soul against one of these that you have in bondage in this place."

" I'll bet it," says the Demon.

The Gambler won the first game, and so he did most of the others, until he had gained every soul in the place but one, and the Devil would not stake that one no matter how hard the Gambler urged him. He gathered them together then, but when the poor soul that was left behind saw them departing it let a screech out of it that would split a stone, but there was no help for it.

He drove them before him then, like a flock of sheep, and said, " What will be done with ye[1] now ? "

" O friend, take us to heaven, take us to heaven," said they.

" It's as good for me, since ye are here," says he, and he drove them away with him until he came to the great white gates of heaven.

The gates opened and they were welcomed, and the souls went in. And the porter-saint said to the Gambler, " Won't yourself come in ? "

---

[1] Anglo-Irish very sensibly uses " ye " for the plural of thou in all cases, " you " having become ambiguous.

" If I get leave to bring in the cards, I'll go," said the Gambler ; " but if I don't, I won't."

" You won't get that permission," said the saint, but leave them on the wall here outside the gate, and go in, till you see those souls counted in their place.   And you can come out after a while for the cards if you wish."

The Gambler did that.   He went in, and has forgotten ever since to come out for them.

That is the way the Gambler of the Branch went to heaven, and that is the reason that when a slow messenger delays in the house he has been sent to with a message, people say, " You forgot to return as the Gambler of the Branch did."

THE BEETLE, THE DHARDHEEL, AND THE PRUMPOLAUN.

PREFACE.

I have often heard versions of the following story. This particular one was written down in Irish by my friend Domhnall O Fotharta of Connemara, who printed it in his " Siamsa an gheimhridh " in 1892.

My friend the O'Cathain tells me that the reason the dardaol (pronounced in Mid-Connacht dhardheel) is burnt, is because if you stamp on it with your foot, or kill it with a stone or a stick, then the next time your foot or the stick or the stone strikes a person or an animal it will give rise to a mortal injury. That is the reason the dardaol is taken up on a shovel and put in the fire, or else destroyed by a hot coal.

The scientific name of the dardaol is " ocypus olens," in English he is sometimes called the " devil's coach-horse." He is really a useful creature and very voracious. He preys on most insects injurious to farm crops. He is very fearless and assumes an attitude of attack when interfered with, opening his jaws and turning his long tail over his back as if to sting. This looks very formidable and intimidating, but the fact is that, in common with the rest of the beetle tribe, he has no sting.

I had the good fortune to twice see a dardaol kill a worm. On each occasion the creature sprang into the air in a manner I could not have conceived possible, and came down on the uphappy worm. It never loosed its hold, but held on for nearly ten minutes, the worm struggling and swelling all the time, until it finally appeared to be dead. One of these dardaols was quite small, not much over three-quarters of an inch, but the other one was very large, an inch and a half or so, and the worm it killed might have been 3½ or 4 inches long.

The ciaróg or keerogue is one of the common species of ground beetles or " carabus," probably " violaceus." He is a large active insect, usually called a "clock " in Anglo-Irish.   " One keerogue knows another," is a common Irish proverb. He is about an inch in length.

The Prumpolaun [priompollán] is the large common dung beetle, " geotrupes stercorarius." It is the heavy, slow-flying beetle, which at dusk flies about searching for dirty places to deposit its eggs, and as its weight and short body render it difficult for it to steer, it is apt to strike the wayfarer in the face. It is the " shard-born beetle " of the poet.

In the south of Ireland the dardaol is generally known as dearg-a-daol, and in the Anglo-Irish of Connacht he is called a " crocodile." There are other allusions to this intimidating insect in this book. Its dull black colour and threatening movements have made the little creature an object of unmerited hatred and superstition in many other countries besides Ireland.

THE STORY.

AT the time that Jesus was flying from those who were betraying Him it chanced that He passed through a field in which was a sower who was sowing wheat-seed. His disciples said to the sower that if any man were to ask him " if Jesus out of Nazareth had passed that way," he was to give them this answer : " He passed through this field the time we were sowing the seed in it [but not since.]"

The next day the farmer went out to look at his field for fear the birds of the air might be doing any damage [to the grain he had sowed the day before]. But astonishment seized him when he beheld the wheat [he had sowed the day before] ripe and yellow and of the colour of gold, and fit to be reaped.

The farmer called on his mêhill [troop of workmen] to bring sickles with them and cut the wheat. And while they were cutting it it chanced that the spies came through it. They asked the man whose the field was, whether he had seen Jesus out of Nazareth going that way. The farmer answered them and told them what he had been bidden to tell : " He went through this field when we were sowing the wheat that we are reaping to-day."

The keerogue put his head out of a hole and said " iné, iné,[1] yesterday ! yesterday ! " to let them know that Jesus had gone past the day before.

As they were talking with the keerogue, the dhardheel put his head out of another hole and said," gér ! gér ! gér ! " " sharp ! sharp, sharp," three times over, to make them feel that if they followed Jesus sharply they would lay hold of Him.

" O vo, vo ! boiling and burning and fire on you," said the prumpolaun, for he was afraid that the spies might understand the words that were said to them, and that they might follow Jesus sharply to lay hold of Him.

It is a fashion still amongst the people of West Connacht when a dhardheel comes into any house to run for the tongs, take a red coal and blow it, and lay it on the dhardheel to burn it, saying at the same time, " the sins of the day, of my life, and of my seven ancestors on you."

---

[1] Pronounce in-yaé.

When they get hold of a keerogue the head is cut off it and they say the same words that it said itself, " iné ! iné " ! while cutting the head off it.   But nothing bad is done to the prumpolaun on account of the pity it had for our Saviour when He was flying from the Jews.

THE LADY OF THE ALMS.

PREFACE.

This was a story told by Michael S. Seoidhigh or Joyce from Turlogh More, Co. Galway, for the Oireachtas many years ago.

The form of the story is obviously corrupt and confused. Why should the woman tell her experiences to the voice above her head. There can be little doubt that it was the voice who directed her and that when she had come home, chastened and enlightened, she then told the story as it is here. Either that, or it is the fragment of a longer story in which both a strange man and the supernatural voice each played a part.

THE STORY.

THERE was once a lady, and there never was such an almsgiver as she was. When her master used to be at home she would go upstairs, and when she had no other way of giving she would take the inside garment off her own body and hand it out to the poor people.

She had three sons and one of them died. He was one and twenty years old when he died. After that she was greatly angered with the Son of God.

It was not long after that until another son went, who was twenty-two years old. And a great trouble fell upon her after their both dying.

Two years after that the third son died on her.

She went away then [half crazed]. She got a bag and began asking alms [like any beggar]. She spent the day going [on her quest] until night came on, and she never found house or wattled-shelter, under which she might put her head. She heard a voice above her, and she wondered. " What has sent you here ? " said the voice, " methinks you had no cause to take up with misery were it not your own senselessness."

" I had not," said she, " but I think I never did anything against the Son of God, and He has taken from me a son who was twenty-one years old, a son as nice as there was in the parish. Well I did not half mind that—the Son of God's taking him from me—until a year from that day He took the second son from me. Two years from that day the third son was taken from me, and then I went and took a bag with me and said that I would never again do another day's service to God. I was [always] so good to the Son of God and the glorious Virgin that I never thought that He would put such punishment upon me. But He put such punishment on me that I went looking for alms. Away [from my home] I went and proceeded to look for alms, and I never met house or wattled-shelter. A man came to me before you [came] and he said to me, ' What has brought you here ? ' I told him that the Son of God had taken my three children from me. ' Go in,' said he, ' into yonder house in which you see the light ? ' I went in, and what should I see there but a corpse and three lighted candles. I remained there watching the body and plenty of grief and fear on me. At the hour of midnight a slumber of sleeping fell upon me, for I was hungry and troubled. When I awoke out of the sleep I found food and drink and everything I desired laid out before me. I ate and drank my enough. After that I fell asleep,

and when I awoke there was nothing there but a bare
field, and my bag laid under my head. I arose and stood
up and threw the bag over my shoulders and turned back
again, and the same man met me a second time. ' Where
did you spend the night ? ' said he. ' I spent it watching
a corpse,' said I. ' Did you get your enough to eat and
drink ? ' ' I did,' said I. ' Why did you take up with
misery ? ' ' Well I did take up with misery,' said I,
' I had a son who was twenty-one years old and he was
taken from me. A year from that day the second son was
taken from me, and two years from that day the third
son was taken. I went off then and I said that I would
not do one morsel of God's rules any more.'

' Go home, now,' said the man, ' God was so good
to you that He did not desire you to find shame or scandal.
That first son that you had—he was to have been hanged
[if he had lived] for slaying a man. And the second son,
he was to have been banished far away to an island in the
sea for stealing cattle [had he lived]. And the third son—
a woman was to have sworn against him that he was the
father of her child, although he never had anything, good
or bad, to do with her. Go home now and mind your own
business. God had so much consideration for you that
He did not wish such pain to come down on you
or your children, since you were yourself so good to the
poor. Those [three sons] shall be three candles before
you, and the three don't know which of them will arrange
your bed under you in the Heaven of God.' "

According to what authors say, there are no other four
who [now] enjoy greater pleasure and happiness than
they !

ST. PATRICK AND HIS GARRON.

PREFACE.

This story of St. Patrick I got from Pronisias O'Conor. It seems to have a certain affinity with the story of Crom Dubh (which see). St. Patrick does not play a very desirable part in this tale. He uses his private knowledge of his garron's capacity as a weight-bearer to the detriment of his neighbour, the story-teller drawing no distinction between what was legal and what was morally equitable !

The story of the serpent's candle must be old and well-known, for it is alluded to in the widely-circulated poem the " Dirge of Ireland," by O'Connell, said to have been a Bishop of Kerry. Talking of St. Patrick's exploits he says it was he who " múċ coinneal na cappaiʒe le na ṛméiꝺeaꝺ," " who quenched the candle of the Rock by his nod."

THE STORY.

WHEN Saint Patrick came to Ireland to kindle the light of Grace in this island, many troubles were coming upon him. The island was filled with snakes, north, south, east and west, but it was God's will that Patrick should put them under foot.

When he came to West Connacht he had a servant whose name was Fintan, a pious and faithful man. One lay when he was drawing towards the Reek, and the

demons running away before him in fear, it chanced that
Fintan was travelling in front of the saint, and the serpents
came round him and killed him. When the saint came
he found Fintan dead on the road. He was grieved, but
he went on his knees and prayed to God to bring his
servant to life again. No sooner had he his prayers finished
than Fintan rose up as well as ever he was. Patrick gave
thanks to God, and said, " In God's name we will set up
a church here as a sign of the great power of God, and
we will call it Achaidh Cobhair." [1]

The saint bought a garron or nag for carrying stones, and
he blessed it ; for no burden had ever been laid upon it that
it was not able to carry. Then he got workmen, masons
and carpenters, and began to found the church. After
a while the men began clamouring that they had nothing
to eat. There was great famine and scarcity in the
country that year. Meal was so scarce that few
people had any to spare, or to sell, either for gold or
silver.

There was a man named Black Cormac living near the
place. He had the full of a barn of bags of meal. The
saint took the men and the garron with him one morning
to the house of Black Cormac, and he inquired how much
would he be asking for as much meal as the garron would
be able to carry on his back. Cormac looked at the garron
and said " so much "—naming his price. " It's a bargain," said the saint, handing him money down. The
men went into the barn and brought out a great bag
and set it on the garron's back. Cormac said that it

---

[1] *i.e.*, Field of Help. This is folk etymology. Now Aughagower, in Mayo

would break the creature's back. " Never mind," said
the saint, " keep packing bags on him until I tell you
to stop." They put bag after bag on him until they had
a pile as big as a small house. " Drive on now," says the
saint. The garron went off as readily and quickly as
though it had only one bag. There was great anger on
Black Cormac, and he said, " My share of trouble on ye,
ye have me destroyed out and out." There was amaze-
ment upon every person who saw the garron and the load
that was on him.

A short time after this the workmen asked the saint for
meat, for they were working very hard. Some of them
said that they heard that Black Cormac had a bull to sell
cheap. The saint sent for Cormac, and asked him how
much would he be wanting for the bull. Now it was a
savage bull who had killed many people, and since Cormac
hated the saint with a great hatred he hoped the bull
would kill him, and he told him, " You can have the bull
for nothing if you go yourself for him." " I'm very
thankful to you," said the saint, " I'll go for him in the
evening when I'll have my work done."

That evening the saint went to Black Cormac's house
and asked him to show him the field where the black bull
was. He was greatly delighted and said, " Follow me ;
the walk is not a long one." He brought the saint down
to a boreen, and showed him the bull in the field and said
to him, " Take him with you now if you can." The
saint went into the field, and when the bull saw him it
raised its head and tail in the air and came towards him
in anger. He raised his crozier and made the sign of
Christ between himself and the bull. The beast lowered

his head and his tail and followed the saint as quietly as a lamb.

When the saint came home he killed the bull and told the men, " Take the flesh with ye, but leave the skin and the bones." They took the flesh with them and ate it.

A week after that Black Cormac came to the saint and said, " I hear people saying that you are an honest man, but I know that you have done me a great wrong." " How so?" said the saint. " About my meal and my bull," said he. " I gave you your own bargain for the meal, and as for your bull, you can have it back if you wish it."

" How could I get it back, and it eaten by you and your workmen ? " said Black Cormac.

The saint called for Fintan and told him, " Bring me the skin and bones of the bull." He brought them to him and he prayed over them, and in a moment the bull leapt up as well as ever he was. " Now," said the saint, " take your bull home with you."

Black Cormac was greatly surprised, and when he went home he told the neighbours that it was an enchanter the saint was, and that his own bull was a blessed bull, and that it was proper that the people should worship it. They believed that, and they said that they would come on Sunday morning.

The saint heard what Cormac had done, and he threatened him saying not to lead the people astray from the true faith that he himself was teaching them ; but Black Cormac would not listen to him. On Sunday morning some of the people gathered along with him to worship the bull, and Black Cormac was the first to go into the field to set an example, and he went to prostrate himself

ST. PATRICK PRAYS OVER THE SKIN OF THE BULL

in presence of the bull, but the beast came and put his two horns under him behind, and tossed him up in the air so high that when he came to the ground he was dead.   The people remember that, still, in West Connacht, as Cormac Dubh's Sunday.

When Saint Patrick finished his church he said Mass in it, and after that he faced for the Reek, for many of the serpents had gone up that hill out of fear of the saint. For that reason he followed them and found that they were up on the top of the Reek.

When he came to the bottom he dug a great hole, and he went up on the Reek and drove the serpents down. They fell into the hole and were all drowned but two. Those two escaped from him.   One of them went into a hole in a great rock near the Mouth of the Ford [1] in Tirawley, and wrought great havoc amongst the people.

Every night when the sun would be going down this serpent used to light a candle, and anybody who would see the light used to fall dead.   The people called this serpent Sercín, and the rock is to be seen to this day, and it, is called Carrig-Sercín.   The saint followed this serpent.

He and his servant, Fintan, came to a little village near Carrig-Sercín, and the saint asked a widow for lodgings for himself and his servant.   " I'll give you that," said she, " but I must close my door before set of sun."   " Why so ? " said the saint.   " There is a serpent in a hole of a rock out in the sea ; he lights a candle every evening before sunset, and anybody who sees that light

---

[1] Ballina, Co. Mayo.

falls dead. He has great destruction made amongst the people."

" Have you a candle in the house ? " said the saint. " Indeed I have not," said she. " Have you the makings of a candle," said the saint. " No," said she ; " but I have dry rushes."

Then the saint drew out a knife and opened Fintan's stomach and took a bit of lard out of it, and gave it to the woman of the house, and told her to make a candle. She did as he had directed, and when the candle was made the saint lit it and stood in the mouth of the door. It was not long until the serpent lit his candle, but no sooner was it lit than it fell dead. The people thanked the saint greatly, and he explained to them the mighty power and the love of God, and baptized them all.

When the other serpent escaped St. Patrick, it never stopped until it went in on a little island that was in the north of the country. The name of this serpent was Bolán Mór, or Big Bolaun. He was as big as a round tower. St. Patrick pursued Bólán ; but when he came as far as the lake he had no boat to take him to the island. He stripped off his clothes, and with his crozier in his hand he leapt into the water and began swimming to the island.

When the serpent saw the saint coming to him he took to the water, and when he came as far as the saint he opened his mouth, and, as sure as I'm telling it, he swallowed the saint. Bolán Mór had a great wide stomach, and when the saint found himself shut up there he began striking on every side with his crozier, and Bólán Mór began to throw a flood of blood out of his mouth, until the water of the lake was red (dearg), and there is no name on the lake from that day to this but Loch Dearg. The saint was beating Bolán Mór with the crozier until he killed him. Then he made a hole in his side and came out, and drew Bolán Mór's body to land after him.

There was wonder and great joy on the people of the villages round about, because neither man, beast, nor bird had come to the lake since Bólán came there but he had swallowed down into his big stomach, and it was great good for them he to be dead.

The next day the saint got a boat, and he and Fintan and a number of the people from the villages went to the island. St. Patrick blessed the little island, and it was not long until a number of pious men came and cut out [the site of] a monastery on the island, and from that time to the present, good people go on a pilgrimage to that blessed island.[1]

St. Patrick remained for a time amongst the people near Loch Derg teaching and baptising them. And as soon as some of them were able to teach the others he returned to Aughagower. While the saint had been away from them some of them had fallen into unbelief, but so soon as he came back they returned to the true faith of St. Patrick and never lost it more. Many people also came to the saint seeking to buy the little garron from him ; but he would not sell it.

One day the king who was over Connacht at that time came and said, " I hear you have a wonderful garron, and that he is able to carry a heavy load."

---

[1] *i.e.*, Lough Derg.

He is a good garron," said the saint, " no load has failed
him since I bought him, and I wouldn't like to part with
him."

" I'll give you as much gold as he will be able to carry
on his back in one load in one day from rise of sun until
it sets.   It is thirty miles from my castle to this place and
he must do the journey in one day."

" Perhaps you have not as much gold in the house as
the garron can carry," said the saint.

" If I haven't," said the king, " I'll give you as much
as will found three churches for you, and you'll have your
garron, too."

" It's a bargain," said the saint.

The king had a coach, a tent and servants, and he said,
" I'll wait here till morning and you can come to my castle
with me, and the morning after you can go home with
your load.

" Very well, let it be so," said the saint.

On the morning of the next day they all departed,
the saint riding on the garron, and the king and his servants in the coach.   The king drove his horses as fast as
they were able to run, to see would the garron be able to
keep up with them.   But if they had to go seven times as
quick the garron was able for them.   St. Patrick remained
that night at the king's castle and next morning before sunrise the king brought himself and his garron to his treasury.
The treasurer was there with his men.   They filled a great
bag with gold and put it on the garron's back.   " Will
he be able to carry it home ? " said the king.   " He will,
and twenty times as much," said the saint.   He filled
another bag and put it on him, and another bag after that.

" Isn't there his enough of a load on him now ? " said the
king. " There isn't a half or a quarter of a load yet on
him," said the saint. They were putting [bags] on him
until every ounce in the treasury was on him. Then
the saint said, " To show that there isn't half a load on
him yet, put two or three tons of iron on top of the gold."
They did that, and the garron walked out as lightly as
though there had been nothing in it but a bag of oats.
" Now," said the saint, " you see that my garron-*een*
hasn't half a load on him yet." " I see he has not," said
the king. " There is more power in your garron than
in all the horses of the Ard-ri.[1] Take your garron home
again, and begin and set up those churches, and I'll pay
the cost."

The saint rode on his garron and came home. He soon
began to put up the three churches, and the king paid the
costs. But the garron carried every stone that went to
the building. The people have the old saying still when
they want to praise anyone, " May you have the strength
of Patrick's garron ! "

When the three churches were finished he bestowed his
garron on the brethren, and he himself went northward,
lighting a coal of faith throughout Ireland which was
never quenched, and never shall be quenched.

When the great judgment shall come it is St. Patrick
who will judge the children of the Gael.

---

[1] *i.e.*, The High King.

HOW SAINT MOLING GOT HIS NAME.

PREFACE.

There is hardly any Irish saint of whom more legends are related, at least in our literature, than of Saint Moling. He was both a poet and a prophet. Some stories bring him into contact with Gobán Saor, the great builder. He figures largely in the extraordinary tale of "Suibhne Geilt." See also the story of the "Death of Bearchán." The following legend was printed by my friend, Seán Tóibín, in the "Lochrann" a couple of years ago. I was sure it was taken from oral sources, but he has just told me to my surprise, that he was only retelling what he had read in Irish, not what he had HEARD or taken down orally. However, as the story had been set up in print, and as I have here no other story about St. Moling it may stay, only the reader must understand that it is not actual surviving folk-lore, but a retelling from an Irish MS.

THE STORY.

[HE was first called Taircheal, and he was pupil to a cleric.] Taircheal went out one day, and he had two bags, one on his back and one in front of him. He took his master's stick in his hand and off he set in this guise. He went round Luachair on pilgrimage, and he was there reciting his rosary when he saw coming towards him the Fuath[1] and his people ; a black, dark, truly

---

[1] Pronounced " Foo-a."   A weird shape, phantom, or spectre.

ugly band were they, and they had the form of demons.
And they used never give quarter to anyone. And this
was the number of those who were there, namely the
Fuath himself, his wife, his gillie, his hound, and nine
others.

Says the Fuath to his people, " Wait ye there and I'll
go talk to yon man who is alone, and since I took up with
a life of plundering and stealing I never felt a desire to
protect any man except that one only." He gripped his
sword and went over to meet Taircheal.

He said to Taircheal, " Whence have you come from,
you eater of beastings ? "

" Whence have you come from yourself, you black
burnt gruagach¹ ? " said the young man.

" I'll take your bags off you, and your head too, unless
you listen to me," said the Fuath.

" By my father's hand you won't unless I wish it myself," said Taircheal.

" By the hand of him who taught me, but I'll ply my
weapon on you," said the Fuath.

" I'd think it easier to put you down than boiled meat,"
said Taircheal.

" Listen or I'll stick this point in through the middle
of your heart," said the Fuath.

" I swear," said the young man, " that I'll strike you
on the head with this stick, it is the crozier of my master
and tutor, and he promised that it should never be broken
in single combat."

Then fear possessed the Fuath, and he called to his

---

¹ Literally, " long-haired one." It is a term for a wizard or warlock.

people to come and help him.   The other Fuaths came.
Then it was plain to Taircheal that he had no way of
escape or of withdrawing.

" We'll kill you now, brown Taircheal," said the
Fuath's hag, " I'll thrust you through with my knife, and
you'll get death and violent dissolution."

" I ask a request of ye," said Taircheal.

" What is it ?" said the Fuaths.

" Let me go to the other side of that ditch, and give
three steps in the path of the King of Heaven and
Earth," said he.

The Fuaths laughed.   " That's all you want ?" said
they.   " That's all," said he.

" Have it then," said the hag, " for you won't go from
us, for we are as swift as the deer of the hill, and this
hound of ours is as swift as the wind."

Then Taircheal walked to the ditch, and gave his three
leaps.   He went so far, of the first leap, that they thought
he was no bigger [when he landed] than a crow on top of
the hill.   The second leap he gave they did not see him
at all, and they did not see whether it was to heaven or
earth he had gone. Of the third leap he landed upon
the wall of his tutor's church.

" That way he's gone," said the Fuath's hag.   Then
they rose up and ran, both hound and person, so that their
cry and yell was heard a mile overhead in the upper air.
The hounds and populace of the village came out each one
of them to protect the youth, for it was plain to them that
he was being pursued by the Fuaths.   But he leapt down
off the wall and ran into the church, and began returning
thanks to God in presence of his tutor.

" What angry madness is on you, son ? " said the tutor.

" Nothing much, my tutor," said Taircheal, " it was the Fuaths who were hunting me ; " and he told him the story how he had leaped [ling] from Luachair in his three leaps.

" Great is your leap [ling] my pupil," said the priest, and it was for you that the angel Victor made the prophecy, and Moling [= my leap] of Luachair shall be your name henceforth from the leaps that you have leapt."

CRÍOCH.

APPENDIX.

NOTE ON THE DEATH OF MULRUANA, p. 33.

This proverb, "as I've burnt the candle I'll burn the inch," must be old, and appears to have been well-known, for Maolmuire Ua hUiginn, Archbishop of Tuam, used it over 300 years ago, in a poem beginning "Slán uaim don da aodhaire," of which I have a manuscript copy.

> Cig ꞃaoiꞃꞃe anꞣiaiꞣ ꞃó-ꞇ́ꞃuiꞣe,
>
> Caꞃ éiꞃ ꞣuꞣuig cig ꞃoineann,
>
> ꝼuilnge ꝼeaꞣ an óꞃlaig-ꞃi,
>
> Maꞃ ꞣo caiꞇeaꞣ an ꞇoineall.

i.e., freedom comes after hard-captivity, after darkness comes fine weather, it is to be endured for the space of this inch, since the [rest of the] candle has been burnt.

NOTE ON THE DEATH OF BEARACHAN, p. 63.

I have found another version of the very curious story of the Death of Bearachan. It was sent in many years ago in a collection by some un-known collector competing for a prize in folk lore at the Oireachtas, under the ainm-bꞃéige of Seaꞡan Cꞃón. In this version Bearachan is not a saint but a druid, and the three kings are Finn Mac Cumhaill king of the Fian, one of the provincial kings, and the hound Bran, the king of all hounds. The thing that wailed so piteously outside the door is called an " iarmhar," pronounced Eervar or Eerwar—there is no such creature known to me. The word is used by Keating as meaning a " remnant." He talks of the Iarmhar or Remnant of the Fir Bolg. I have never met the word in any other sense. There is nothing said in this version about its growing large when it got the heat, and the relationship to the Breton Buguel Noz is not so apparent as in the other story.

bÁs bheaRacháin na Ráiḋte gcliste.

Ḃí sean-draoi ann, fad ó, gur ḃ'é ainm a ḃí air ná Ḃearacán, agus táinig Fionn Mac Cúṁaill agus ríg eile d'á ḟiosrugaḋ, oiḋce áiriġte.

Do ḃíodar ag caiteaṁ na h-oiḋce leó féin ann—ag déanaṁ gac aon caiteaṁ-aimsire d' ḟeadadar dóiḃ féin.

I gcaiteaṁ na h-oiḋce dóiḃ d'iarr Fionn de Ḃearacán an fada an saoġal a ḃí geárrta amac dó nó an raiḃ aon ḟios aige air.

Duḃairt Ḃearacán d'á ḟreagairt go raiḃ, go mait—go maireaḋ sé go brát cun go dtiucfaḋ trí niġte gan cuireaḋ cum a tiġe i gcóṁair na h-oiḋce,—ar an oiḋce sin go dtiucfaḋ mac tíre cuige do ṁar'óċaḋ é.

" Déan t'anam, mar sin", arsa Fionn, " mar tá trí niġte gan cuireaḋ ann ro anoct."

" Cionnas a ḃéaḋ "? arsa Ḃearacán, " agus gan ann act beirt agaiḃ."

"Τά," αππα Ϝιοnn, "mιre ριζ na Ϝéιnne, αζυρ é reo Lem' coιr ριζ cúιζεαϋ ιr εαϋ é, αζυρ Ϸrαn ατά 'na ριζ αρ ζαϋαραιϋ an ϋοrhαιn."

" O ! Ϋια Le m' αnαm"! αππα Ϸεαραcάn, τά mo ζnó ϋéαnτα mαρ ριn."

"Νι ϋαοζαL ϋυιτ αnoċτ pé rζéαL é," αππα Ϝιοnn, "no τειρϝιϋ ré οππαιnn-ne."

Sé ριο ϋο ϋειneαϋαρ, ná é ϋο ċυρ ϝα ϋéαL τοϋάιn, αζυρ an ϋειρτ eιLe ϋειτ αζ ιmιρτ ϝιτċιLLe αρ ċóιn an τοϋάιn αρ eαζLα ζο ϋτυιτϝεαϋ ριαϋ 'na ζcοϋLαϋ an ϝαιϋ ϋο ϋειϋιρ αζ ϝαιρe αρ Ϸεαραcάn. Ϋο ϋιοϋαρ αζ ιmιρτ Leó.

Ϸυϋ ζαιριϋ ϋόιϋ ζυρ αιριζεαϋαρ an τ-ιαρrhαρ α' Lαϋαιρτ αmυιζ, αζυρ ϋ'ιαππ ré οπτα ζο h-ιαιrhéιLeαċ é ϋο Leοζαιnτ ιρτεαċ.

Ϋυϋrαϋαρ Leιr ζο ϋοιτċεαLLαċ, ι mϋαρα, ná Leοζϝαιϋιρ.

Ϋο Leαn ré οππα, ϝαιϋ ζαċ n-ϝαιϋ, αζυρ é nιορα τρυαιζrhéιLιζe ζαċ υαιρ 'ná α ċéιLe.

Ϋυϋαιρτ Ϝιοnn ré ϋειneαϋ τιαρ ċαLL ζυρ ċóιρ ζυρ cυιρεαϋαρ ϋιοϋ cαταnnα ϋα cruαιϋe 'ná pé ιαρrhαρ α ϋι αmυιζ ϋο rmαċτυζαϋ ζο mαιϋιn.

Ϋ'ορζLαϋαρ an ϋορυρ αζυρ ϋο rζαοιLeαϋαρ ιρτεαċ é, αζυρ ϋο ϝυιϋ ré ϝα' cúιnne αζυρ ϋο Leoζ (Leιζ) ré αιρ ϋο ϋειτ ϋά Leιζεαϋ (Leαζαϋ) αζ an Ϸϝυαċτ. Ιr ζεαρρ ζυρ ταρραιnζ ré cυιζe pιοϋ, αζυρ ϋο τορnαιζ ré αρ an ζcεόL ϋο rρρεαζαϋ ϋο ϋ'υαιϋριζe αζυρ ϋ' αιριζ αοn neαċ ριαrh. Αζυρ ϋα ζεαρρ 'na ϋιαιϋ ριn ζυρ τυιτ ϋυιne αcα na cοϋLαϋ ċαLL αζυρ ϋυιne eιLe, αϋορ, αζυρ αρ mαιϋιn nυαιρ ϋúιριζεαϋαρ nι ραιϋ ϝe ϋéαL an τοϋάιn αċτ cαιρnιn cnάrh. Sιn é ϋάρ Ϸεαραcάιn αζαιϋ.

DATE DUE